Adobe® InDesign™

Classroom in a Book®

Adobe

Contents

Getting Started

Welcome to Adobe® InDesign™— the future of professional publishing, and your solution for creating graphics-intensive documents. InDesign is an extremely capable design and production tool with unparalleled precision and control, and seamless integration with Adobe's professional graphics applications, including Adobe Photoshop® and Adobe Illustrator®. When you have special requirements, you can enhance or customize almost any part of InDesign using plug-in software from Adobe and other vendors. InDesign is capable of producing professional-quality, full-color output on high-volume color printing presses, and also supports a wide range of output devices and formats such as desktop printers, PDF files, and HTML files.

About Classroom in a Book

Adobe InDesign 1.0 Classroom in a Book® is part of the official training series for Adobe graphics and publishing software developed by experts at Adobe Systems. The lessons are designed to let you learn at your own pace. If you're new to Adobe InDesign, you'll learn the fundamental concepts and features you'll need to master the program. If you've been using Adobe InDesign for a while, you'll find Classroom in a Book teaches many advanced features, including tips and techniques for using this exciting design tool.

Although each lesson provides step-by-step instructions for creating a specific project, there's room for exploration and experimentation. You can follow the book from start to finish or do only the lessons that correspond to your interests and needs. Each lesson concludes with a review section summarizing what you've covered.

Prerequisites

Before beginning to use *Adobe InDesign 1.0 Classroom in a Book*, you should have a working knowledge of your computer and its operating system. Make sure you know how to use the mouse and standard menus and commands, and also how to open, save, and close files. If you need to review these techniques, see the printed or online documentation included with your system.

Installing the program

You must purchase the Adobe InDesign software separately. For complete instructions on installing the software, see the Introduction to the *Adobe InDesign 1.0 User Guide*.

Installing the Classroom in a Book fonts

To ensure that the lesson files appear on your system with the correct fonts, you may need to install the Classroom in a Book font files. The lessons fonts are located in the Fonts folder on the InDesign Classroom in a Book CD. If you already have these on your system, you do not need to install them. If you have ATM, see its documentation on how to install fonts. If you do not have ATM, installing it from the CIB CD will automatically install the necessary fonts.

You can also install the Classroom in a Book fonts by copying all the files in the Fonts folder on the InDesign Classroom in a Book CD to the Fonts folder within the folder in which you installed InDesign on your hard disk. Doing so makes the fonts available to InDesign but not to other applications.

Copying the Classroom in a Book files

The Classroom in a Book CD includes folders containing all the electronic files for the lessons. Each lesson has its own folder. You must install these folders on your hard drive to use the files for the lessons. To save room on your drive, you can install the folders for each lesson as you need them.

1 Insert the Adobe InDesign Classroom in a Book CD into your CD-ROM drive.

2 Create a folder on your hard disk and name it **IDCIB**.

3 Do one of the following:

• Copy the Lessons folder into the IDCIB folder.

• Copy only the single lesson folder you need.

Restoring default preferences

To ensure that the tools and palettes function exactly as described in this lesson, you must delete or deactivate (by renaming) the InDesign Defaults file and the InDesign SavedData file.

The InDesign Defaults file and the InDesign SavedData file control how palettes and command settings appear on your screen when you open the Adobe InDesign program. Each time you exit Adobe InDesign, the position of the palettes and certain command settings are recorded in these files. To ensure that the tools and palettes function exactly as described in this book, you can delete the current InDesign Defaults and InDesign SavedData files at the beginning of each lesson. (If they don't already exist, Adobe InDesign creates new versions of these files the next time you start the program and save a file.)

Important: *If you want to save the current settings, rename the defaults files rather than deleting them. When you are ready to restore the settings, change the names back and make sure that the files are located in the InDesign 1.0 folder (Windows®) or the Preferences folder (Mac OS).*

1 If InDesign is running, choose File > Exit.

2 To locate the InDesign defaults files, do one of the following:

• (Windows) Choose Start from the Windows taskbar, and then choose Find > Files or Folders. For Named, type **"InDesign Defaults", "InDesign SavedData"** (including the quotation marks). For Look In, select Local Hard Drives (or the drive that contains Windows). Then click Find Now. Drag the InDesign Defaults and InDesign SavedData files to the Recycle Bin (or rename them). Do not delete any other InDesign file. Close the Find dialog box.

• (Mac OS) Choose File > Find from the Finder menu. For Find Items, choose On Local Disks, Except CD-ROMS. In the text box, type **InDesign Defaults**. Then click Find. Drag the InDesign Defaults file to the Trash or rename it. In the same way, search for **InDesign SavedData** and delete or rename this file. Do not delete any other InDesign file. Close the Find windows.

 If you renamed the defaults files to preserve them, you can return to your previous settings by first deleting the newest copies of the InDesign Defaults and InDesign SavedData files. Then restore the original names of the files you renamed in the steps above.

Additional resources

Adobe InDesign 1.0 Classroom in a Book is not meant to replace documentation that comes with the program. Only the commands and options used in the lessons are explained in this book. For comprehensive information about program features, refer to these resources:

• The User Guide. Included with the Adobe InDesign software, the User Guide contains a complete description of all features. For your convenience, you will find excerpts from these guides, including the Quick Tours for the software, in this Classroom in a Book.

• The Web Tour, available on the application CD.

• The Quick Reference Card, a useful companion as you work through the lessons.

• Online Help, an online version of the User Guide and Quick Reference Card, which you can view by choosing Help > Contents. (For more information, see Lesson 1, "Getting to Know the Work Area.")

• The Adobe Web site, which you can view by choosing File > Adobe Online if you have a connection to the World Wide Web.

Adobe certification

The Adobe Training and Certification Programs are designed to help Adobe customers improve and promote their product proficiency skills. The Adobe Certified Expert (ACE) program is designed to recognize the high-level skills of expert users. Adobe Certified Training Providers (ACTP) use only Adobe Certified Experts to teach Adobe software classes. Available in either ACTP classrooms or on site, the ACE program is the best way to master Adobe products. For Adobe Certified Training Programs information, visit the Partnering with Adobe website at partners.adobe.com.

A Quick Tour of
Adobe InDesign

This interactive demonstration of Adobe InDesign provides an overview of key features of the program. It should take you approximately 30 minutes to complete.

Getting started

You'll start the tour by opening a partially completed document. You'll add the finishing touches to this 6-page article on Mexican folk art written for an imaginary travel magazine. Before you begin, you'll need to restore the default preferences for Adobe InDesign.

1 To ensure that the tools and palettes function exactly as described in this lesson, delete or deactivate (by renaming) the InDesign Defaults file and the InDesign SavedData file. See "Restoring default preferences" on page 2.

2 Start Adobe InDesign.

3 Choose File > Open, and locate the Tour folder on your hard disk:

• (Windows) The tour files are typically found in C:\Program Files\Adobe\InDesign\Learning Adobe InDesign\Tour.

• (Mac OS) The tour files are typically found in Adobe InDesign: Learning Adobe InDesign: Tour.

4 In the Tour folder, double-click ID_01.indd.

Note: In Windows, your extensions may be hidden. If this is the case, the file will appear as ID_01 (not ID_01.indd) in the Open a File dialog box.

5 Choose File > Save As, and rename the file **Tour** in the Tour folder. If someone else has created this file, choose Yes to replace it.

For a color version of the finished document, see the color section.

Viewing the document

The first spread (pages 2 and 3) appears on your screen. You'll now look at the rest of the 6-page article using several navigation methods. First, you'll use the Navigator palette, which is useful for changing the view magnification. As in Adobe Illustrator and Adobe Photoshop, palettes are often grouped with other palettes. However, you can move, separate, and combine these palettes any way you like.

1 Choose View > Fit Spread in Window.

2 Click the Navigator palette tab to bring it to the front of the palette group.

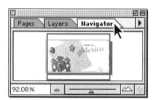

3 Position the pointer on the black triangle to the right of the Navigator tab, and choose View All Spreads from the Navigator palette menu. If you can't see the three spreads well, drag the lower right corner of the palette down to resize it; drag it back up when you're finished.

Like many palettes, the Navigator palette has a
menu that displays additional options.

Notice that the red view box in the Navigator palette determines which area of the document is displayed.

4 In the Navigator palette, click the middle spread to view pages 4 and 5. If necessary, drag the red box so that you can see pages 4 and 5.

Now we'll look at the Pages palette, which is another useful tool for turning pages. You'll be using the Pages palette throughout this tour, so you'll separate the Pages palette from the other two palettes.

5 Click the Pages palette tab, and then drag the Pages tab below the other palettes.

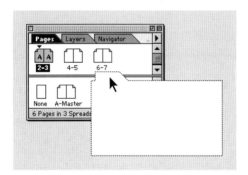

Feel free to move and rearrange palettes in this Quick Tour as needed. If the palettes are blocking your work area, you can move a palette by dragging its top bar, or you can click the minimize button or close button on the top bar. When you need to use the palette again, click the restore button or choose the appropriate menu command (such as Window > Pages to display the Pages palette).

6 In the Pages palette, double-click the numbers 6-7 below the page icons to view the last spread in the document.

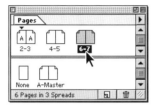

Double-clicking the numbers below the page icons centers the full spread in the document window. Double-clicking a page icon centers the page in the document window.

Now that you've seen all three spreads, let's go back to page 3 and start working.

7 In the Pages palette, double-click the page 3 icon to move to page 3.

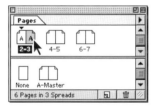

Turning on guides

In this document, the guides are hidden. You'll turn on the guides to make it easy to see your layout grid and snap objects into place.

Choose View > Show Guides.

Before and after turning on guides

Threading text in frames

In InDesign, all text exists inside frames. You can either add text to a frame that has already been created, or you can create the frame while you import text.

Placing and flowing text

An article describing Judith and Clyde's trip to Oaxaca has been saved in a word processor file. You'll place this file on page 3 and then thread it throughout your document.

1 Make sure no objects are selected, and choose File > Place. Double-click 01_a.doc in the Tour folder.

The pointer takes the shape of a loaded text icon (⊞). With a loaded text icon, you can drag to create a text frame, click inside an existing frame, or click to create a frame within a column. You'll add a column of text to the lower half of page 3.

2 Position the loaded text icon just below the fourth guide from the bottom margin and just to the right of the left margin, and click.

The text flows into a new frame in the lower half of the first column on page 3. When a text frame has more text than can fit, the frame is said to have *overset* text. Overset text is indicated by a red plus symbol in the out port of the frame.

💡 *If the text box is not placed in the left column, click the selection tool (▸) and drag the sizing handles to move it to the proper location.*

3 Click the out port in the selected frame.

The pointer becomes a loaded text icon. Now you'll add a column of text to the lower half of the second column.

4 Position the loaded text icon just below the fourth guide from the bottom margin and just to the right of the second column guide, and click.

Threading text

Clicking the out port to flow text is called *manual threading*. You can also hold down Shift to thread text automatically so that all the overset text is flowed into the columns, but you don't want to do that in this document because the text frames should not appear on every page. However, you can hold down Alt (Windows) or Option (Mac OS) to thread text one frame at a time without having to reload the text icon.

1 Click the out port in the second column.

2 To center page 4 in the document window, double-click the page 4 icon in the Pages palette.

3 Holding down Alt (Windows) or Option (Mac OS), position the loaded text icon in the upper left corner of the first column, and click. Release the Alt/Option key.

The text flows into the left column. Because you held down Alt/Option, the pointer is still a loaded text icon.

4 Position the loaded text icon in the upper left corner of the second column on page 4, and click.

Whenever the pointer is a loaded text icon, you can click any tool in the toolbox to cancel. No text will be lost.

Now you'll flow the text into the bottom of the two columns on page 7.

5 Click the out port in the second column, and then double-click the page 7 icon in the Pages palette to center page 7 in the document window.

6 Holding down Alt/Option, position the loaded text icon in the left column below the guide on page 7, and click. Release the Alt/Option key.

7 Position the loaded text icon in the second column below the guide, and click.

You have just finished threading text frames. A threaded set of frames is called a *story*.

8 Choose File > Save.

Adding a pull quote

To enhance the design on page 4 of your document, you'll add a pull quote. We copied text from the article and placed it into a frame on the pasteboard. You will position this pull-quote text frame in the middle of page 4 and finish formatting it.

1 In the Pages palette, double-click the page 4 icon. If you cannot see the pull-quote text frame to the left of page 4, locate the scroll box on the horizontal scroll bar and drag it to the left.

2 Using the selection tool (↖), drag the text frame from the pasteboard so that it's centered between the columns of text on page 4. If necessary, use the arrow keys to nudge the frame. The bottom of the frame should pass through the middle of the red star.

3 Choose View > Fit Page in Window. Then choose File > Save.

Wrapping text around an object

The text in the pull quote is difficult to read because the main story text does not wrap around the text frame. You'll wrap the main story text around the pull-quote frame.

1 Make sure the pull-quote frame is selected.

2 Choose Object > Text Wrap.

3 In the Text Wrap palette, click the third wrap option to wrap text around the object's shape.

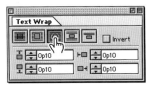

4 Click the Close button to close the Text Wrap palette.

5 Choose File > Save.

Adding a stroke to the frame

Now you'll change the color of the text frame so that the stroke (border) matches the color of the red star. When you apply colors in InDesign, it's a good idea to use the Swatches palette instead of the Colors palette. Using the Swatches palette to name colors makes it easy to apply, edit, and update colors efficiently for all objects in a document.

The magazine in which the article will appear will be sent to a commercial press, so we're using CMYK process colors. We've already added the set of necessary colors to the Swatches palette.

1 With the text frame still selected, click the Stroke box (⬚) in the toolbox. Selecting the Stroke box will allow the frame of the image to be affected by the color you select.

2 Choose Window > Swatches, and then select PANTONE® Warm Red CVC in the Swatches palette.

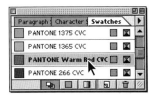

3 To change the weight of the stroke, choose Window > Stroke.

4 For Weight, select 0.5 pt.

5 Click the Close button to close the Stroke palette.

6 Choose Edit > Deselect All.

The text frame now has a thin red stroke.

7 Choose File > Save.

Changing the frame inset

The text in the pull-quote frame is too close to the edge, making it unattractive and difficult to read. You'll now change the frame inset.

1 Using the selection tool ( ), click the pull-quote text frame to select it, and then choose Object > Text Frame Options.

2 Under Inset Spacing, type **1** for Top, Left, Bottom, and Right. (Pressing Tab moves the focus to the next option in a dialog box.)

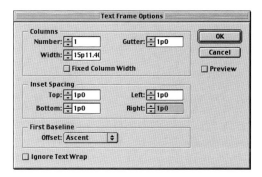

3 Click OK.

The pull-quote text is pushed away 1 pica from the inside edges of the frame.

Changing the margin alignment

To make the opening quotation mark appear outside the frame inset, you can change the optical margin alignment.

1 With the pull-quote frame still selected, choose Type > Story.

2 Select Optical Margin Alignment.

Selecting this option causes punctuation and edges of wide characters (such as W, X, and Y) to "hang" outside the margins.

3 For font size, select 18 pt.

As a general rule, you get the best margin alignment when you select the same size font that the text in your story uses. In this case, the pull quote uses an 18-point font.

4 Click the Close button to close the Story palette. Choose Edit > Deselect All to view the completed pull-quote frame.

5 Choose File > Save.

Working with styles

InDesign includes two kinds of styles. A *paragraph* style includes both character and paragraph formatting attributes. A *character* style includes only character attributes, making it useful for formatting words and phrases within a paragraph.

Applying paragraph styles

To save time, we created paragraph styles that you'll apply next. These styles will help you format the body text in the article.

1 In the Pages palette, double-click the page 3 icon to center page 3 in the document window.

2 Select the type tool (T), and then click anywhere in the columns of text.

3 Choose Edit > Select All to select the text in all the frames of the story.

4 Choose Type > Paragraph Styles to display the Paragraph Styles palette.

5 In the Paragraph Styles palette, select Body Text to format the entire story with the Body Text style.

6 Choose Edit > Deselect All to deselect the text.

Now you'll apply a different paragraph style to the first paragraph of the story.

7 Using the type tool (T), click anywhere in the first paragraph on page 3.

8 In the Paragraph Styles palette, select Body Text / Drop Cap.

Like other options in the Paragraph and Character palettes, drop caps can be part of a style.

9 Choose File > Save.

Formatting text for the character style

Now you'll create and apply a character style to emphasize page references within paragraphs. Before you create this character style, you'll use the Character palette to italicize the text and make it one point smaller. You'll then base the character style on this formatted text.

1 In the Pages palette, double-click the page 7 icon to center page 7 in the document window. To make sure you can read the text at the bottom of this page, press Ctrl++ (Windows) or Command++ (Mac OS) and use the scroll bars as necessary.

You should be able to see three references to other pages: (page 7), (page 2), and (page 5).

2 Using the type tool (T), select the "(page 7)" reference.

3 Choose Type > Character to display the Character palette (grouped with the Transform and Paragraph palettes).

4 Select Italic from the Type Style menu. For font size (T), select 11 pt.

The page reference is now formatted.

5 Choose File > Save.

Creating and applying a character style

Now that you have formatted the text, you are ready to create a character style.

1 Make sure the text you formatted is still selected, and choose Type > Character Styles to display the Character Styles palette.

2 Click the New Style button at the bottom of the Character Styles palette.

A new character style named Character Style 1 is created. This new style includes the characteristics of the selected text.

3 In the Character Styles palette, double-click Character Style 1 to open the Modify Character Style Options dialog box.

4 For Style Name, type **Emphasis** and click OK.

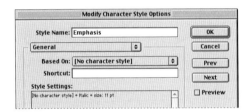

5 Using the type tool (T), select "(page 2)" in the next paragraph, and then select Emphasis in the Character Styles palette.

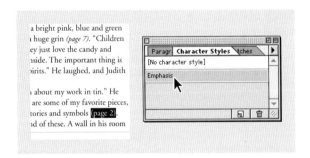

6 Apply the character style to "(page 5)" in the same paragraph.

Because you used a character style instead of a paragraph style, the style you applied affected only the selected text, not the entire paragraph.

7 Choose File > Save.

Placing graphics

Graphics you insert are automatically placed inside frames. When dealing with graphics, you should become familiar with the two selection tools.

The selection tool ( ) is used for general layout tasks, such as positioning and sizing objects. The direct-selection tool ( ) is used for tasks involving drawing and editing paths or frames; for example, to select frame contents or to move an anchor point on a path. The direct-selection tool is also used for selecting objects within frames or groups.

Working with grouped objects

The three stars on page 5 are grouped together. You'll select the right-most star so that you can change its color.

1 In the Pages palette, double-click the page 5 icon to center page 5 in the document window. Choose View > Fit Page in Window.

2 Using the selection tool ( ), click the black star on page 5 to select it.

Notice that the star is part of a group. Instead of having to ungroup the objects to select only the black star, you can use the direct-selection tool ( ) to select the object within a group.

3 Click the direct-selection tool (↖), and then click the black star.

The anchor points of the selected object appear.

4 To change the fill color to purple, select the Fill box (⬚) in the toolbox, choose Window > Swatches, and then select PANTONE 265 in the Swatches palette.

Using the pen tool to reshape an object

The purple star you selected needs another ray to match the other stars. You'll use the pen tool to add anchor points so that you can create a new ray in the star.

1 Position the pointer over the pen tool in the toolbox, and then click and hold down the mouse button to display additional tools. Select the add anchor point tool.

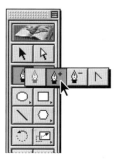

2 Click the edge of the star twice to add two anchor points.

3 Select the direct-selection tool (⬐), and then drag the lower of the two anchor points away from the star to create another ray.

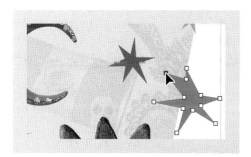

4 Use the direct-selection tool (⟨) to drag anchor points as needed to reshape the star.

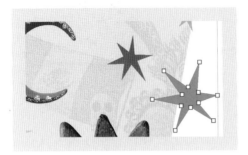

5 Choose File > Save.

Targeting layers when placing

Like Illustrator and Photoshop, InDesign lets you place objects on different layers. Think of layers as sheets of transparent film that are stacked on top of each other. By using layers, you can create and edit objects on one layer without affecting—or being affected by— objects on other layers. Layers also determine the stacking position of objects.

Before you place a photograph of an armadillo, you'll make sure you'll add the frame to the appropriate layer.

1 In the Pages palette, double-click the page 3 icon to center page 3 in the document window.

2 Choose Window > Layers to display the Layers palette.

3 Click the word "Photos" in the Layers palette to target the Photos later. (Do not click the boxes to the left of the Photos layer, or you'll hide or lock the layer.)

4 Select the selection tool (⟨).

5 Choose File > Place, and double-click the 01_b.tif file located in the Tour folder.

6 With the loaded graphics icon (), click above the top margin to place the armadillo at the top of the page. You'll move the graphic later, after you rotate and crop it.

Notice that the armadillo frame is the same color as the Photos layer in the Layers palette. An object's frame color tells you which layer it belongs to.

7 In the Layers palette, click the box next to the Text layer name so that the crossed-out pencil icon (✗) appears.

By locking the objects on the Text layer, you will be able to edit the frame containing the armadillo without accidentally selecting the frame containing "Hecho en Mexico."

Rotating the photograph

Because the frame and photo are independent of each other, you can rotate the photo without rotating the frame.

1 Click outside the armadillo to deselect it.

2 Select the direct-selection tool (▹), and then click the armadillo to select it.

Using the direct-selection tool to select the object lets you rotate only the armadillo photograph, not the entire frame.

3 Select the rotate tool (⟳) in the toolbox.

The crosshair icon, which appears in the upper left anchor point of the frame, determines the point of rotation. You can change the crosshair location using the proxy icon in the Transform palette.

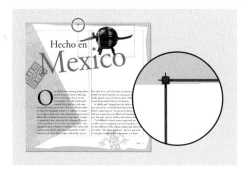

4 In the Transform palette, click the center point of the proxy icon to move the crosshair icon to the center of the selected frame.

5 Drag any of the selection handles to rotate the object clockwise.

6 Choose File > Save.

Cropping and moving the photograph

You'll now use the selection tool to crop and move the photograph.

1 Choose Edit > Deselect All. Select the selection tool (↖) in the toolbox, and then click the armadillo.

Notice that the frame enclosing the armadillo has not been rotated—the frame and photo are separate objects.

2 Position the pointer over the middle handle on the right side of the armadillo frame and hold down the mouse button. Drag the frame toward the center of the armadillo to crop it.

3 Using the selection tool (↖), position the pointer over the center of the armadillo frame and drag the object so that it snaps to the right edge of the page.

Notice that the edge of the armadillo is behind the decorative border. This is because the Photos layer is below the Graphics layer in the Layers palette.

4 Choose File > Save.

Working with master pages

A master page is like a background that you can quickly apply to many pages. You can apply master page formatting to any of the pages in your document.

In this document, the master page includes a border and page numbers for facing pages. You may have noticed that the master pages are applied to pages 2 and 3 (as indicated by the letter A), but the master pages are not applied to pages 4–7.

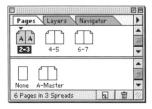

Editing master pages

On the A-Master pages, the right footer has placeholder text for the magazine issue. You'll edit this text and then apply the A-Master to pages 4–7.

1 In the lower half of the Pages palette, double click the right A-Master page icon to center the right master page in the document window.

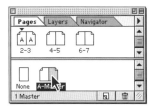

This master page includes a decorative border surrounding the spread and text frames at the bottom of each master page. You'll edit the footer on the right master page to change "Issue" to "Fall/Winter." However, this text frame belongs to the Text layer, which is currently locked.

2 In the Layers palette, click the lock icon next to the Text layer so that the lock icon is removed.

3 Select the zoom tool (🔍), and then drag across the lower right corner of the master page to zoom in on the footer text.

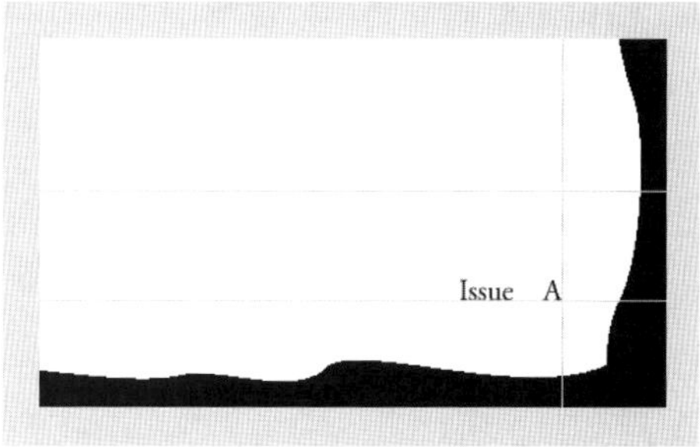

4 Select the type tool (T), and then drag across the word "Issue." (Do not select the em space after the word or the letter A, which is the page number marker.)

5 Type **Fall/Winter**.

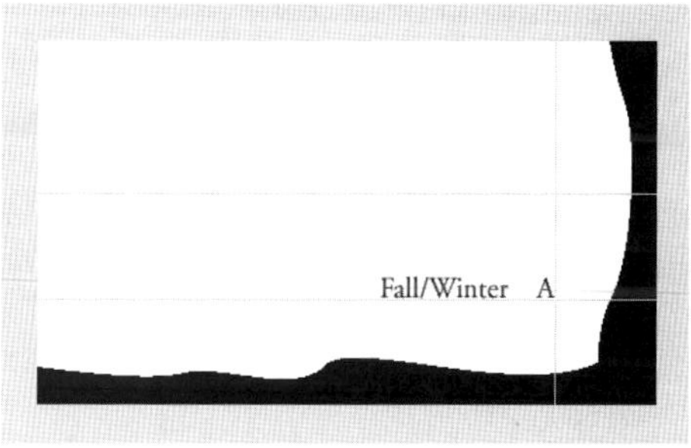

Applying master pages to document pages

Now you'll apply the A-Master pages to the spreads on pages 4–5 and 6–7.

1 Select the selection tool (➤).

2 In the Pages palette, double-click pages 4–5 below the page icons. Choose View > Fit Spread in Window to see both pages of the spread.

3 In the Pages palette, click A-Master below the A-Master icons so that both A-Master pages are highlighted, and drag the hand pointer over pages "4–5" until you see a box around both page icons; release the mouse button.

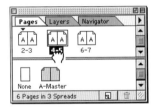

When you drag a master over the page numbers below the page icons, the master is applied to both pages in the spread.

4 Repeat step 3 to apply the A-Master to the page 6–7 spread.

The A-Master is now applied to all the pages in the document.

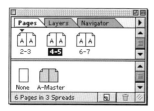

5 Choose File > Save.

Overriding master page items

To vary the design, we want to change the color of the border on pages 4–7 to match the background color of each spread. Instead of re-creating these items on a new master page, you can alter them on the actual pages.

1 Click the black decorative border surrounding pages 4–5 to try to select it.

You cannot select the object by clicking it because the object belongs to the master page. However, you can override the master page object.

2 Using the selection tool ( ), hold down Shift+Command (Mac OS) or Shift+Ctrl (Windows) and click the black border surrounding pages 4–5 to select it.

3 Make sure the Fill box ( ) is selected in the toolbox, and then select PANTONE 116 in the Swatches palette.

4 In the Pages palette, double-click pages 6–7 below the page icons to center the spread in the document window.

5 Using the selection tool ( ), hold down Shift+Command (Mac OS) or Shift+Ctrl (Windows) and click the black border surrounding pages 6–7 to select it.

6 Make sure the Fill box () in the toolbox is selected, and then select PANTONE 390 in the Swatches palette.

When you changed the color of the master page object on the layout page, you did not break the connection between the master page object and the layout page object; only the color is different. If you decided to move the object on the master page, the object on the layout page would also move.

Viewing your document

Now let's take a look at your completed document.

1 Choose Edit > Deselect All. Then choose View > Hide Guides.

2 From the zoom pop-up menu in the lower left corner of the document window, select 25% to view all the spreads. If necessary, select a different zoom percentage so that you can view all three spreads.

3 Press Tab to hide palettes.

When you want to see an unobstructed view of your document, pressing Tab will remove the palettes.

4 Press Tab again to show palettes.

5 Choose File > Save.

On your own

Congratulations! You've completed the InDesign tour. You're now ready to create your own InDesign documents. To learn more about InDesign, you may want to try the following:

• Continue experimenting with the travel document. Add new pages, edit the master pages, move items among the layers, create text frames, and adjust the graphics using the tools in the toolbox.

• Choose Help > Help Topics to use online Help.

• Go through the lessons in the rest of this book.

Lesson 1

1 | Getting to Know the Work Area

To make the best use of the extensive drawing, layout, and editing capabilities in Adobe InDesign, it's important to learn how to navigate the work area. The work area consists of the document window, the pasteboard, the toolbox, and the floating palettes.

In this lesson, you'll learn how to do the following:

- Work with tools, document windows, the pasteboard, and palettes

- Change the magnification of the document

- Navigate through a document

- Work with layers

- Use context menus and online Help

- Use Adobe online services

Note: This lesson covers tasks that are common to Adobe products such as Photoshop, Illustrator, and Acrobat. If you are familiar with these Adobe products, you may want to skim through this lesson and move ahead to the next lesson.*

Getting started

In this lesson, you'll practice using the work area and navigating through pages of the *Exploring the Library* booklet. This is the final version of the document—you won't be changing or adding text or graphics, only checking to make sure everything is ready for print. Before you begin, you'll need to restore the default preferences for Adobe InDesign.

1 To ensure that the tools and palettes function exactly as described in this lesson, delete or deactivate (by renaming) the InDesign Defaults file and the InDesign SavedData file. See "Restoring default preferences" on page 2.

2 Start Adobe InDesign.

To begin working, you'll open an existing InDesign document.

3 Choose File > Open, and open the 01_a.indd file in the ID_01 folder, located inside the Lessons folder within the IDCIB folder on your hard disk.

4 Choose File > Save As, rename the file **01_Library.indd**, and save it in the ID_01 folder.

Note: This document was saved with the frame edges hidden (View > Hide Frame Edges). By default, frame edges are visible in all documents.

Looking at the work area

InDesign's work area encompasses everything you see when you first open or create a document: the toolbox, document window, pasteboard, and palettes. You can customize the work area to suit your work style. For example, you can display only the palettes you frequently use, minimize and rearrange palette groups, resize windows, add additional document windows, and so on.

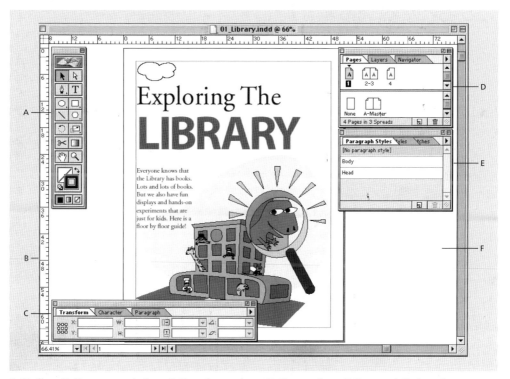

A. *Toolbox* **B.** *Document window* **C.** *Transform palette* **D.** *Pages palette* **E.** *Paragraph Styles palette*
F. *Pasteboard*

Toolbox

The InDesign toolbox contains tools for selecting objects, working with type, drawing, and viewing, as well as controls for applying and changing color fills, strokes, and gradients.

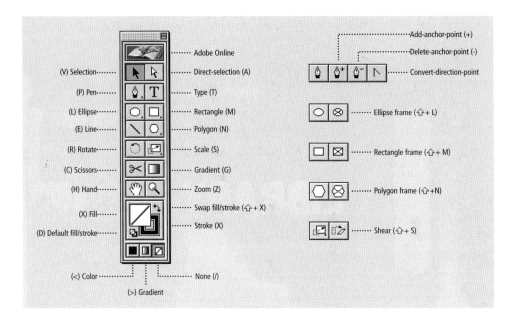

As you work through the lessons, you'll learn about each tool's specific function. Here you'll familiarize yourself with the toolbox and the tools.

1 Position the pointer over the selection tool ( ) in the toolbox. Notice the name and shortcut are displayed. You can select a tool by either clicking the tool in the toolbox or pressing the tool's keyboard shortcut.

2 Position the pointer over the pen tool and hold down the mouse button—additional pen tools appear. Drag to the right and release the mouse button over one of the additional tools to select it. Any tool that displays a small black triangle at the bottom right corner contains additional tools.

3 Select the selection tool again; then click the little cloud in the top left corner of page 1 to select it.

Now you'll use the color controls, which are located on the bottom half of the toolbox.

4 Select the Fill box to make sure any changes you make affect the center portion of the object and not its stroke.

5 Click the Color box (■) in the toolbox. The object becomes filled with solid black. Click the Gradient box (▤). The object becomes filled with a white-to-black gradient. Click the None box (☒) to return the object to its original unfilled state.

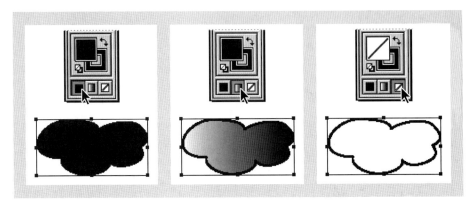

Object filled with black (left), filled with a gradient (center), and reset to no fill (right).

Note: *If you accidently double-click a Fill or Gradient box, the Fill or Gradient palette will open. Close the palette to continue with the lesson.*

6 Now select the Stroke box (▣) so that any changes you make affect the object's stroke.

7 Click the Gradient box (▣) in the toolbox. The solid stroke becomes a gradient stroke. Click the Color box (■) to return to the object to its original stroke.

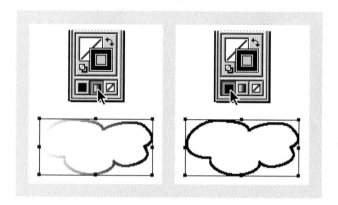

To learn how to change the color of a fill, stroke, or gradient, see "Creating and Applying Colors, Tints, and Gradients" on page 127.

Document window

The document window contains your document pages. All palettes and tools float on top of the document window. You set margins for the document when you first open a new document, and then you place, type, or create all text and artwork on the document pages. You can have more than one document window open at a time. Here, you'll open a second window so you can see two different views of the document at the same time as you work.

1 Choose Window > New Window. A new window titled 01_Library.indd:2 opens.

2 To view both windows simultaneously, choose Window > Tile.

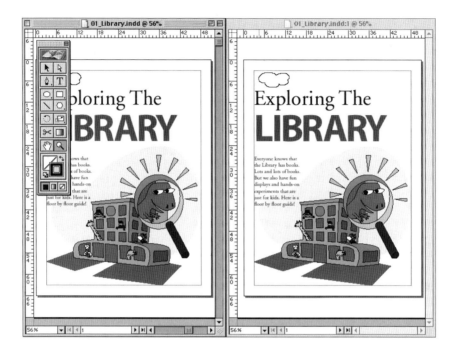

3 Now select the zoom tool in the toolbox (🔍) and click twice on the dinosaur in the 01_Library.indd:2 document window. Notice how the original document window remains at the original magnification. This arrangement lets you work closely on details and see the overall results on the rest of the page.

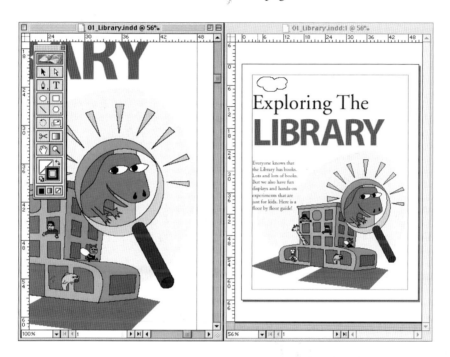

4 Close the 01_Library.indd:2 document window, and click the maximize button for the remaining document window to return it to full size.

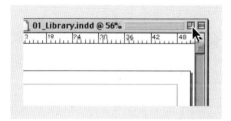

Pasteboard

Each page or spread in your document has its own pasteboard surrounding it, where you can store objects before positioning them. Pasteboards also provide the additional space along each edge of the document for extending objects past the edge of the page (also known as creating a bleed).

1 To see the full size of the pasteboard for the pages in this document, choose View > Entire Pasteboard.

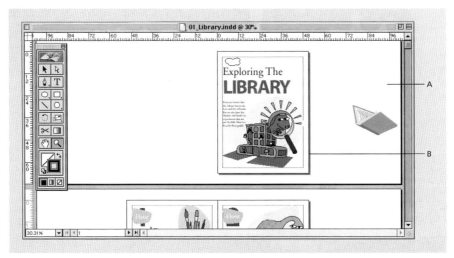

A. Pasteboard B. Document

Notice the book graphic on the pasteboard for page 1. This graphic was originally placed in the document, but then moved to the pasteboard in anticipation that it would be used somewhere else in the document. It is no longer necessary to keep this image with the document.

2 Using the selection tool, select the book image on the pasteboard and press Delete.

3 Choose View > Fit Page in Window to restore the window to its previous size.

4 Choose File > Save.

Palettes

Palettes provide a quick access to commonly used tools and features in InDesign. By default, palettes appear in stacked groups, which you can reorganize in various ways. Here you'll experiment with hiding, closing, and opening palettes.

1 Press Tab to hide all open palettes and the toolbox. Press Tab again to display them all again.

Note: you can hide or display just the palettes (not the toolbox) by pressing Shift+Tab.

2 Choose Window > Stroke to open the Stroke palette group. Click the Attributes tab in the Stroke palette group to make the Attributes palette appear at the front of the group.

Now you'll reorganize a palette group.

3 From the Stroke palette group, drag the Attribute palette's tab outside of the group to create a new group.

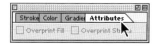 

Palettes are grouped (left). Drag the palette tab to separate a palette from the group (right).

4 Now drag the Attribute palette's tab into the Pages palette group. Then drag the tab back to the Stroke palette group. You can combine any palette with any palette group or create your own palette group consisting of the palettes you use most.

5 Close the Stroke palette group.

Now you'll organize the palettes to create more space in your work area.

6 Drag the lower right corner of the Pages palette to change the height of the palette. Then click the minimize/maximize box (Windows) or the resize box (Mac OS) to collapse the group to the palette titles only. Click the box again to expand the group.

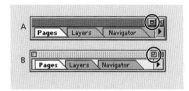

Click to collapse or expand palette in
Windows (A) or Mac OS (B).

Some palettes, such as the Transform palette, have a triangle in the upper right corner, from which you can access a menu containing additional commands and features.

7 In the Transform palette group, position the pointer on the triangle in the upper right corner of the palette, and hold down the mouse button to display the palette menu.

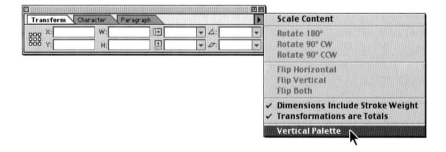

8 Choose Vertical Palette. This command changes the orientation of the Transform palette, but not the other palettes in the group. The commands in the palette menu apply only to the active palette.

9 From the Transform palette menu, choose Horizontal Palette to return the palette to its original size.

Changing the magnification of your document

You can reduce or enlarge the view of the document to any magnification level from 5% to 4000%. InDesign displays the percentage of the document's actual size in the title bar, next to the filename, and at the lower left corner of the document window.

Using the view commands and magnification menu

You can easily enlarge or reduce the view of a document by doing one of the following:

• Choose a percentage from the magnification menu at the lower left corner of the document window to enlarge or reduce the display by any preset increment.

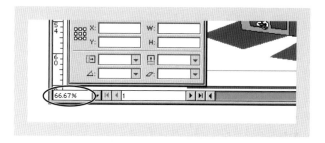

• Type a percentage in the magnification menu.

• Choose View > Zoom In to enlarge the display by one preset increment.

• Choose View > Zoom Out to reduce the display by one preset increment.

Note: *Preset sizes are those listed in the magnification menu.*

• Choose View > Actual Size to display the document at 100%. (Depending on the dimensions of your document and your screen resolution, you may or may not see the entire document on-screen.)

• Choose View > Fit Page in Window to display the targeted page in the window.

• Choose View > Fit Spread in Window to display the targeted spread in the window.

Using the zoom tool

In addition to the view commands, you can use the zoom tool to magnify and reduce the view of a document.

1 Select the zoom tool (⚲) in the toolbox and position it over the dinosaur on page 1. Notice that a plus sign appears at the center of the zoom tool (⚲).

2 Click once. The view changes to the next preset magnification.

3 Click again over the dinosaur on page 1. The view of the area you clicked is magnified again. Notice that the page is centered on the point where you clicked. Now you'll reduce the view.

4 Position the zoom tool pointer over the dinosaur and hold down Alt (Windows) or Option (Mac OS). A minus sign appears at the center of the zoom tool (⚲).

5 With Alt/Option still held down, click twice over the dinosaur; the view is reduced.

In addition to clicking the zoom tools, you can drag a marquee to magnify a specific area of your document.

6 With the zoom tool still selected, hold down the mouse button and drag a marquee around the dinosaur; then release the mouse.

The percentage by which the area is magnified depends on the size of the marquee (the smaller the marquee, the larger the level of magnification).

Dragging a marque with the zoom tool (left) and the resulting view (right)

Note: *You can also draw a marquee to reduce the view.*

7 Double-click the zoom tool in the toolbox to return to a 100% view.

Because the zoom tool is used frequently during the editing process to enlarge and reduce the view of your document, you can temporarily select it from the keyboard at any time without deselecting any other tool you may be using. You'll do that now.

8 Click the selection tool in the toolbox and position it in the document window.

9 Hold down Ctrl+spacebar (Windows) or Command+spacebar (Mac OS). The selection tool icon becomes the zoom tool icon.

10 Click on the dinosaur to magnify the view, and release the keys. The pointer returns to the selection tool icon.

11 Hold down Ctrl+Alt+spacebar (Windows) or Command+Option+spacebar (Mac OS) and click to zoom out, returning to a 100% view.

12 Choose View > Fit Spread in Window to center the page.

Navigating through your document

InDesign provides several options for viewing and navigating through a document, including the Pages and Navigator palettes, and the scroll bars.

Turning pages

You can turn pages using the Pages palette, the page buttons at the bottom of the document window, the scroll bars, or a variety of commands.

The Pages palette provides page icons for all the pages in your document. Double-clicking on any page icon or page numbers brings that page or spread into view. Double-clicking the numbers below the page icons centers a spread in the document window; double-clicking one page icon for a spread centers that page in the document window.

Targeting and selecting spreads using the Pages palette

You can target or select spreads, depending on the task at hand:

• Target a spread where the next new object should appear. For example, this is helpful when several spreads are visible in the document window and you want to paste an object on a specific spread. Only one spread can be the target at any time. By default, the target spread currently occupies the center of the document window. The target spread is indicated by the highlighted page numbers (not highlighted page icons) in the Pages palette and by a vertical ruler that is not dimmed.

• Select a page or spread when your next action will affect a page or spread rather than objects, such as setting margin and column options for a specific page only. When all pages of a spread are highlighted in the Pages palette, that spread is selected. You can select multiple spreads in a document. The selected spread is indicated by the highlighted page icons (not highlighted page numbers) in the Pages palette.

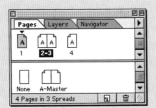

Page 1 selected; pages 2 and 3 targeted.

–From the Adobe InDesign User Guide, Chapter 3

1 Make sure the selection tool (↖) is still selected.

2 In the Pages palette, double-click the 2–3 page numbers below the page icons to target and view the spread on pages 2 and 3. The spread opens and appears centered in the document window.

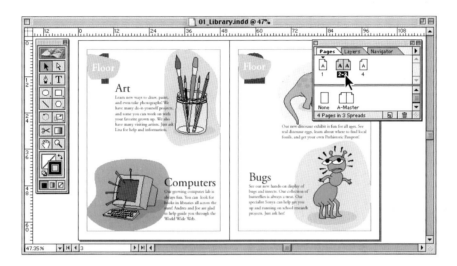

3 Double-click the page 3 icon to select and center only that page in the document window.

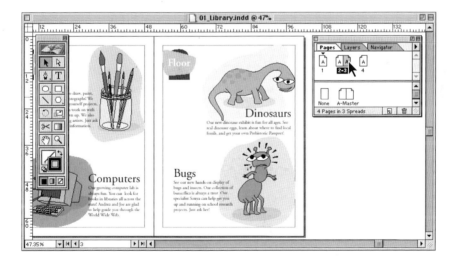

Now you'll use the page buttons at the bottom of the document window to change pages.

4 Click the next-page button (▶) at the lower left corner of the document window to go to page 4.

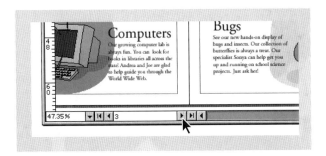

You can also turn to a specific page number by typing the number in the page box.

5 Select 4 in the page box at the lower left of the document window, type **1**, and press Enter or Return.

Now you'll change pages using a menu command.

6 Choose Layout > Go Back to return to page 4.

7 Choose Layout > Previous Page to turn to page 3.

You can experiment with all the different methods. For a full list of commands used for turning pages, see "Turning pages" in Chapter 2 of the InDesign User Guide.

Scrolling through a document

You can also use the hand tool and the scrollbars along the side of the document window to move to different areas or pages of a document. Here you'll use both methods to navigate through the document.

1 Drag the scrollbar along the right side of the document window all the way to the top to view page 1.

2 With the selection tool selected in the toolbox and the pointer positioned over the document, hold down the spacebar on the keyboard. Notice that the selection tool icon changes to the hand tool. You can use this shortcut when you don't want to change tools while moving through the document. You can also simply select the hand tool (✋) in the toolbox.

3 With the spacebar still held down, drag upward in the document window until the page 2–3 spread appears on-screen. As you drag, the document moves with the hand.

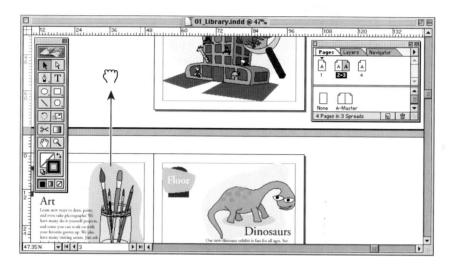

You can also use the hand tool as a shortcut to fit the page or spread in the window.

4 Double-click the hand tool in the toolbox to fit the spread in the window.

5 Using the hand tool, click on or near the bug in the lower right corner and drag to center it in the window.

Using the Navigator palette

The Navigator palette provides several navigation and view tools in one location so you can quickly and easily magnify and scroll to a desired location.

1 Click the Navigator palette tab (or choose Window > Navigator) to make sure it is at the front of the palette group.

2 In the Navigator palette, drag the slider to the right to magnify the view. As you drag the slider to increase the level of magnification, the red outline in the Navigator window decreases in size, showing you the area of view.

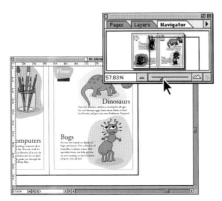 

Increasing the magnification using the Navigator palette

3 In the Navigator palette, position the pointer inside the red outline. The pointer becomes a hand, which you can use to scroll to different areas of the page or spread.

4 Drag the hand to scroll to the upper left corner of page 2.

5 Save the file.

 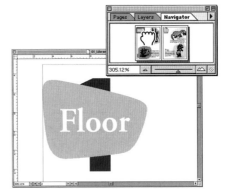

Scrolling to a different area using the Navigator palette

Working with layers

By default, a new document contains just one layer (named Layer 1). You can rename the layer and add more layers at any time as you create your document. Placing objects on different layers lets you organize them for easy selection and editing. Using the Layers palette, you can select, display, edit, and print different layers individually, in groups, or all together.

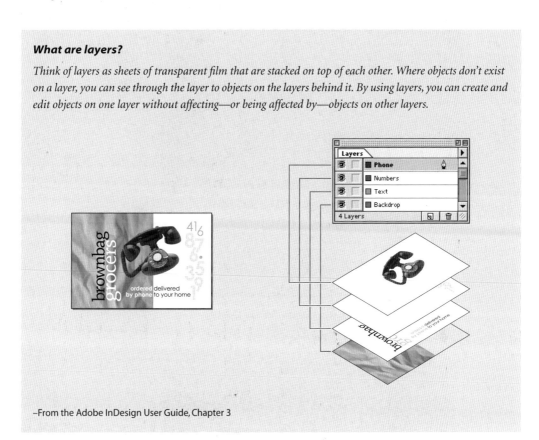

What are layers?

Think of layers as sheets of transparent film that are stacked on top of each other. Where objects don't exist on a layer, you can see through the layer to objects on the layers behind it. By using layers, you can create and edit objects on one layer without affecting—or being affected by—objects on other layers.

–From the Adobe InDesign User Guide, Chapter 3

For a color version of document layers, see figure 1-1 in the color section.

The 01_Library.indd document has three layers. You'll experiment with these layers to learn how the order of the layers and the placement of objects on layers can greatly affect the design of your document.

1 Click the Layers palette tab in the Pages palette group, or choose Window > Layers.

2 In the Layers palette, select the Number layer. Notice that a pen icon (✎) appears to the right of the layer name. This icon indicates that this layer is the target layer and anything you import or create will belong to this layer. The highlight indicates that the layer is selected.

3 In the Layers palette, drag the Number layer between the Floor layer and the Graphics layer; when you see a black line, release the mouse. Notice how the objects now appear in a different order in your document.

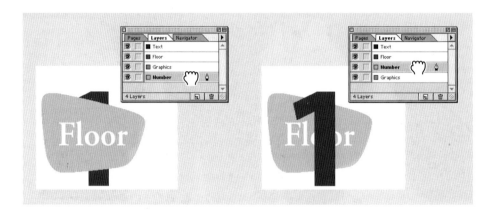

4 Click the empty square to the left of the Number layer name. This square lets you lock a layer so it cannot be edited. When you lock a layer, the palette displays a crossed-out pencil icon in the square.

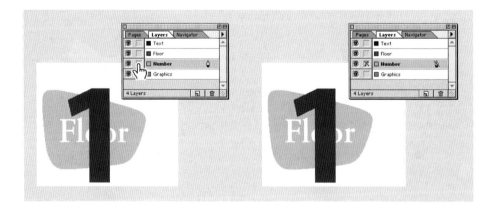

5 Using the selection tool ( ), click the word "Floor" in the document window. Notice in the Layers palette that the Graphics layer is selected and a dot appears to the right of the layer name. This indicates that the selected object belongs to this layer. You can move objects from layer to layer by dragging the dot.

6 In the Layers palette, drag the dot from the Graphics layer to the Floor layer. The word "Floor" now belongs to the Floor layer and appears in the stacking order in the document accordingly.

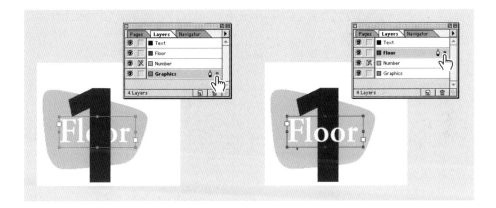

For a color version of moving an object to another layer, see figure 1-2 in the color section.

7 Now that you're done editing the layers, you can click the crossed-out pencil icon for the Number layer to unlock this layer.

8 Save the file.

Using context menus

In addition to the menus at the top of your screen, you can use context-sensitive menus to display commands relevant to the active tool or selection.

To display context-sensitive menus, position the pointer over an object or anywhere in the document window, and click with the right mouse button (Windows) or press Control and hold down the mouse button (Mac OS).

1 Make sure the word "Floor" is still selected.

2 With the selection tool, right-click (Windows) or Control-click (Mac OS) the word. Options for the text under the tool are displayed in the context-sensitive menu. (These same options are in the Object menu.)

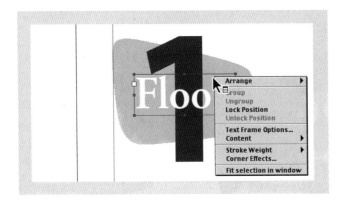

3 Now click in the pasteboard, and then right-click (Windows) or Control-click (Mac OS) the pasteboard. Notice the context menu items change according to what is directly behind the tool.

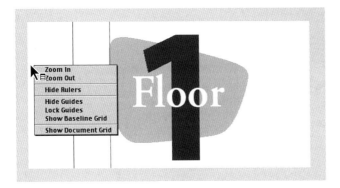

Using online Help

You can use online Help to find all of the information from the InDesign User Guide, plus keyboard shortcuts and additional information.

First you'll look for a topic using the online Help Contents screen.

1 Choose Help > Help Topics. The Adobe InDesign Help Contents screen appears.

2 If necessary, click the Contents tab at the upper left of the Help screen to see a list of topics.

3 Drag the scroll bar or click the arrows to navigate through the contents. The contents are organized in a hierarchy of topics, much like the chapters of a book. Each book icon represents a chapter of information in Help.

 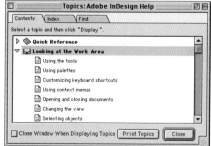

Book icons representing chapters (left); topics and subtopics (right)

4 To display the contents of Looking at the Work Area, double-click that book icon.

5 Locate the "Selecting objects" topic, and double-click to display it. A description of the topic appears along with a color illustration. All illustrations in the user guide appear in color in online Help.

You can click any red underlined text, called a *link*, to jump to another topic. The pointing finger icon ( ) indicates links and appears when you move the pointer over a link or a hotspot.

6 Position the pointer over the red text "Using the selection bounding box, and click. That topic appears.

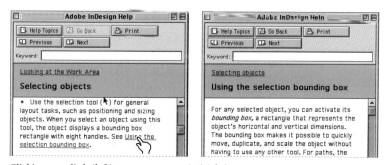

Clicking on a link (left) opens a new topic (right).

7 At the top of the Help window, click >> (Windows) or Next (Mac OS) to display the next topic.

8 To return to the Contents menu, do one of the following:

• In Windows, click Help Topics.

• In Mac OS, close the active Help window.

9 Double-click the Looking at the Work Area book icon to collapse the topic.

Using keywords, links, and the index

If you can't find the topic you are interested in by scanning the Contents page, then you can try searching using links, the index, or a keyword.

1 In the Help Topics window, click the Index tab to display index entries. These entries appear alphabetically by topic and subtopic, like the index of a book.

2 In the Index window, type the term **palettes** in the text box under the instructions for step 1. Then find the subentry "using" (Windows) or "Using palettes" (Mac OS) and select it. The subentries are indexed differently for each platform, but the contents are identical.

3 Click Display to display the entry.

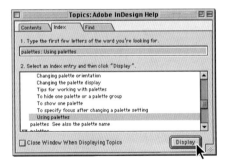

4 Click the Help Topics button at the top of the window to return to the main Help window.

Now you'll search using the Find option. This option creates a list of all the words in the Help system and lets you search by those words rather than just by the words included in topic headings. Here you'll search for text relating to the word "hybrid."

5 Click the Find tab.

6 In Windows, in the Find Setup Wizard dialog box, click Next. Then click Finish.

Windows creates a list of words in your InDesign Help files. It is only necessary to create this list the first time you use InDesign Help.

7 In Windows and Mac OS, type the word **hybrid** in the empty text box under step 1. Notice that you can refine your search by selecting matching words under step 2 (Windows) or by choosing an option from the pop-up menus to the left of the step 1 text box (Mac OS).

8 In Mac OS, click Search.

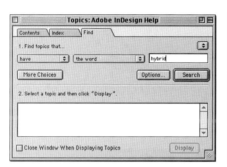 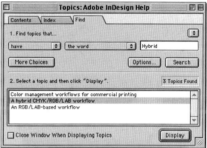

9 In Windows and Mac OS, select "A hybrid CMYK/RGB/LAB workflow" in the list that appears, and then click Display. (You can also double-click the entry to display it.)

10 When you have finished with that topic, you can click the link at the top of the Help window to view more links associated with the topic.

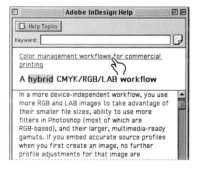 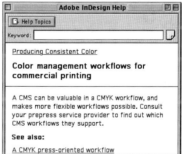

11 When you have finished, close all remaining Help windows.

Using Adobe online services

Another way to get information on Adobe InDesign or on related Adobe products is to use Adobe online services. If you have an Internet connection and a Web browser installed on your system, you can access the Adobe Systems Web site (www.adobe.com). Now you'll take a look at what Adobe Online has to offer:

1 Choose File > Adobe Online, or click the icon at the top of the toolbox.

2 In the Adobe Online window, click Preferences.

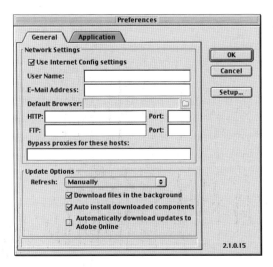

3 Click Setup and follow the prompts to set your Internet connection preferences correctly. See the ReadMe file in your Adobe InDesign folder for more details on setting up your Internet connection.

4 Click OK to accept the preferences and return to the Adobe Online window.

5 Click Refresh. If a message appears asking if you want to update Adobe Online components, click Yes.

A progress bar indicates that the Adobe Online components are being updated.

6 The splash screen for Adobe InDesign online services appears, with buttons linking to topics on the Adobe Web site and links to related sites.

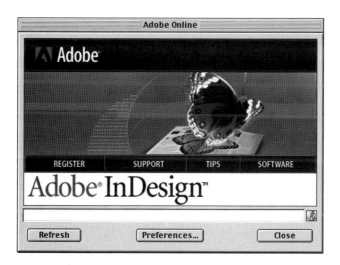

7 Click a topic button to go to the corresponding Adobe Web site.

Using Adobe Online, you can easily find information about InDesign—including tips and techniques, and troubleshooting and technical information. You can also learn about other Adobe products and news.

8 When you have finished browsing the Adobe site, exit from the browser, and then click the Close button in the Adobe Online window.

You've explored the most common aspects of the InDesign work area and should now be able to use the tools and palettes, navigate through your document, and find the help you need to use Adobe InDesign.

9 Save the file, and then close the document window.

On your own

Now that you have explored the work area, try some of the following tasks using either the Library_01.indd document or your own.

1 Display the document in four tiled document windows.

2 Using the Navigator palette, display all the pages of the document simultaneously in the document window.

3 Find information on layers using each of the different search options in online Help: Contents, Index, Keywords (Mac OS only), and Find.

4 Open the links in the Adobe Online window and explore the information available.

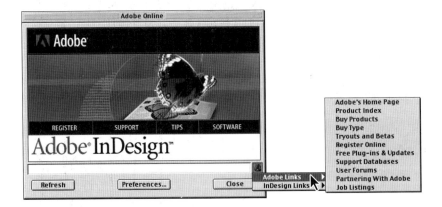

Review questions

1 Describe two ways to change your view of a document.

2 How do you select tools in InDesign?

3 Describe three ways to change the palette display.

4 Describe two ways to get more information about the InDesign program.

Review answers

1 You can select commands from the View menu to zoom in or out of a document, or fit it to your screen; you can also use the zoom tools in the toolbox, and click or drag over a document to enlarge or reduce the view. In addition, you can use keyboard shortcuts to magnify or reduce the display. You can also use the Navigator palette to scroll through a document or change its magnification without using the document window.

2 To select a tool, you can either click the tool in the toolbox or you can press the tool's keyboard shortcut. For example, you can press V to select the selection tool from the keyboard. You select hidden tools by clicking the triangle on a tool in the toolbox and dragging to select from the additional tools that appear.

3 To make the palette appear, you can click a palette's tab or choose a palette name from a menu, for example, Window > Align. You can drag a palette's tab to separate the palette from its group and create a new group, or drag the palette into another group. You can drag a palette group's title bar to move the entire group. Double-click a palette's tab to display palette titles only. You can also press Shift+Tab to hide or display all palettes.

4 Adobe InDesign contains online Help, with all the information in the Adobe InDesign User Guide, plus keyboard shortcuts and full-color illustrations. InDesign also has online services with links to the Adobe Systems Web site for additional information on services, products, and InDesign tips.

Lesson 2

2 | Setting Up Your Document

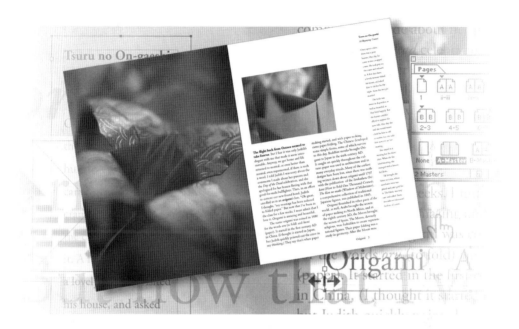

By taking advantage of the tools that help you set up your document, you can ensure a consistent page layout and simplify your work. In this lesson, you'll learn how to create master pages and set columns and guides.

In this introduction to setting up your document, you'll learn how to do the following:

- Start a new document
- Create and edit master pages
- Create additional masters
- Apply the masters to document pages
- Add sections to change page numbering
- Override master page items on document pages
- Add graphics and text to document pages

Getting started

In this lesson, you'll set up a 24-page magazine article about origami, and then you will place text and graphics on one of the spreads. Before you begin, you'll need to restore the default preferences for Adobe InDesign. Then you'll open the finished document for this lesson to see what you'll be creating.

1 To ensure that the tools and palettes function exactly as described in this lesson, delete or deactivate (by renaming) the InDesign Defaults file and the InDesign SavedData file. See "Restoring default preferences" on page 2.

2 Start Adobe InDesign.

3 If you want to see what the finished document will look like, open the 02_b.indd file in the ID_02 folder, located inside the Lessons folder within the IDCIB folder on your hard disk. You can leave this document open to act as a guide as you work .

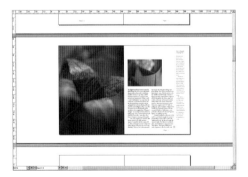

 For a color version of the finished document, see the color section.

The document window shows several spreads, including pages 2–3, which is the only spread that you'll complete in this lesson. You can refer to this document throughout this lesson.

Note: As you work through the lesson, feel free to move palettes around or change the magnification to a level that works best for you. For more information, see "Changing the magnification of your document" on page 50 and "Using the Navigator palette" on page 57.

Starting a new document

When you first start a new document, the Document Setup dialog box appears. You'll use this dialog box to specify the number of pages, the page size, and the number of columns.

1 Choose File > New.

2 Make sure the Facing Pages option is selected. For Number of Pages, type **24**. For Width, type **50p3** (the abbreviation for 50 picas and 3 points). For Height, type **65p3**. Under Margins, type **4** for Bottom and leave the Top, Inside, and Outside margins at 3 picas (3p0). Under Columns, type **5** for Number.

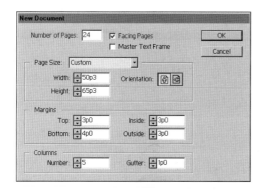

*Note: When you type numbers in a dialog box or palette, you don't need to type the unit of measurement (such as **p** for picas or **pt** for points) if the measurement you're typing is the default. After you type a value and press Tab or click another option, the measurement is applied automatically.*

3 Click OK.

The document window appears, displaying page 1, as indicated in the Pages palette. The Pages palette is divided into two sections. The top half displays icons for document pages in your document. The bottom half displays icons for the master pages. In this document, the master consists of a two-page spread for facing pages.

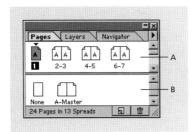

A. Document pages B. Master pages

4 Choose File > Save As, name the file **02_Setup** in the ID_02 folder, and then click Save.

Editing master pages

Before you add graphics and text frames to the document, you'll set up the master pages. A *master page* is like a background that you can apply to pages in your document. Any object you add to master pages will appear on document pages to which the master pages are applied. You'll now add guides and insert footers with page numbering on the master.

Adding guides to the master

Guides are non-printing lines that help you lay out your design precisely. Guides you place on master pages appear on any document pages to which the master is applied. For this document, you'll add a series of guides that, along with the column guides, will act as a grid to which you can snap graphics and text frames into place.

1 In the bottom half of the Pages palette, double-click the A-Master name below the A-Master icon.

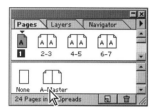

Double-clicking the text below the icons displays both facing pages of the A-Master.

The left and right master pages appear centered in the document window. The highlighted page numbers below the icons in the Pages palette indicate the active page or spread.

2 Choose Layout > Create Guides. Under Rows, type **8** for Number and type **0** for Gutter. For Fit Guides To, select Margins.

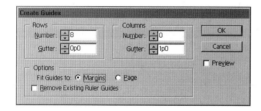

Selecting Margins instead of Page causes the guides to fit within the margin boundaries rather than the page boundaries. You won't add column guides because column lines already appear in your document.

3 Click OK.

A series of horizontal guides appears on your master pages.

Using grids and guides

Two kinds of nonprinting grids are available: A baseline grid for aligning columns of text, and a document grid for aligning objects. To view either grid type, choose View > Show Baseline Grid or View > Show Document Grid. On the screen, a baseline grid resembles ruled notebook paper, and a document grid resembles graph paper. You can customize both kinds of grids.

Ruler guides are different from grids in that they can be positioned freely on a page or on a pasteboard. You can create two kinds of ruler guides: page guides, which appear only on the page on which you create them, or spread guides, which span all pages and the pasteboard of a multiple-page spread.

Take advantage of the following tips as you work with grids and guides:

• To create a spread guide, you can drag the guide from the horizontal or vertical ruler, keeping the pointer in the pasteboard, or you can hold down Ctrl (Windows) or Command (Mac OS) as you drag from the ruler.

• To make guides snap to ruler tick marks, press Shift as you drag.

• To change the color of guides, select the guides and then choose Layout > Ruler Guides. To change the color of grids, choose File > Preferences > Grids, and then specify the new grid colors.

—From Adobe InDesign User Guide, Chapter 3

Dragging guides from rulers

To position the footers accurately, you will add a horizontal guide and two vertical guides.

1 Make sure the A-Master pages are still in view (the page box near the bottom left corner of the document window indicates which page is displayed).

2 Without clicking in your document, move the pointer around the document window, and notice how the hairline indicators in the vertical and horizontal rulers correspond to the pointer's position. The dimmed X and Y values in the Transform palette also indicate the position of the pointer.

3 To zoom out so that you can see both pages, press Ctrl+- (Windows) or Command+- (Mac OS).

Now you will drag a guide from the ruler. Holding down Ctrl (Windows) or Command (Mac OS) while dragging a guide applies the guide to the spread instead of the individual page.

4 Holding down Ctrl (Windows) or Command (Mac OS), position the pointer in the horizontal ruler and drag to the 62 pica marker to create a ruler guide. (You can look in the Transform palette to see the current position.)

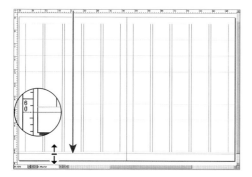

5 To make sure the guide is at the 62 pica location, select the selection tool ( ) in the toolbox, click the guide to select it (the guide changes color), type **62p** in the Y box of the Transform palette, and then press Return or Enter.

6 Drag a ruler guide from the vertical ruler to the 20p1.2 pica marker (the ruler guide will snap to the column guide at that location). Drag another guide from the vertical ruler to the 80p4.8 marker.

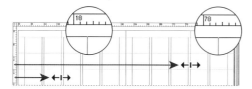

When you are selecting and dragging frames, it's common to drag guides accidentally. To prevent guides from being dragged, you'll lock guides.

7 Choose View > Lock Guides. Then choose File > Save.

Creating a footer text frame in the master

Any text or graphics that you place on the master page will appear on pages to which the master is applied. To create a footer, you'll add a publication title ("Origami") and a page-number marker to the bottom of both master pages.

1 Make sure that you can see the bottom of the right master page. If necessary, zoom in, use the scroll bars or hand tool, and move any palette that is in the way.

2 Select the type tool (T) in the toolbox. On the right master page, drag to create a text frame below the fourth column, as shown. Don't worry about drawing the frame in exactly the right location—you'll snap it into place later.

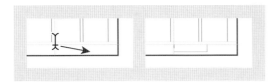

3 Type **Origami**.

4 To add an em space, right-click (Windows) or Control-click (Mac OS) the text frame to display a context menu, and then choose Insert Special Character > Em Space.

5 Choose Layout > Insert Page Number.

The letter A appears after the word "Origami" in your text frame. This character will reflect the current page number in your document pages. For example, the bottom of page 3 will display "Origami 3." Next, you'll change the font and size of the text in the frame.

6 With the insertion point still in the text frame, choose Edit > Select All to select the text and page number marker.

7 In the Character palette, choose Adobe Garamond® from the Font Family menu (you may need to scroll through the menu). For Size, choose 10 pt.

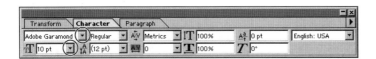

Note: *It's easy to confuse the Size menu (⊤) with the Leading menu (⅄). Make sure you change the font size, not the leading.*

8 Select the selection tool (▶). If necessary, drag the footer frame so that it snaps to the horizontal and vertical guides, as shown.

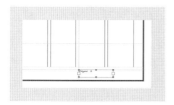

9 Click a blank area of your document window or choose Edit > Deselect All to deselect the footer frame.

Notice that part of the footer frame is hidden by the guides. You will change a preferences setting to place the guides in back and change the column guide color.

10 Choose File > Preferences > Guides. Under Guide Options, select Guides in Back. Under Columns, select Cyan for Color (you may need to scroll through the menu). Click OK.

Notice that the guides are now behind the footer frame.

Copying and pasting to create a second footer

You have created a footer text frame on the right master page. Unless you insert a similar footer on the left master page, only the right-facing pages in your document will have page numbers. You'll copy and paste the text frame to the left master page.

1 Using the selection tool (▶), select the footer frame, and then choose Edit > Copy. Choose View > Fit Spread in Window to show both master pages, and then choose Edit > Paste.

The text frame is pasted into the middle of the spread.

2 Click inside the pasted text frame and drag it to the left master page so that it snaps to the guides, mirroring the right master page.

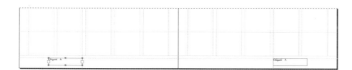

💡 *If any palettes are in the way, you can move them by dragging their top bars.*

3 Select the type tool (**T**), and then click anywhere inside the text frame on the left master page to place an insertion point.

4 Click the Paragraph palette tab (or choose Type > Paragraph), and then click Align Right (≡).

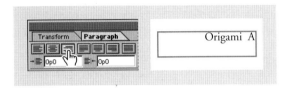

The text is now right aligned within the footer frame on the left master page.

5 Choose File > Save.

Creating a B-Master based on the A-Master

The changes you've made to the master so far are necessary for most of the pages in the document. However, the document pages containing the articles require placeholder frames not needed on other pages. To accommodate these different designs, you'll create a separate master for the article pages that is based on the A-Master.

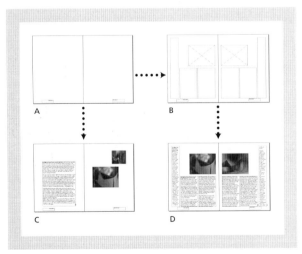

A. *A-Master* **B.** *B-Master* **C.** *Document pages based on A-Master*
D. *Document pages based on B-Master*

1 Position the pointer on the black triangle to the right of the Pages tab, and choose New Master from the Pages palette menu.

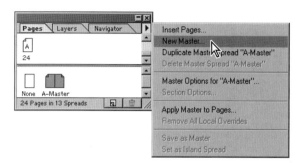

2 For Based on Master, choose A-Master, and then click OK.

You're now working on a separate master page spread, as indicated by the selected B-Master icons that appear in the bottom half of the Pages palette. The items you added to the A-Master appear on the new master spread, but you cannot select them by clicking them.

Creating placeholder frames

Next, you'll add placeholders for the text and graphics that will appear in your articles. By creating placeholders on the master pages, you won't need to create text frames for each page in your document.

1 To center the left page in the document window, double-click the left page icon of the B-Master in the Pages palette.

2 Select the type tool (**T**). Drag to create a box that fills the left column of the left master page. If a palette blocks the left column, drag its top bar to move it out of the way.

When you use the type tool to create a text frame, the box is drawn from the crosshair of the insertion point, not from the top of the insertion point.

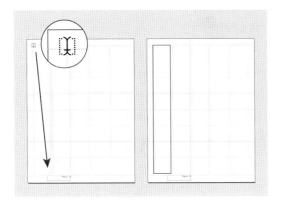

💡 *If the edges of the text frame do not snap to the guides inside the first column of the left master page, select the selection tool (▸), select the text frame, and then drag a selection handle to resize the frame.*

3 Double-click the right page icon of the B-Master in the Pages palette, and then use the type tool to drag a frame that fills the right column of the right master page.

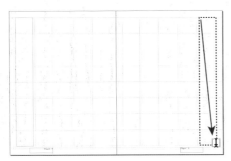

You have now created the text frame placeholders in the outside columns. These place-holders will act as sidebars in your document.

Adding inset spacing

When text is placed in these sidebar frames, the text will be easier to read if there is space between the text and the edge of the frame. Space between the frame and the text is called *inset spacing*.

1 Choose View > Fit Spread in Window. Select the selection tool ( ) in the toolbox.

2 Holding down Shift, click the text frame on the left master page so that both sidebar frames are selected.

3 Choose Object > Text Frame Options. Under Inset Spacing, type **0p9** for Top, Bottom, Left, and Right. Click OK.

Notice that a hairline appears inside the edges of the text frame. This shows the inset spacing.

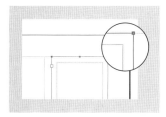

4 Choose File > Save.

Creating text frames with columns

Now that you have created the text frames for the sidebars in your article pages, you'll create the text frames for the main story of the B-Master.

1 Press Shift+Tab to hide all palettes except the toolbox.

2 Select the type tool (T), and then drag to create text frames four columns wide on the lower half of each master page, snapped to the guides.

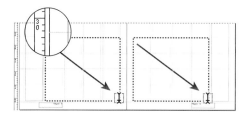

Next, you'll make sure each of the main story text frames has two columns.

3 Select the selection tool ( ). Holding down Shift, click the main story text frame on the left master page so that both main story text frames are selected.

4 Choose Object > Text Frame Options. Under Columns, type **2** for Number, and then click OK.

Each of the main story text frames will include two columns of text.

Adding placeholder frames for graphics

You have added text frame placeholders to the B-Master. To finish the B-Master, you'll add graphics frames to the top of the pages. Similar to text frames, graphics frames act as placeholders for the document pages, helping you maintain a consistent design.

First, let's create a guide to make it easy to position the graphics frames.

1 To unlock guides, choose View > Lock Guides to uncheck the menu command. Press Tab to view palettes.

2 Holding down Ctrl (Windows) or Command (Mac OS), drag a ruler guide from the horizontal ruler to the marker at 30 picas (you can look in the Transform palette to see the current position).

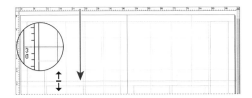

 To make sure the guide is at the 30 pica location, select the selection tool ( ) in the toolbox, click the guide to select it (the guide changes color), and then type 30p in the Y box of the Transform palette. Press Enter or Return.

3 Choose View > Lock Guides to lock the guides again. Press Shift+Tab to hide the palettes.

Two tools let you create rectangles: the rectangle tool and the rectangle frame tool. Although they are more or less interchangeable, the rectangle frame tool—which includes a non-printing X—is commonly used for creating placeholders for graphics.

4 Position the pointer on the rectangle tool in the toolbox and then drag to select the rectangle frame tool (⊠).

5 Draw a frame in the upper portion of the right page in the spread that is three columns wide. Snap the edges of the frame to the guides. The bottom of the frame should snap to the guide you set at 30 picas.

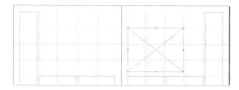

6 Select the selection tool (↖), and make sure the rectangle frame is selected.

7 To copy the frame, hold down Alt (Windows) or Option (Mac OS) and drag the frame to the left master page in the same relative position, as shown.

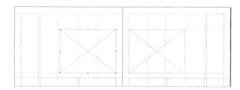

8 Press Shift+Tab (or Tab) to show palettes. Choose File > Save.

Applying the masters to document pages

Now that you have created all your master pages, it's time to apply them to the pages in your layout. All the pages are formatted with the A-Master by default. However, most of the pages will use the B-Master. You can apply master pages by dragging the master page icons onto the document page icons or by using a palette menu option.

Guidelines for working with masters

Keep the following guidelines in mind as you work with masters:

• *For best results, apply a master to a spread of the same number of pages. For example, design and apply a three-page master to your three-page spreads for a consistent look.*

• *If you want to create a set of masters that are slight variations on one main design, don't re-create each master completely; instead, create a main master and base design variations on it.*

• *If you don't specify options for a new master, it uses a default prefix and name, and is not based on any other master.*

• *Masters cannot contain sections. Set up sections in regular pages.*

• *If Layout Adjustment is on, applying a different master may alter the positions and sizes of objects in your layout. When used properly, Layout Adjustment can automatically adjust objects to fit the new master.*

—From Adobe InDesign User Guide, Chapter 3

1 Drag the lower right corner of the Pages palette down until you can see all the spreads.

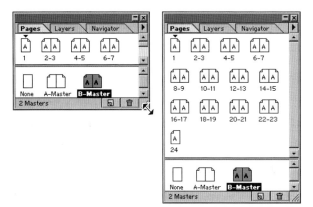

First you'll use the mouse to apply the B-Master to pages in the document that will contain articles.

2 Click the B-Master name below the page icons to select the B-Master spread, and then drag it over the 6–7 page numbers below the page icons. When a box appears around both pages in the spread, release the mouse button.

The B-Master pages are applied to pages 6 and 7, as indicated by the letter B in the page icons. Instead of dragging the B-Master to the remaining spreads, you'll use a different method to apply master pages.

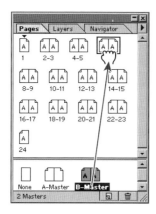 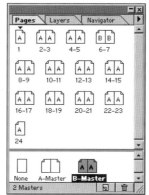

3 Choose Apply Master to Pages from the Pages palette menu. For Apply Master, choose B-Master. For To Pages, type **8-23**. Click OK.

Notice that pages 6–23 in the Pages palette are now formatted with the B-Master.

4 Drag the None master to page 1 and then to page 24.

Pages 1 and 24 will require individual formatting without page numbering, so no master page is desired. Make sure A-Master pages are assigned to pages 2–5 and B-Master pages are assigned to pages 6–23; pages 1 and 24 should not have master pages assigned to them.

5 Choose File > Save.

Adding sections to change page numbering

The magazine you're working on requires introductory material that should be numbered with lowercase roman numerals (i, ii, iii, and so on). You can change the page number by adding a section. You'll start a new section on page 2 to create roman numeral page numbering, and then you'll start another section on page 6 to revert to arabic numerals and restart numbering.

1 Double-click the page 2 icon in the Pages palette.

Notice that because the A-Master is assigned to page 2, the page includes the guides and footer information, but it does not include any of the placeholder frames that you added to the B-Master.

2 Choose Section Options from the Pages palette menu. Make sure Start Section is selected.

3 For Style, choose i, ii, iii, iv... (lowercase). For Page Numbering, make sure Continue from Previous Section is selected, and then click OK.

Starting with page 2, the page numbering occurs in roman numerals, as shown in the Pages palette. Now you'll number the other pages in arabic from page 6 through the rest of the document.

4 Click page 6 (vi) in the Pages palette to select it.

5 Choose Section Options from the Pages palette menu. Make sure Start Section is selected. For Style, choose 1, 2, 3, 4.... For Page Numbering, select Start at and type **2**. Click OK.

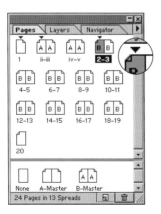

Now your pages are renumbered properly. Notice that a black triangle appears above pages 1, ii, and 2 in the Pages palette. These triangles indicate the start of a new page numbering section.

6 Choose File > Save.

Placing text and graphics on the document pages

Now that the framework of the 24-page publication is in place, you're ready to format the individual articles. To see how the changes you made to the master pages affect document pages, you'll add text and graphics to the spread on pages 2 and 3.

1 In the Pages palette, double-click the page 3 icon (not page iii) to center the page in the document window.

Notice that because the B-Master is assigned to page 3, the page includes the items placed on the right A-Master page as well as the placeholder frames from the right B-Master page.

When you want to import text and graphics from other applications, you can copy and paste, or you can use the Place command. You'll use the Place command to insert text in the sidebar frame.

2 Choose File > Place. Double-click 02_d.doc in the ID_02 folder.

The pointer takes the shape of a loaded text icon ( ). With a loaded text icon, you can drag to create a text frame or click inside an existing text frame. When you hold the loaded text icon over a text frame, the icon appears in parentheses ( ).

3 Click the loaded text icon anywhere inside the sidebar text frame on the right side of page 3.

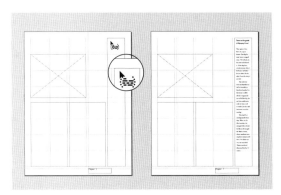

Before and after placing text

The text is placed in the text frame. Now you'll add text to the main story text frame.

4 Choose Edit > Deselect All to make sure no frames are selected.

If a frame is selected when you place a file, the contents of the file will be added to the selected frame.

5 Choose File > Place. Double-click 02_e.doc in the ID_02 folder. Click the loaded text icon anywhere inside the text frame at the bottom of page 3.

The columns in the text frame are filled with text. When a text frame has more text than can fit in the frame, the frame is said to have *overset text*, as indicated by a red plus sign in the lower right part of the frame. Because we're completing only the first spread of this article, you won't thread this overset text into the text frame on page 4.

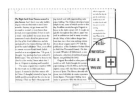

Next, you'll place a graphic into the placeholder frame on page 3.

6 Choose Edit > Deselect All, and then choose File > Place. Double-click 02_f.tif in the ID_02 folder. The pointer takes the shape of a loaded graphics icon ( ).

7 Position the loaded graphics icon over the graphics frame placeholder on page 3 so that the pointer appears in parentheses (), and click.

The photograph is placed inside the graphics frame. For convenience, this Photoshop image has been scaled to fit within the placeholder frame.

You are done with page 3. Now let's work on page 2 to finish the spread.

Overriding master page items on document pages

The placeholders you added to the master pages appear on the document pages, but you cannot select them simply by clicking them. InDesign works this way so that you won't accidentally remove or edit master page objects. However, you can override items on a master page to make it available on your document pages. You'll now delete the footer information at the bottom of page 2.

1 To view page 2, scroll in the document window to view the left half of the spread. If necessary, adjust your view or move palettes so that you can see the footer ("Origami 2") at the bottom of page 2. Click it to try to select it.

You cannot select master page items on the document pages simply by clicking. You'll now override the frame so that you can delete it.

2 While holding down Shift+Ctrl (Windows) or Shift+Command (Mac OS), click the footer at the bottom of page 2 to select it. Press Backspace or Delete.

The footer frame is now deleted from the document page, but it still appears on all the other pages to which the A- or B-masters are applied. You don't need to delete the placeholder frames on page 2 because these frames contain no text or graphics, and will not be printed.

Now you'll add a full-page image to page 2.

3 Choose File > Place. Double-click 02_g.tif in the ID_02 folder. With the loaded icon, click the upper left corner of page 2. If necessary, use the selection tool (▶) to drag the image so that it fills page 2, as shown.

Viewing the completed spread

Now you'll hide guides and frames to see what the completed spread looks like.

1 Choose Edit > Deselect All. Choose View > Fit Spread in Window. Choose View > Hide Frame Edges. Choose View > Hide Guides. Press Tab to hide palettes.

You have formatted enough of the 24-page document to see how adding objects to the master pages will let you maintain a consistent design throughout your document.

2 Choose File > Save.

Congratulations. You have finished the lesson.

Review questions

1 What are the advantages of adding objects to master pages?

2 How do you change the page numbering scheme?

3 How do you override a master page item on a document page?

Review answers

1 By adding objects such as guides, footers, and placeholder frames to master pages, you can maintain a consistent layout on the pages to which the master is applied.

2 In the Pages palette, select the page icon where you want new page numbering to begin. Then choose Section Options from the Pages palette menu and specify the new page numbering scheme.

3 Hold down Shift+Ctrl (Windows) or Shift+Command (Mac OS), and then click the object to select it. You can then edit, delete, or otherwise manipulate the object.

Lesson 3

3 | Working with Frames

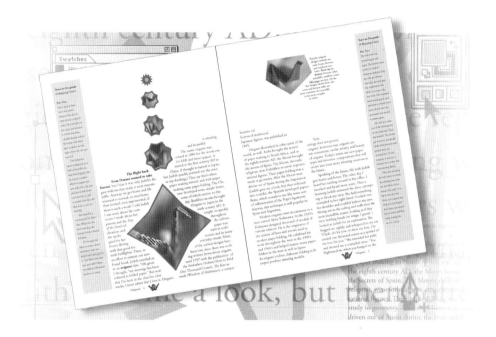

InDesign frames can hold either text or graphics. As you work with frames, you'll notice that InDesign provides a great amount of flexibility and control over your design.

In this introduction to working with frames, you'll learn how to do the following:

- Resize text frames

- Use anchor points to reshape a text frame

- Copy a graphic into a frame

- Convert a graphics frame to a text frame

- Wrap text around an object

- Create and rotate a polygon frame

- Center and scale an object within a frame

Getting started

In this lesson, you'll work on a two-page magazine article on origami. Before you begin, you'll need to restore the default preferences for Adobe InDesign. Then you'll open the finished document for this lesson to see what you'll be creating.

1 To ensure that the tools and palettes function exactly as described in this lesson, delete or deactivate (by renaming) the InDesign Defaults file and the InDesign SavedData file. See "Restoring default preferences" on page 2.

2 Start Adobe InDesign.

To begin working, you'll open an existing InDesign document.

3 Choose File > Open, and open the 03_a.indd file in the ID_03 folder, located inside the Lessons folder within the IDCIB folder on your hard disk.

4 Choose File > Save As, rename the file **03_frames.indd**, and save it in the ID_03 folder.

About paths and frames

You can draw objects in your document and use them as paths or as frames:

• ***Paths*** *are vector graphics like those you create in a drawing program such as Adobe Illustrator.*

• ***Frames*** *are identical to paths, with only one difference—they can be containers for text or other objects. A frame can also exist as a **placeholder**—a container without contents. As containers and placeholders, frames are the basic building blocks for your document's layout.*

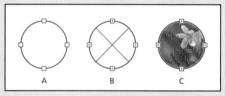

A. Path **B.** *Frame as a graphic container* **C.** *Frame with a placed graphic*

You can draw both paths and frames using tools in the toolbox. You can also create frames simply by placing (importing) or pasting contents into a path.

Because a frame is simply a container version of a path, you can do all of the things to a frame that you can do to a path, such as add a color or a gradient to its fill or stroke, or use the pen tool to edit the shape of the frame itself. You can even use a frame as a path, or vice versa, at any time. This flexibility makes it extremely easy to change your mind and provides a wide range of design choices.

—— From the Adobe InDesign 1.0 User Guide, chapter 6

5 If you want to see what the finished document will look like, open the 03_b.indd file in the same folder. You can leave this document open to act as a guide as you work. When you're ready to resume working on the lesson document, choose its name from the Window menu.

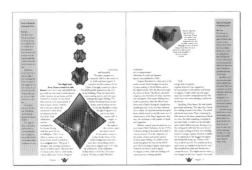

For a color version of the finished document, see the color section.

Note: As you work through the lesson, feel free to move palettes around or change the magnification to a level that works best for you. For more information, see "Changing the magnification of your document" on page 50 and "Using the Navigator palette" on page 57.

Modifying text frames

You can move, resize, and manipulate text frames. The tool you use to select a frame determines how you can change it:

• The type tool (**T**) lets you type or edit text within the frame.

• The selection tool (↖) lets you move or resize the text frame using its bounding box. The *bounding box* is a rectangle that represents the object's horizontal and vertical dimensions. When you select a text frame, it appears as a bounding box with eight solid handles.

• The direct-selection tool (↘) lets you select and edit a frame's individual *anchor points* (hollow handles that determine a frame's shape).

This document includes two layers: Art and Text. You'll lock the objects on the Art layer so that you won't accidentally select the shapes while you resize the text frames.

Resizing text frames

If you want to resize a text frame and the text inside simultaneously, you use the scale tool. You'll use the scale tool later in this lesson. For now, you'll resize a text frame using the selection tool. That way, the text inside remains the same size but may wrap differently (have different line breaks) or display more or less text than before.

1 Click the Layers palette tab, and then click the lock box to the left of the Art layer.

 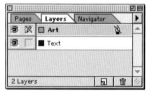

The objects on the Art layer are now locked. You'll now resize the bounding box of a text frame.

2 To hide all palettes except the toolbox, press Shift+Tab.

3 Using the selection tool ( ), click anywhere in the main story text frame on the left page. Notice that the text frame has eight solid handles.

4 Drag the top center handle up to resize the height of the frame so that it snaps to the next horizontal guide above (near 22 picas on the vertical ruler).

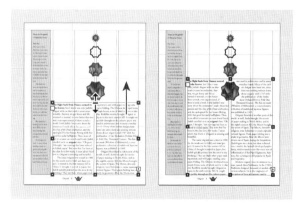

Before and after resizing text frame

Notice that after you resized the frame, text flows throughout the entire frame. Also, the bottom image has a text wrap applied to it, so the text flows around the image.

Selecting objects

Two tools are available for selecting objects: the selection tool and the direct-selection tool. Switching between the two tools changes the appearance of the selection. By paying attention to the handles or points that appear on a path, you can instantly tell if a path is properly selected for the task you want to perform:

• *Use the selection tool ( ) for general layout tasks, such as positioning and sizing objects. When you select an object using this tool, the object displays a bounding box rectangle with eight handles.*

• *Use the direct-selection tool ( ) for tasks involving drawing and editing paths, frames or frame contents, or to move anchor points on a path. When you select an object using this tool, it displays special handles called anchor points that make up the path.*

Imported images do not have anchor points, so when selected with the direct-selection tool they always display a rectangle with eight handles. Images are always contained inside a frame; if you see anchor points, you've selected an image's frame, not the image itself.

With rectangular objects, it can be difficult to tell the difference between the object and its bounding box. A path always displays hollow anchor points, while a bounding box always displays eight solid handles. If you see hollow anchor points, you've selected a path with its anchor points ready for editing.

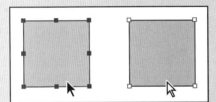

Rectangular path selected with selection tool
(left) and direct-selection tool (right)

If you see a dot in the middle of each anchor point or bounding box handle, you've selected a frame or its bounding box. If the frame contains graphics or text, you can use the direct-selection tool or text tool to select the contents.

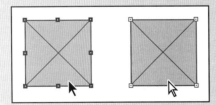

Rectangular frame selected with selection tool
(left) and direct-selection tool (right)

---From the Adobe InDesign User Guide, Chapter 2

Using anchor points to reshape a text frame

When working with frames, it is important to pay attention to which selection tool you're using. When you use the selection tool to resize a text frame, the text frame maintains its rectangular shape. When you use the direct-selection tool, dragging the anchor points will change the shape of the frame.

1 With the text frame on page 4 selected, click the direct-selection tool ( ) in the toolbox.

Four hollow handles, called *anchor points*, now appear on the selected text frame.

2 Position the pointer over the upper left anchor point and then click and hold down the mouse button until the pointer becomes a triangle ( ). Drag the anchor point so that it snaps to the horizontal guide below it, and release the mouse button.

Make sure you drag only the anchor point—if you drag just below the anchor point, you'll move the text frame.

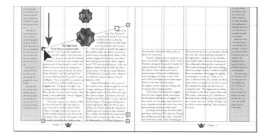

3 Select the selection tool ( ).

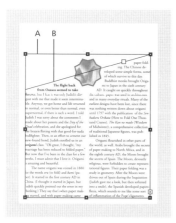

A. Bounding box B. Frame

Now you can see the difference between the bounding box and the path of the text frame. Notice that the bounding box is a rectangle with eight solid handles.

Next, you'll resize the text frame on the right page of the spread so that it mirrors the text frame on the left page.

4 Select the direct-selection tool, and click anywhere in the main story text frame on the right page to display the anchor points on the text frame.

5 Drag the upper left handle of the text frame up to the next horizontal guide so that the text frame on the right page mirrors the left page. Again, make sure you drag only the anchor point, not the entire text frame.

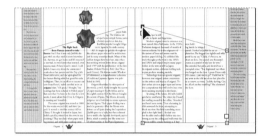

6 Choose File > Save.

💡 *When no insertion point is placed, you can press **a** or **v** to toggle between the selection and direction-selection tools. Your Quick Reference Card provides a list of many other shortcut keystrokes.*

Modifying graphics frames

To understand the difference between resizing a frame and resizing the bounding box, you'll import an image and then resize the frame. First you'll unlock the Art layer and lock the Text layer.

1 Press Tab to show the hidden palettes. In the Layers palette, unlock the Art layer and lock the Text layer. Click the Art layer to select it.

2 To center the right page in the document window, click the Pages palette tab, and then double-click the page 5 icon. If the toolbox covers the top of the left-most column on page 5, drag the toolbox out of the way.

3 Choose View > Hide Guides. You won't be snapping the object to any guides.

4 Choose Edit > Deselect All to make sure no items are selected (if another frame is selected, the graphic you place will be inserted into the selected frame).

5 Select the selection tool ( ). Choose File > Place, and then double-click 03_c.tif in the ID_03 folder.

The pointer changes to a loaded graphics icon ( ).

Note: *If the pointer appears with a line through it ( ) when you try to use the selection tool, the current layer is locked but still selected. You cannot add objects to a locked layer. Select and unlock the Art layer in the Layers palette and proceed.*

6 Click near the top of page 5 to place the graphic.

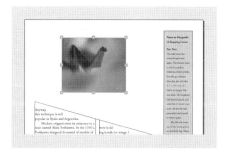

When you place a graphic in your document, the content fits within a frame. The content and the graphics frame are separate items, each with its own bounding box.

7 Using the selection tool, make sure the placed graphic is selected. Drag the lower right handle away from the center of the graphic to enlarge the frame. Don't worry about dragging a precise distance.

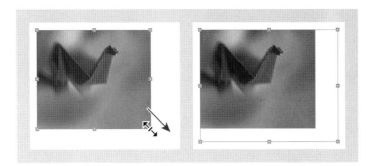

You have just resized the bounding box of the frame, but the content remains the same size. The content and frame are separate objects; the frame determines which part of the content is shown. Now you will crop the image by resizing the frame.

8 Drag the lower right handle toward the center of the frame to crop the photograph so that the origami image is centered within the frame.

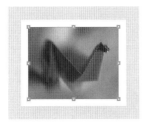

9 Choose File > Save.

Changing the shape of the frame

When you resized the frame using the selection tool, the frame maintained its rectangular shape. Now you will use the direct-selection tool to reshape the frame.

1 With the image still selected, click the direct-selection tool ( ). Notice that the selected object now has hollow points, indicating that the frame is selected.

Now you will use the pen tool to add a new anchor point to the frame.

2 Click the pen tool (✏). Hold the pointer over the center of the bottom line of the object so that the pen tool has a plus sign (✏₊), and click. A new point is added.

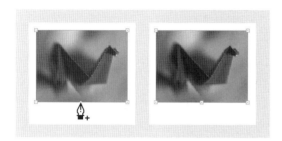

The pen tool lets you add or remove points. To move these points, you must use the direct-selection tool.

3 Select the direct-selection tool. While holding down Shift, drag the lower right anchor point approximately halfway toward the top of the image.

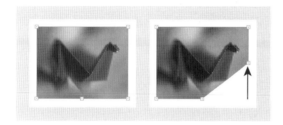

The Shift key constrains the point on the line.

4 Holding down Shift, drag the lower left anchor point the same distance so that the shape looks like a home plate in baseball.

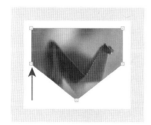

5 Holding down Shift, drag the upper left point a short distance to the right. Then drag the upper right point an equal distance to the left.

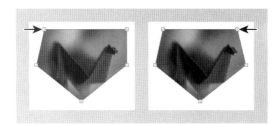

Now you will center the image within the frame.

6 With the direct-selection tool still selected, click the image inside the frame to select it.

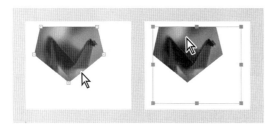

Selected frame (left) and selected content (right)

In general, when you select an object with the direct-selection tool, hollow points appear. The exception is imported graphics, which always display a rectangle with eight handles. This is a reminder that you can only move or resize imported bitmaps, not radically alter their shape as you can with frames.

7 Drag the selected object up and to the left so that the origami figure is centered within the frame.

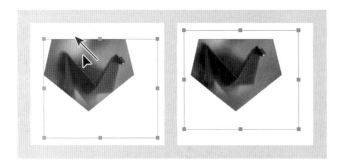

The frame acts as a mask to the content. As you can see, the content and frame of a graphic can be manipulated independently.

Resizing the graphic and frame simultaneously

Now you'll make the graphic and frame a bit smaller. You can use the Control or Command key to resize the frame and content simultaneously. As is true in most graphics programs, you can hold down the Shift key while dragging to resize an object proportionally.

1 Select the selection tool (▶), and select the graphic on page 5.

2 Holding down Shift+Ctrl (Windows) or Shift+Command (Mac OS), drag the lower right handle toward the center of the object to reduce its size.

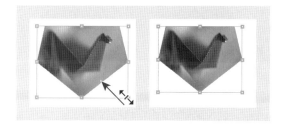

Notice that both the content and the frame are resized. As you can see, the Ctrl or Command key is useful for resizing the content and frame simultaneously.

3 Choose File > Save.

Converting a graphics frame to a text frame

Frames can hold either text or graphics. Next, you'll copy and paste the graphics frame so that you can replace the image in the copied frame with text.

1 With the frame still selected with the selection tool (▶), choose Edit > Copy.

2 Choose Edit > Paste, and then drag the pasted graphic so that it overlaps the lower right area of the original frame.

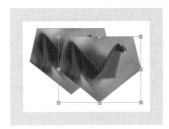

3 Select the direct-selection tool (⬚), and click the image in the pasted frame. Choose File > Place, and then double-click 03_d.doc in the ID_03 folder.

When you place a text file, it flows into the selected frame and replaces the contents.

As you can see, frames can contain either text or graphics. Now you'll make sure the text frame belongs to the Text layer instead of the Art layer.

4 Click the Layers palette tab. Click the lock icon (⬚) next to the Text layer to unlock objects on the Text layer.

In the Layers palette, the small dot to the right of the layer name indicates which layer the selected object belongs to. You can change an object's layer by dragging this dot to a different layer.

5 With the text frame selected, drag the small dot from the Art layer to the Text layer.

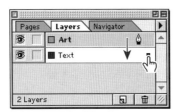

The text frame now belongs to the Text layer. The Art layer is above the Text layer in the Layers palette, so the object on the Art layer hides part of the object on the Text layer.

Wrapping text around an object

You can wrap text around the frame of the object or around the object itself. Now you'll see the difference between wrapping text around the bounding box and wrapping text around the graphic.

1 Using the selection tool ( ), select the five-sided graphics frame (not the text frame) on page 5.

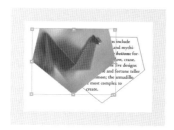

2 Choose Object > Text Wrap. Select the second wrap option so that the text wraps around the bounding box.

The text wraps around the bounding box of the image, not around the image itself.

3 Next, select the third wrap option so that the text wraps around the contour of the image.

The text wraps around the graphic instead of the bounding box.

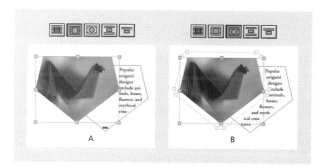

A. *Text wrapped around bounding box* **B.** *Text wrapped around content*

4 Close the Text Wrap palette.

The text frame is not large enough to hold all the text in the frame, so you will resize it.

5 Using the selection tool, click the text frame to select it. Holding down Shift, drag the lower right handle away from the center of the frame to enlarge it until you can see all the text.

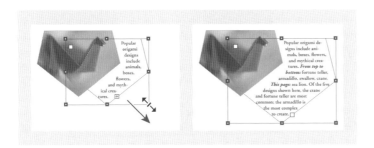

6 Choose File > Save.

Fitting the content to the frame

Now that you have completed page 5, you will turn your attention to page 4. Because the four objects on page 4 are grouped, you cannot use the selection tool to select one of the frames unless you ungroup the objects first. However, you can use the direct-selection tool to select an object within a group. You'll add a photograph to the second shape from the top.

1 Click the Pages palette tab, and then double-click the page 4 icon. To zoom in, select the magnification tool ($\mathbb{Q}$), and then drag across the top three shapes.

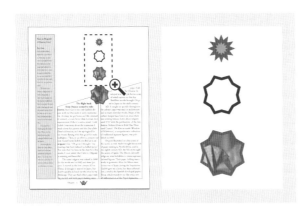

2 Select the direct-selection tool (⤢), and then select the frame with the black stroke. Choose File > Place, and then double-click 03_e.tif in the ID_03 folder.

The object is placed within the frame. However, because the graphic is much larger than the frame that masks it, you can see only a small part of the graphic. To fix this, you'll fit the content within the frame.

3 With the frame still selected, choose Object > Fitting > Fit Content to Frame to resize the graphic so that it fits in the frame.

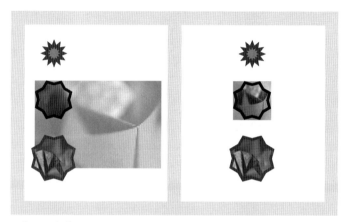

Before and after using Fit Content to Frame

Modifying the stroke of a frame

A frame's outline is called a *stroke*. A color or gradient applied to a frame's enclosed area is called a *fill*. The icons in the toolbox determine whether the fill or stroke is affected.

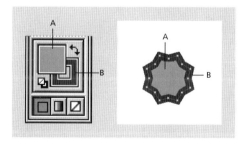

A. *Fill* **B.** *Stroke*

Changing the stroke color of the frame

Now you'll change the stroke color of the shape to red.

When a frame contains a bitmap graphic like this one, you must click the edge of the frame to select the frame; selecting inside the frame selects the graphic.

1 Using the direct-selection tool (![arrow]), click the graphic within the second frame. Notice that the graphic is selected, not the frame.

2 Using the direct-selection tool, click the edge of the black frame to select the frame instead of the graphic.

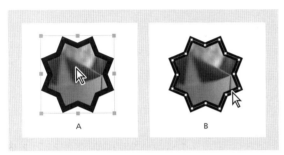

A. Selected graphic B. Selected frame

3 Select the Stroke box (![stroke box]) in the toolbox. Choose Window > Swatches, and then select Red in the Swatches palette (you may need to scroll).

4 Choose File > Save.

Drawing a polygon

Now you'll draw a polygon. A polygon, like any graphic composed of paths, can act as a frame. To see this, you'll place a graphic within the polygon. To make the page less cluttered, you'll hide objects on the Text layer.

1 Choose View > Fit Page in Window. Click a blank area of your document window to make sure no objects are selected.

2 Click the Layers palette tab, and then click the eye icon next to the Text layer to hide the Text layer. Make sure the Art layer is selected.

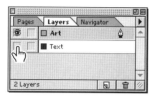

Objects on the Text layer are hidden.

3 Choose View > Show Guides.

4 Double-click the polygon tool (⬠) in the toolbox.

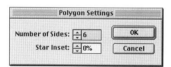

You can change the number of sides as well as the inset percentage, which bends the polygon lines inward to form a star-shaped object in some cases.

5 For Number of Sides, type **4**. For Star Inset, type **15** and then click OK.

6 Holding down Shift to maintain an equal height and width, drag to create a shape that is the width of two columns, as shown below.

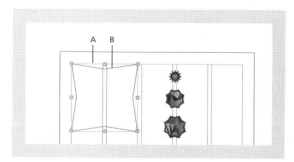

A. Bounding box B. Frame

Note: *If the pointer appears with a line through it (⨳) when you try to use the polygon tool, the Text layer is hidden but still selected. You cannot add objects to a hidden layer. Select the Art layer in the Layers palette and try again.*

Changing the weight of the stroke

Now you'll change the stroke thickness of the polygon's frame and place a graphic within the polygon. You'll open the Stroke palette to change the weight, or thickness, of the stroke.

1 With the polygon still selected, choose Window > Stroke. For Weight, type **4** and press Return or Enter. Close the Stroke palette.

2 Make sure the Stroke box (⬓) in the toolbox is selected. Then select Red in the Swatches palette.

Next, you'll place a graphic within the frame.

3 With the object still selected, choose File > Place.

4 Double-click 03_f.tif in the ID_03 folder.

The graphic is placed within the selected frame. You'll scale this graphic after you rotate the frame.

5 Choose File > Save.

Transforming a frame

You use the Transform palette to view or modify an object's location and dimensions and to transform it in various ways, such as shearing or rotating. You can transform frames just as you would any graphic object.

Rotating the frame

The content resides within the polygon frame. The frame and content are independent of each other, so you can rotate the frame without rotating the content. If you use the selection tool, you can rotate both frame and content. If you use the direct-selection tool, you can rotate either.

1 Select the direct-selection tool (⇖), and then click the edge of the polygon frame (not inside the frame).

The selection tool that is used to select the object determines which object will be rotated.

2 Select the rotation tool (⟳).

The crosshair icon, which appears in the upper left handle, determines the point of the rotation. You can change the crosshair location by clicking the corresponding point in the proxy icon of the Transform palette.

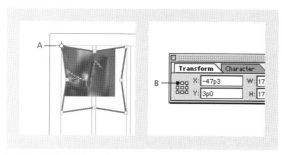

A. Crosshair B. Proxy icon

3 Click the center point in the proxy icon of the Transform palette to move the crosshair icon to the center of the selected frame.

4 Drag any handle to rotate the object 45° in either direction. To be precise, you can type **45** in the Rotation box of the Transform palette and press Return or Enter.

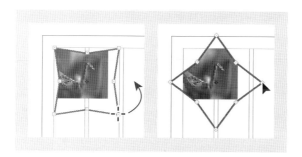

♀ *If you hold down Shift while dragging the point, the object snaps to 45° increments.*

Notice that the polygon shape rotates around its center. This is because you selected the center point in the proxy icon.

5 Choose File > Save.

Centering and scaling the graphic

Now you'll center the graphic within the frame and then scale the graphic so that it fills the frame.

1 Select the selection tool (↖), and then click a blank area of your document window or choose Edit > Deselect All to make sure no objects are selected.

2 Using the selection tool, click the polygon to select it. Choose Object > Fitting > Center Content.

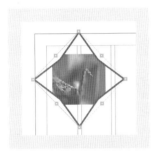

The graphic is centered within the frame.

3 Select the direct-selection tool (↘), and click the center of the graphic to select the content (not the frame).

Now you'll use the scale tool to resize the graphic. Unlike the selection tool, the scale tool lets you resize an object from the center outward. Using the scale tool also displays the change in size as a percentage as you drag.

4 Select the scale tool (▱). In the Transform palette, select the center point in the proxy icon.

5 Holding down Shift, drag a corner handle outward until the graphic fills the polygon frame. Release the Shift key.

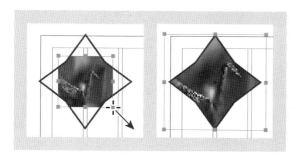

6 Choose Edit > Deselect All.

Finishing up

Now you'll place the graphic at the bottom of the page and wrap the text around it. Then you'll hide guides and palettes to look at the finished spread.

1 In the Layers palette, click the left-most box next to the Text layer to show objects on the Text layer.

2 Select the selection tool (⬆), and drag the polygon to the bottom of page 4, centered between the grouped objects and the bottom margin, as shown.

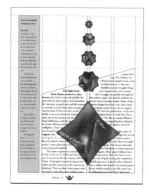

Notice that this object is overlapping the text. You'll wrap text around it.

3 With the object still selected, choose Object > Text Wrap. Select the third wrap option.

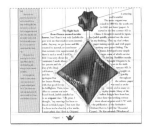 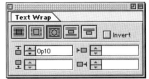

4 Close the Text Wrap palette, and then choose Edit > Deselect All.

Now you'll hide guides, frame edges, and palettes to view your spread.

5 Choose View > Fit Spread in Window. Choose View > Hide Frame Edges, and then choose View > Hide Guides.

6 Press Tab to hide the toolbox and palettes. Choose File > Save.

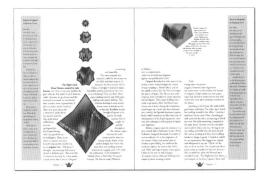

Congratulations. You have finished the lesson.

On your own

One of the best ways to learn about frames is to experiment on your own. In this section, you will learn how to nest an object inside a shape you create. Follow these steps to learn more about selecting and manipulating frames:

1 Using the direct-selection tool ( ), select and copy any image on page 4 or 5.

2 To create a new page, choose Insert Pages from the Pages palette menu and then click OK.

3 Use the polygon tool to draw a shape on the new page (use any number of sides or star inset). Select the shape using the direct-selection tool, and then choose Edit > Paste Into to nest the image inside the frame. (If you choose Edit > Paste, the object will not be pasted inside the selected frame.)

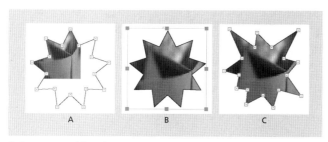

A. Image pasted into frame **B.** *Image moved and scaled within the frame* **C.** *Polygon frame reshaped*

4 Use the direct-selection tool to move and scale the image within the frame.

5 Use the direct-selection tool to change the shape of the polygon frame.

6 Use the selection tool ( ) to rotate both the frame and the image. Use the direct-selection tool to rotate only the image within the frame.

7 When you are done experimenting, close the document without saving.

For more information on nesting frames within frames, see Lesson 9.

Review questions

1 When should you use the selection tool ( ) to select an object, and when should you use the direct-selection tool ( ) to select an object?

2 How do you resize a frame and its contents simultaneously?

3 How do you rotate a graphic within a frame without rotating the frame?

4 Without ungrouping objects, how do you select an object within a group?

Review answers

1 Use the selection tool (↖) for general layout tasks, such as positioning and sizing objects. Use the direct-selection tool (↘) for tasks involving drawing and editing paths or frames; for example, to select frame contents or to move anchor point on a path.

2 To resize a frame and its contents simultaneously, select the selection tool (↖), hold down Ctrl (Windows) or Command (Mac OS), and then drag a handle. Hold down Shift to maintain the object's proportions.

3 To rotate a graphic within a frame, use the direct-selection tool to select the graphic within the frame. Select the rotation tool (◌), and then drag one of the handles to rotate only the graphic, not the frame.

4 To select an object within a group, select it using the direct-selection tool.

Lesson 4

4 Creating and Applying Colors, Tints, and Gradients

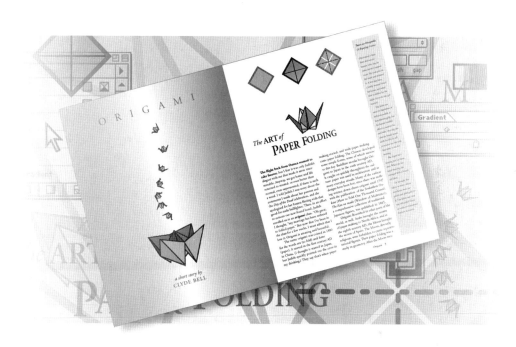

The Swatches palette lets you apply, modify, and save colors, tints, and gradients in your document. You can apply LAB, RGB, or CMYK colors, process and spot colors, tints, and gradients of blended colors to your text and graphics.

In this introduction to working with colors, you'll learn how to do the following:

- Add colors to the Swatches palette

- Apply colors to objects

- Create dashed strokes

- Create and apply a gradient swatch

- Adjust the direction of the gradient blend

- Create a tint

- Create a spot color

Getting started

In this lesson, you'll work on a 2-page spread for a magazine article about origami. If you've gone through the two previous lessons, the design of this document will look somewhat familiar. The document includes two layers (Art and Text), two master pages (B is based on A), and a separate main story and sidebar. Before you begin, you'll need to restore the default preferences for Adobe InDesign. Then you'll open the finished document for this lesson to see what you'll be creating.

1 To ensure that the tools and palettes function exactly as described in this lesson, delete or deactivate (by renaming) the InDesign Defaults file and the InDesign SavedData file. See "Restoring default preferences" on page 2.

2 Start Adobe InDesign.

3 Choose File > Open, and open the 04_a.indd file in the ID_04 folder, located inside the Lessons folder within the IDCIB folder on your hard disk.

4 Choose File > Save As, rename the file **04_color.indd**, and save it in the ID_04 folder.

5 If you want to see what the finished document will look like, open the 04_b.indd file in the same folder. You can leave this document open to act as a guide as you work. When you're ready to resume working on the lesson document, choose its name from the Window menu.

 For a color version of the finished document, see the color section.

Note: As you work through the lesson, feel free to move palettes around or change the magnification to a level that works best for you. For more information, see "Changing the magnification of your document" on page 50 and "Using the Navigator palette" on page 57.

Defining printing requirements

It's a good idea to know printing requirements before you start working on a publication. This magazine article was designed to be printed by a commercial printer using the CMYK color model. You also need to know the color printing requirements.

Adding colors to the Swatches palette

You add color to objects using a combination of palettes and tools. The InDesign color workflow is centered around the Swatches palette. Using the Swatches palette to name colors makes it easy to apply, edit, and update colors for objects in a document. Although you can also use the Color palette to apply colors to objects, there is no quick way to update these colors, called *unnamed colors*. Instead, you'd have to update the color of each object individually.

You'll now create most of the colors you'll use in this document. Since this document is intended for a commercial press, you'll be creating CMYK process colors.

About color modes and models

When you create a color in a document, you can choose from the LAB, RGB, or CMYK color modes. Each color mode corresponds to the standard L*a*b, RGB, or CMYK color model for describing and reproducing color. In the Swatches palette, you can identify the color mode of a color using icons that appear next to the name of the color.

L*a*b color consists of a luminance or lightness component (L) and two chromatic components: the a component (from green to red) and the b component (from blue to yellow). L*a*b color is designed to be device-independent, creating consistent color regardless of the device (such as monitor, printer, or scanner) used to create or reproduce the image.

A large percentage of the visible spectrum can be represented by mixing red, green, and blue (RGB) colored light in various proportions and intensities. Because RGB colors combine to create white, they are called additive colors. Additive colors are used for lighting, video, and monitors.

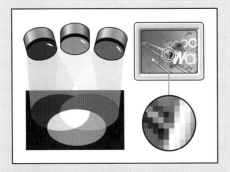

Whereas the RGB model depends on a light source to create color, the CMYK model is based on the light-absorbing quality of the paper. As white light strikes translucent inks, a portion of the spectrum is absorbed. Color that is not absorbed is reflected back to your eye. In theory, pure cyan (C), magenta (M), and yellow (Y) pigments should combine to absorb all color and produce black; for this reason they are also called subtractive colors. (The letter K is used to avoid confusion, because B also stands for blue.) Combining these inks to reproduce color is called four-color process printing.

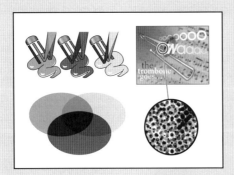

---From Adobe InDesign User Guide, Chapter 9

1 Make sure no objects are selected, and then click the Swatches palette tab. (If the Swatches palette is not visible, choose Window > Swatches.)

The Swatches palette stores the colors that have been preloaded into InDesign, as well as the colors, tints, and gradients you create and store for reuse.

2 Choose New Color Swatch from the Swatches palette menu. For Swatch Name, type **Purple**. Make sure Color Type and Color Mode are set to Process and CMYK, respectively.

3 For the color percentages, type the following values: Cyan = **67**, Magenta = **74**, Yellow = **19**, Black = **12**, and then click OK.

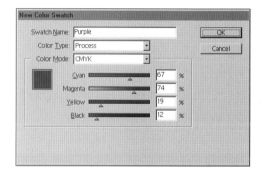

4 Repeat the previous two steps to name and create the following colors:

	C	M	Y	K
Red	0	69	60	12
Green	51	19	91	12
Gold	0	31	81	4

If you forgot to type the name for a color or if you typed an incorrect value, double-click the swatch, change the name or value, and then click OK.

New colors added to the Swatches palette are stored only with the document they are created in. You'll apply these colors to text, graphics, and frames in your document.

Applying colors to objects

There are three general steps to applying a swatch color: (1) select the text or object, (2) specify in the toolbox whether you'll change the stroke or fill, and (3) select the color in the Swatches palette.

1 Select the selection tool ( ), and click one of the diamond shapes at the top of the right page to select the group of objects.

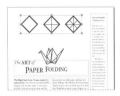

Notice that these three objects are grouped. You will ungroup these objects and lock them in place. Locking these objects will prevent them from being moved accidentally.

2 With the group of objects still selected, choose Object > Ungroup. Choose Object > Lock Position.

3 Click a blank area in your document window or choose Edit > Deselect All to deselect the objects.

4 To zoom in on the diamonds, click the zoom tool ( ), and drag across the three diamonds. Make sure you can see all three diamond shapes.

To zoom in, you can press Ctrl++ (Windows) or Command++ (Mac OS). To zoom out, you can press Ctrl+- (Windows) or Command+- (Mac OS).

5 Select the selection tool ( ), and then click the border of the middle diamond to select it. Select the Stroke box ( ) in the toolbox, and then select Purple in the Swatches palette.

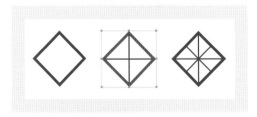

The stroke of the diamond shape is now purple. However, the color is not applied to the lines inside the shape because they are separate objects.

6 Deselect the object.

💡 *To deselect an object, you can choose Edit > Deselect All, you can click a blank area in your document window, or you can press Shift+Ctrl+A (Windows) or Shift+Command+A (Mac OS).*

7 Holding down Shift, click the borders of the two outer diamonds to select them. Release Shift. Select Red in the Swatches palette to apply a red stroke.

8 With the objects still selected, select the Fill box (■) in the toolbox, and then select Gold in the Swatches palette (you may need to scroll through the swatches).

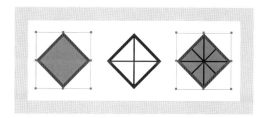

The left and right diamonds have a red stroke and gold fill. Now you'll change the color of the two diagonal lines in the right diamond.

9 Deselect the objects. Holding down Shift, select the two diagonal lines inside the right diamond. Release Shift. Select the Stroke box (▣) in the toolbox, and then select [Paper] in the Swatches palette.

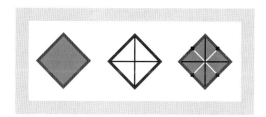

[Paper] is a special color that simulates the paper color on which you're printing. Objects behind a paper-colored object won't print where the paper-colored object overlaps them. Instead, the color of the paper on which you print shows through.

Creating dashed strokes

You'll now change the lines in the center and right diamonds to a custom dashed line.

1 Click a blank area of your document to deselect the lines. Holding down Shift, use the selection tool (▸) to select the four vertical and horizontal lines in the middle and right diamonds. Release Shift.

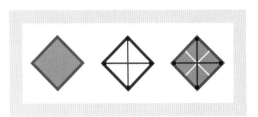

2 Choose Window > Stroke to display the Stroke palette. For Type, select Dashed. (If you cannot see the Type option, select Show Options from the Stroke palette menu.)

Six dash and gap boxes appear at the bottom of the Stroke palette. To create a dashed line, you specify the length of the dash, and then the gap, or spacing, between the dashes.

3 Type the following values in the Dash and Gap boxes: **6, 4, 2, 4** (press Tab after you type each value to move to the next box). Leave the last two dash and gap boxes empty.

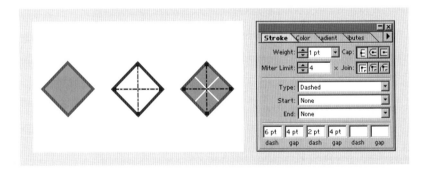

4 Close the Stroke palette, and then choose File > Save.

Working with gradients

A *gradient* is a graduated blend between two or more colors, or between tints of the same color. You can create either a linear or a radial gradient.

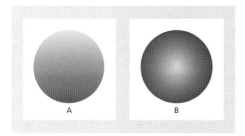

A. Linear gradient B. Radial gradient

Creating and applying a gradient swatch

Every gradient in InDesign has at least two color stops. By editing the color mix of each stop and by adding color stops in the Gradient palette, you can create your own custom gradients.

1 Click a blank area in your document window.

2 Choose New Gradient Swatch from the Swatches palette menu.

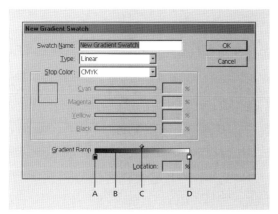

A. Left stop B. Gradient bar C. Ramp slider D. Right stop

Gradients are defined by a series of color stops in the gradient bar. A *stop* is the point at which a gradient changes from one color to the next and is identified by a square below the gradient bar.

3 For Swatch Name, type **Green/Gold Gradient**.

4 Click the left stop marker (⬕), and select Named Color for Stop Color. Select Green in the list box.

Notice that the left side of the gradient ramp is green.

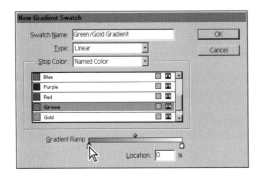

5 Click the right stop marker (⬕), select Named Color for Stop Color, and select Gold in the list box.

The gradient ramp shows a color blend between green and gold.

6 Click OK.

Now you'll apply the gradient to the fill of the middle diamond.

7 Click the border of the middle diamond to select it.

8 Select the Fill box (■) in the toolbox, and then click Green/Gold Gradient in the Swatches palette.

Adjusting the direction of the gradient blend

Once you have filled an object with a gradient, you can modify the gradient by using the gradient tool (▭) to "repaint" the fill along an imaginary line you drag. This tool lets you change the direction of a gradient and change the beginning point and endpoint of a gradient. You'll now change the direction of the gradient.

1 Make sure the middle diamond is still selected, and then select the gradient tool (▱) in the toolbox.

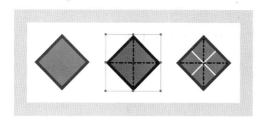

Now you'll experiment with the gradient tool to see how you can change the direction and intensity of the gradient.

2 To create a more gradual gradient effect, place the pointer an inch or so outside the selected diamond and drag past it.

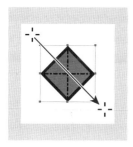

When you release the mouse button, you'll notice that the blend between green and gold is more gradual than it was before you dragged the gradient tool.

3 To create a sharper gradient, drag a small line in the center of the diamond. Continue to experiment with the gradient tool so that you understand how it works.

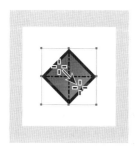

4 When you have finished experimenting, drag from the top corner of the diamond to the bottom corner. That's how you'll leave the gradient of the middle diamond.

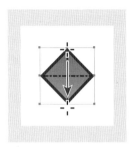

5 Choose File > Save.

Creating a tint

In addition to adding colors, you can also add tints to the Swatches palette. A *tint* is a screened (lighter) version of a color. You'll now create a 30% tint of the green swatch you created earlier in this lesson.

1 Select the selection tool ( ), and click a blank area in your document window to deselect the object.

2 Click Green in the Swatches palette. Choose New Tint Swatch from the Swatches palette menu. For Tint percentage, type **30** and then click OK.

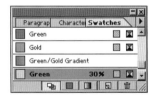

Notice that a new tint swatch appears at the bottom of the Swatches palette. This tint is based on the original Green color swatch. If you change the Green color swatch to a different color, for example, the tint swatch you just created would be a lighter version of the new color.

3 Choose View > Fit Page in Window to center the right page of the spread in the document window. Using the selection tool ( ), click the sidebar text frame on the right side of the page.

4 Make sure the Fill box () is selected, and then click the Green tint you just created in the Swatches palette.

Before and after adding fill tint

Creating a spot color

This publication will be printed to a commercial printer using the standard CMYK color model, which requires four separate plates for printing—one for cyan, one for magenta, one for yellow, and one for black. However, the CMYK color model has a limited range of colors, which is where spot colors come in handy.

In this publication, the title design calls for a metallic ink not found in the CMYK color model. You'll now add a metallic spot color from a color library.

1 Click a blank area in your document window to make sure no objects are selected.

2 Choose Window > Swatch Libraries > PANTONE Coated.

The Swatch Libraries command lets you import entire color libraries from color systems such as the PANTONE Coated and PANTONE Process systems, as well as from other InDesign and Adobe Illustrator documents.

3 Locate and double-click PANTONE 876 CVC.

*To select an item in a palette using the keyboard, hold down Ctrl+Alt (Windows) or Command+Option and click an item in the palette. Then quickly type the color number. In this case, you would quickly type **876** to select PANTONE 876 CVC.*

About spot and process color types

A spot color is a special premixed ink that is used instead of, or in addition to, CMYK inks, and that requires its own plate on a printing press. Use spot color when few colors are specified and color accuracy is critical. Spot color inks can accurately reproduce colors that are outside the gamut of process colors. However, the exact appearance of the printed spot color is determined by combination of the ink as mixed by the commercial printer and the paper it's printed on, so it isn't affected by color values you specify or by color management. When you specify spot color values, you're describing the simulated appearance of the color for your monitor and composite printer only (subject to the gamut limitations of those devices).

A process color is printed using a combination of four standard process inks: cyan, magenta, yellow, and black (CMYK). Use process colors when a job requires so many colors that using individual spot inks would be expensive or impractical, such as when printing color photographs. Keep the following guidelines in mind when specifying a process color:

• Don't specify a process color based on how it looks on your monitor unless you have set up a color management system properly and you understand its limitations for previewing color. For best results in a printed document, specify process colors using CMYK values printed in process-color reference charts, such as those available from a commercial printer.

• The final color values of a process color are its values in CMYK, so if you specify a process color using RGB or LAB, those color values will be converted to CMYK when you print color separations. These conversions will work differently if you turn on color management; they'll be affected by the profiles you've specified.

• Avoid using process colors in documents intended for online viewing only, because CMYK has a smaller color gamut than a typical monitor.

Sometimes it's practical to print process and spot inks on the same job. For example, you might use one spot ink to print the exact color of a company logo on the same pages of an annual report where photographs are reproduced using process color. You can also use a spot color printing plate to apply a varnish over areas of a process color job. In both cases, your print job would use a total of five inks—four process inks and one spot ink or varnish.

—From Adobe InDesign User Guide, Chapter 9

The metallic spot color is added to your Swatches palette. Notice the icon (⊚) next to the color name in the Swatches palette. This icon indicates that it is a spot color.

4 Close the PANTONE Coated palette.

Note: The color you see on your monitor does not reflect the actual printed color. To determine the color you want to use, look at a chart provided by the color system, such as the PANTONE Color Formula Guide 747XR, or an ink chart obtained from your printer. It's a good idea to minimize the number of spot colors you use. Each spot color you create will generate an additional spot color plate for the press, increasing your printer costs.

Applying color to text

As with frames, you can apply a stroke or fill to text itself. You'll apply colors to the text inside the frames on page 2 of the document.

1 In the Pages palette, double-click the page 2 icon to center page 2 in the document window.

2 Select the type tool (T) in the toolbox, and then double-click "Origami" to select the title.

3 Make sure the Fill box (▇) in the toolbox is selected, and then click PANTONE 876 CVC in the Swatches palette. Click a blank area to make sure no objects are selected.

Your monitor probably shows the text in a dull brown shade, but the actual printed color of the text will be the metallic spot color. Next, you'll insert another text frame and apply colors to the text.

4 Using the type tool (T), triple-click "a short story by" at the bottom of the page to select the line. If the Character palette is in the way, drag its top bar to move it.

5 Make sure the Fill box (▇) is selected in the toolbox, and then click Purple in the Swatches palette.

6 Triple-click "Clyde Bell" to select the name, and then click Red in the Swatches palette.

7 Choose File > Save.

Applying colors to additional objects

Now you'll apply the same colors used by the small cranes to the large crane image at the bottom of the page. First you'll look at a magnified view of one of the small cranes to see which colors are used.

1 Click a blank area to make sure no objects are selected. Click the magnification tool (🔍), and then drag across one of the small cranes to zoom in.

2 Select the direct-selection tool (⬚), and then click any of the objects in the crane image. Notice that the corresponding swatch in the Swatches palette becomes highlighted when you select the object the swatch is applied to.

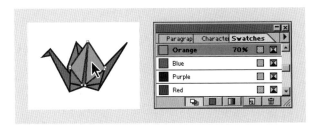

Now you'll apply these colors to the larger image at the bottom of the page.

3 Choose View > Fit Page in Window. Select the selection tool (▶), and click the large image at the bottom of page 2 to select the object. Choose Object > Ungroup.

Notice that the image consists of many smaller shapes grouped together. Now you'll apply orange to two of these shapes.

4 Deselect all objects, and then select the Fill box (◼) in the toolbar. Holding down Shift, click the two objects indicated below, and apply the Orange fill color (not the Orange tint).

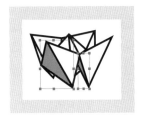

5 Deselect all objects, select the object indicated below, and then apply the Orange 70% fill.

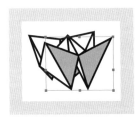

6 Deselect all objects, select the object indicated below, and apply the Blue fill.

💡 *If you applied the color to the wrong object, choose Edit > Undo Swatch and try again.*

Creating another tint

You'll now create a tint based on the Blue color. When you edit the Blue color, the tint that is based on the color will also change.

1 Deselect all objects.

2 Click Blue in the Swatches palette. Choose New Tint Swatch from the Swatches palette menu. Type **70** in the Tint box, and then click OK.

3 Select the object shown below and apply the Blue 70% fill.

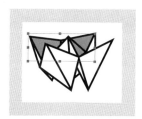

Notice how the large image shares the same colors with the small cranes you imported. Next you'll change the Blue color. Blue 70% is based on the Blue swatch, so the tint will also change.

4 Deselect all objects.

5 Double-click Blue (not the Blue tint) to change the color. For Swatch Name, type **Violet Blue**. For the color percentages, type the following values: Cyan = **59**, Magenta = **80**, Yellow = **40**, Black = **0**. Click OK.

Notice that the color change affects all objects to which Blue and Blue 70% were applied. As you can see, adding colors to the Swatches palette makes it easy to update colors in multiple objects.

6 Choose File > Save.

Using advanced gradient techniques

Earlier you created and applied a gradient and adjusted its direction using the gradient tool. InDesign also lets you create gradients of multiple colors and control the point at which the colors blend. In addition, you can apply a gradient to individual objects or to a collection of objects to make it appear as if each object were revealing more of the gradient.

Creating a gradient swatch with multiple colors

Earlier in this lesson, you created a gradient with two colors—green and gold. Now you'll create a gradient with three stops so that a green color on the outside will fade to white in the middle.

1 Choose Edit > Deselect All. Then choose New Gradient Swatch from the Swatches palette menu, and then type **Green/White Gradient** for Swatch Name.

The colors from the previous blend appear in the dialog box.

2 Click the left stop marker (▩), select Named Color for Stop Color, and make sure Green (not the tinted Green) is selected in the list box. Click the right stop marker (▩), select Named Color for Stop Color, and make sure Green (not the tinted Green) is selected in the list box.

The gradient ramp is now entirely green. Now you'll add a stop marker to the middle so that the color fades towards the center.

3 Click just below the center of the gradient bar to add a new stop. For Location, type **50** to make sure the stop is centered. For Stop Color, select Named Color, and then select [Paper] in the list box.

4 Click OK, and then choose File > Save.

Applying the gradient to an object

To finish page 2, you'll create a full-page box and then apply the gradient to its fill. First, let's change the view size so that you can see all of page 2.

1 Choose 50% from the magnification pop-up list at the bottom of the document window.

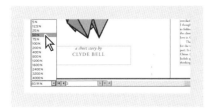

Before you create the graphics frame, make sure the Art layer is selected. It's a good idea to get into the habit of making sure your objects are placed on the appropriate layer so that you can hide or lock a set of objects easily.

2 Choose Edit > Deselect All. Click the Layers palette tab to bring the Layers palette to the front, and then select Art. (Do not select either box to the left of Art, or you'll hide or lock the objects on the Art layer.)

3 Select the Fill box (■) in the toolbox, and then select Green/White Gradient in the Swatches palette, if it's not already selected. Select the Stroke box (▣) in the toolbox, and then click the None button (▨) at the bottom of the toolbox.

A. Apply last-used color
B. Apply last-used gradient
C. Remove color or gradient

Now that the Fill box is set to the gradient and the Stroke box is set to none, the next object you draw will contain the gradient fill with no stroke.

4 Select the rectangle tool (▢), and then draw a frame that covers all of page 2, including the margins.

5 With the frame still selected, choose Object > Arrange > Send to Back (not Send Backward).

You are now finished with page 2.

Applying a gradient to multiple objects

Previously in this lesson, you used the gradient tool (▣) to change the direction of a gradient and to change the gradient's beginning and end points. You'll now use the gradient tool to apply a gradient across multiple objects in the crane on page 3.

1 Double-click the zoom tool (◉) to change the view to 100%. Click the Pages palette tab to display the Pages palette, and then double-click the page 3 icon.

2 Click the Layers palette tab to display the Layers palette. Click the empty box just to the left of the Text layer name to prevent you from selecting the text frame accidentally. A crossed-out pencil icon appears in the box.

3 Select the selection tool (↖), and then click the crane image above "The Art of Paper Folding."

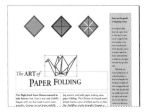

4 With the object selected, choose Object > Ungroup, and then deselect all the objects.

5 To zoom in, hold down Ctrl+spacebar (Windows) or Command+spacebar (Mac OS), and drag across the crane object above "The Art of Paper Folding."

Holding down Ctrl+spacebar or Command+spacebar toggles temporarily to the zoom tool. When you release the keys, the previous tool is selected.

6 Select the object shown below, make sure the Fill box (■) in the toolbox is selected, and apply the Red swatch.

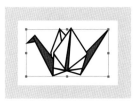

7 Select the object shown below and apply the Green swatch (not the Green tint) as a fill.

Now you'll apply the Green/White gradient to three different objects.

8 Deselect all objects. Holding down Shift, select the three objects shown below, and then apply the Green/White Gradient.

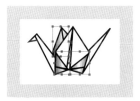

Notice that the gradient affects each object on an individual basis. Now you'll use the gradient tool to apply the gradient across the three selected objects as one.

9 With the three objects still selected, select the gradient tool (▦) in the toolbox. Drag an imaginary line as shown.

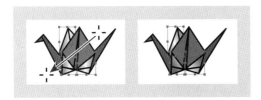

Now the gradient runs across all three selected objects.

Viewing the completed spread

You have finished the spread. Now you'll look at the spread without frame edges or palettes.

1 Choose Edit > Deselect All.

2 To view your spread, choose View > Fit Spread in Window. Then choose View > Hide Frame Edges.

3 Press Tab to hide the palettes. Save the file.

Congratulations. You have completed the lesson.

On your own

Follow these steps to learn more about importing colors and working with gradients.

1 To create a new document, choose File > New, and then click OK.

2 To import the colors from a different InDesign document, choose Window > Swatch Libraries > Other Library. Double-click Work04 (or 04_b.indd). Notice that the colors you created appear in a palette.

3 Make sure the Swatches palette is visible. Double-click Green/Gold Gradient to add it to the Swatches palette. Add a few of the other colors to the Swatches palette.

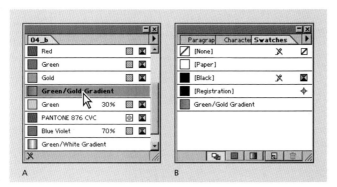

A. *Colors, tints, and gradients imported from another InDesign document*
B. *Swatch added to Swatches palette*

4 Use the ellipse tool (○) to draw a shape. Apply the Green/Gold Gradient to the shape's fill.

5 Double-click Green/Gold Gradient in the Swatches palette to change it. Drag the diamond-shaped slider above the gradient ramp to the right so that the gradient is mostly green, and click OK. Notice that the gradient in the ellipse changes.

6 Create a new gradient swatch that is radial instead of linear. Apply the new gradient to the fill of a different shape you draw. Use the gradient tool to change the gradient.

7 When you are done experimenting with colors, close the document without saving it.

Review questions

1 What is the advantage of applying colors using the Swatches palette instead of the Color palette?

2 What are the pros and cons of using spot colors versus process colors?

3 After you create a gradient and apply it to an object, how do you adjust the direction of the gradient blend?

Review answers

1 If you apply a color to several objects and then decide you want to use a different color, you don't need to update each object individually. Instead, change the color in the Swatches palette and the color of all the objects will be updated automatically.

2 By using a spot color, you can ensure color accuracy. However, each spot color requires its own plate at the press, so using spot colors is more expensive. Use process colors when a job requires so many colors that using individual spot inks would be expensive or impractical, such as when printing color photographs.

3 To adjust the direction of the gradient blend, use the gradient tool to repaint the fill along an imaginary line in the direction you want.

Lesson 5

5 | Importing and Editing Text

One of the most powerful features of Adobe InDesign is the ability to import text, thread it through frames, and edit text within the frames. Once you import text, you can create and apply styles, find and replace text and formatting, and use different language dictionaries to spell-check any part of your document.

In this introduction to importing and editing text, you'll learn how to do the following:

- Flow text manually and automatically
- Load styles from another document and apply them
- Thread text
- Use semi-autoflow to place text frames
- Find and change text and formatting
- Find and change a missing font
- Spell-check a document

Getting started

In this lesson, you'll work on an 8-page newsletter for the Sonata Cycles, a fictitious chain of bicycle stores. Several pages of the newsletter have already been completed. Now that the final article for the newsletter has been written, you're ready to flow the article into the document and add the finishing touches to the newsletter. Before you begin, you'll need to restore the default preferences for Adobe InDesign.

1 To ensure that the tools and palettes function exactly as described in this lesson, delete or deactivate (by renaming) the InDesign Defaults file and the InDesign SavedData file. See "Restoring default preferences" on page 2.

Note: Before you go through this lesson, make sure you have installed the Classroom in a Book fonts. For more information, see "Installing the Classroom in a Book fonts" on page 2.

2 Start Adobe InDesign.

To begin working, you'll open an existing InDesign document. We have added a font to this document that you do not have on your system. You will replace this font later in this lesson.

3 Choose File > Open, and open the 05_a.indd file in the ID_05 folder, located inside the Lessons folder within the IDCIB folder on your hard disk.

When you open a file that includes fonts not installed on your system, an alert message indicates which font is missing. The text that uses this missing font will be highlighted in pink. You will fix this missing font problem later in this lesson by replacing the missing font with an available font.

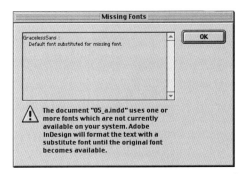

4 Click OK to close the alert message.

If you turn the pages in the document, you will notice that pages 5 through 8 have already been completed. The missing font is found on page 8. In this lesson, you will complete the first four pages of the newsletter.

5 Choose File > Save As, name the file **05_News**, and save it in the ID_05 folder.

6 If you want to see what the finished document will look like, open the 05_b.indd file in the same folder. If you prefer, you can leave the document open to act as a guide as you work. When you're ready to resume working on the lesson document, choose its name from the Window menu.

For a color version of the finished document, see the color section.

Flowing text

The process of making imported text appear in designated parts of a page or pages is called *flowing* text. InDesign lets you flow text manually for greater control or automatically for greater time-saving.

> **Tips on flowing text**
>
> *When you flow text into your document, the loaded text icon can appear in one of three forms, corresponding to the method you choose to control the flow of text on your pages:*
>
> *( ) Manual text flow adds text one frame at a time. It stops flowing text at the bottom of a text frame or at the last of a series of linked frames. You must reload the text icon to continue flowing text.*
>
> *( ) Semi-autoflow works the same as manual text flow, except that the pointer reloads as a loaded text icon each time the end of a frame is reached until all text is flowed into your document. Use Alt (Windows) or Option (Mac OS) to semi-autoflow text.*
>
> *( ) Autoflow adds pages and frames until all the text is flowed into your document. Use Shift to autoflow.*
>
> —From Adobe InDesign User Guide, Chapter 4

Flowing text manually

To flow text manually, you can drag to create a frame, or you can click anywhere on the page to create a text frame in a column. Now you will use both methods to flow the text into the columns on the first page of the newsletter.

1 In the Pages palette, double-click the page 1 icon to make sure the first page of the newsletter is visible.

2 Choose File > Place. Make sure Retain Format is selected. When this option is selected, the text will be imported with the formatting that was applied in the word-processing application.

3 Locate and double-click 05_c.doc in the ID_05 folder. The pointer becomes a loaded text icon.

You will now create a text frame between the light blue guides below the banner.

4 Create a text frame in the left column of page 1 by positioning the loaded text icon next to the left margin just below the 21p (21-pica) guide and dragging down to the right side of the first column at the 30p guide.

Dragging to create a text frame

Notice that the out port of the text frame has a red plus sign, which indicates overset text. You will now flow this text into the second column on page 1.

5 Using the selection tool (↖), click the out port of the frame you just created.

♀ *If you change your mind and decide you don't want to flow overset text, you can click any tool in the toolbox to cancel the loaded text icon. No text will be deleted.*

6 Position the loaded text icon in the upper left corner of the second column just below the 21p guide, and click.

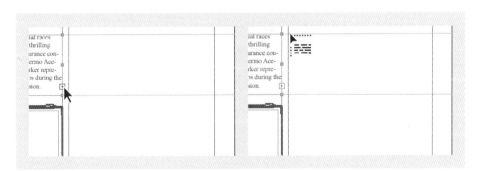

The text flows into a new frame from where you clicked to the bottom of the second column. The out port contains a red plus sign, indicating that there is more overset text.

Flowing text automatically

You will use autoflow to flow the rest of the overset text into the document. When you autoflow text, InDesign creates new text frames within column guides on subsequent pages until all the overset text is flowed in. If there are not enough pages in your document when you use autoflow, InDesign adds new pages until all the text is placed. A connected series of text frames is called a *story*.

1 Using the selection tool (▶), click the out port of the frame you just created in the second column on page 1.

While the loaded text icon is active, you can do many actions, including turning pages, creating new pages, and zooming in and out.

2 In the Pages palette, double-click the page 2 icon to center page 2 in view. Notice that there are no text frames on page 2. Also notice that the text icon is still loaded.

3 Holding down Shift, position the loaded text icon in the upper left corner of the left column on page 2, and click. Release the Shift key.

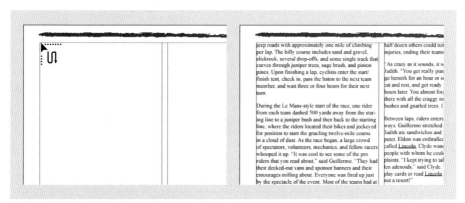

Holding down Shift lets you autoflow text into your document.

Notice that two new text frames were added to each page within the column guides. This is because you held down Shift to autoflow text. All the text in the story is now placed on pages 2 through 4.

Note: *If text frames do not appear on pages 2 and 3, you did not autoflow the text. If this is the case, click the outport in the last text frame that contains text, and hold down Shift as you click in the upper left corner of the next column. Make sure all the text flows into the document pages.*

Resizing a text frame

When you create a text frame by clicking the loaded text icon, InDesign bases the width of the new text frame on the column width. Although these frames are placed within the column margins, you can move, resize, and reshape any of these text frames.

1 In the Pages palette, double-click the page 4 icon to turn to page 4.

Notice that the text frame in the left column covers the photograph that was placed on this page. When you autoflow text, the text frames are created within the column settings regardless of whether objects appear in those columns. You can fix this overlap problem by adding a text wrap or by resizing the text frame.

2 Using the selection tool ( ), click the text frame in the left column on page 4 to select the text frame, and then drag the lower middle handle of the text frame above the photograph to approximately the 31p location (you can look at the vertical ruler as you drag).

Before and after resizing text frame

3 Choose File > Save.

About updating linked text files

When you place text, InDesign adds the text file to the Links palette, which you can use to update and manage the file. (You can choose File > Links to view the Links palette.) When you update a linked text file, any editing or formatting changes applied within InDesign are lost. Because of this risk, linked text files are not automatically updated when the original file is edited, unlike graphics files you place. However, you can easily update the linked file using the Links palette. Just remember that if you update the link, you'll lose any text or formatting changes you've made in InDesign.

—From Adobe InDesign User Guide, Chapter 4

Flowing text into an existing frame

When you place text, you can flow text into a new frame or into an existing frame. To flow text into an existing frame, you can click an insertion point to flow text at that point, or you can click the loaded text icon in an existing frame, which replaces its contents.

The first page of the newsletter includes a placeholder frame for a sidebar. You'll place the text in this frame that announces upcoming cycling events.

1 In the Pages palette, double-click the page 1 icon to turn to the first page of the newsletter.

2 Choose Edit > Deselect All.

If you place text when a frame is selected, the text replaces the frame; if you place text with an insertion point, the placed text appears at the insertion point. If you forget to deselect while placing text, choose Edit > Undo Replace, and then click the loaded text icon where you want the text to appear.

3 Choose File > Place. Locate and double-click 05_d.doc in the ID_05 folder.

The pointer becomes a loaded text icon ( ). When you move the loaded text icon over a text frame, parentheses enclose the icon ( ).

4 Position the loaded text icon over the placeholder frame near the bottom of page 1, and click.

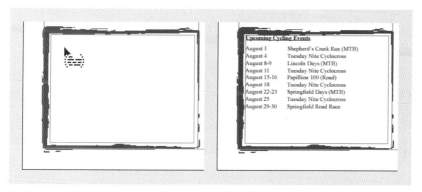

Placing a text file into an existing frame

You will apply styles to this sidebar text later in this lesson.

5 Choose File > Save.

Working with styles

Styles make it easy to format documents that repeat characteristics in several places. Styles can save time when you apply and revise text formatting and can help provide a consistent look to your documents.

Applying a style

To make the appearance of the article consistent with the other articles in the newsletter, you will apply a paragraph style called Body Copy. We created this style for formatting the body text of the main articles in the newsletter.

1 Click the Paragraph Styles palette (or choose Type > Paragraph Styles) to make the palette visible.

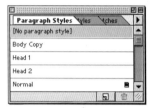

The Paragraph Styles palette includes four styles: Body Copy, Head 1, Head 2, and Normal. The Normal style has a disk icon next to it, indicating that the style was imported from a different application. In this case, Normal is a Microsoft Word style that was imported when you placed the article. You'll now apply the InDesign style, Body Copy, to the text.

2 Using the type tool (**T**), click an insertion point anywhere in the main article you placed. Then choose Edit > Select All to select all the body text in the story. Notice that the sidebar text is not selected; this text belongs to a different story.

3 Once all the text is selected, select Body Copy in the Paragraph Styles palette.

4 Choose Edit > Deselect All. The article is now formatted in a different font, and each paragraph is now indented.

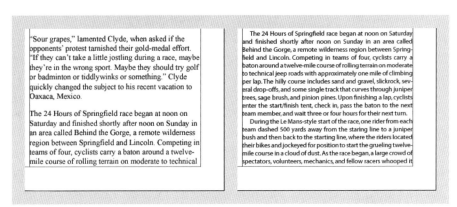

Before and after style is applied

Creating a headline and applying a style

In the blank area between the banner, "Sonata Cycles News," and the beginning of the article, you'll create a text frame for the article headline, "Team Sonata Captures 24 Hours Race." This headline text frame will span the two columns. You'll then apply a headline style to the newsletter.

1 Drag a guide from the horizontal ruler to the 18p6 (18 picas, 6 points) location on page 1. To help you position the guide, watch the Y value in the Transform palette as you drag. Holding down Shift lets you drag in 6-point increments.

2 Using the type tool (T), position the type cursor next to the left margin over the 18p6 guide. The horizontal crossbar on the type cursor should be at 18p6.

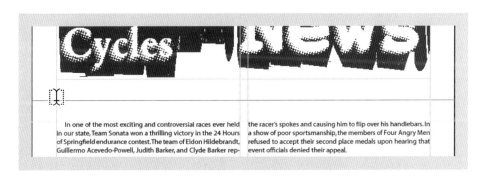

3 Drag to create a text frame in the blank area below the 18p6 guide and above the 21p guide. The text frame should span the two columns, and the top of the frame should snap to the 18p6 guide.

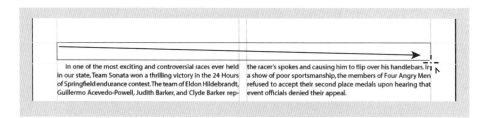

💡 *If you need to resize the frame, select the selection tool, and drag the top edge of the frame to snap to the 18p6 guide. Then select the type tool and click inside the frame.*

After you draw a text frame, the insertion point appears, ready for you to begin typing.

4 In the text frame you just created, type **Team Sonata Captures 24 Hours Race**.

To make this headline consistent with other headlines used in the newsletter, you'll apply the Head 1 style. When you apply a paragraph style, you can place the insertion point anywhere in the paragraph or select any part of the paragraph.

5 With the insertion point anywhere in the headline text you just typed, select Head 1 in the Paragraph Styles palette.

6 Save the file.

Loading styles from another document

Styles appear only in the document in which you create them. However, it's easy to *load*, or import, styles from other InDesign documents. Another Sonata Cycles document includes a couple of sidebar styles that will work well for the sidebars in this newsletter. Instead of re-creating these styles, you'll load the styles from the other document and apply them to text in the newsletter.

1 Position the pointer on the black triangle to the right of the Paragraph Styles tab, and choose Load All Styles from the Paragraph Styles palette menu.

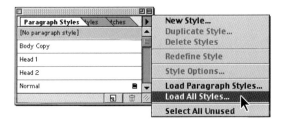

2 Double-click Styles.indd from the ID_05 folder. In the Paragraph Styles palette, notice the new styles called Sidebar Copy and Sidebar Head (you may need to scroll through the list or resize the palette).

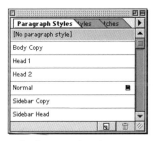

Styles from another document loaded into the Paragraph Styles palette

3 In the document window, change the view so that you can see the sidebar ("Upcoming Cycling Events") on page 1.

4 Using the type tool (**T**), click an insertion point in the sidebar, and then choose Edit > Select All.

5 Select the Sidebar Copy style in the Paragraph Styles palette. Notice that a plus sign appears next to the Sidebar Copy style in the Paragraph Styles palette.

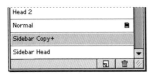

A plus sign next to a style indicates additional formatting. When you apply a style to text, the font and size may change, but some less-common formatting attributes such as super-script, subscript, and underline are automatically preserved. When you applied the Sidebar Copy style in this case, the underlining in the sidebar heading was preserved, as indicated by the plus sign next to the style name.

You can choose to override all formatting when you apply a style. Here you'll override the underline used in the heading as you apply the Sidebar Head style.

6 Using the type tool, click an insertion point in the sidebar heading, "Upcoming Cycling Events."

7 In the Paragraph Styles palette, hold down Alt (Windows) or Option (Mac OS) and select Sidebar Head in the Paragraph Styles palette.

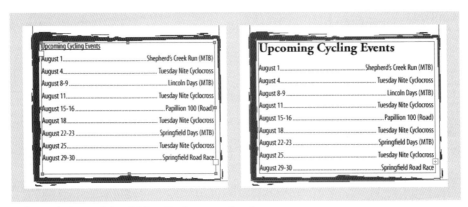

Before and after applying Sidebar Head paragraph style

The underlining disappeared when you applied the style because you held down Alt/Option.

💡 *While applying a style, you can also hold down Shift+Alt (Windows) or Shift+Option (Mac OS) to preserve common formatting such as bold and italics.*

Showing hidden characters

Notice that the red plus sign in the out port of the sidebar indicates overset text. A hard return at the end of the last paragraph causes this. You can see this end-of-paragraph marker and other nonprinting characters by showing hidden characters.

1 Choose Type > Show Hidden Characters. Notice the end-of-paragraph marker at the end of the last line.

```
..................................»...................................Springfield·Days·(MTB)¶
.......................»...................... Tuesday·Nite·Cyclocross¶
......................».......................... Springfield·Road·Race¶
```

2 With the insertion point still in the sidebar frame, press Ctrl+End (Windows) or Command+End (Mac OS) to move the insertion point to the end of the text in the story (you may not be able to see the insertion point, as it is hidden in the overset text).

3 Press Backspace (Windows) or Delete (Mac OS) until the end-of-paragraph character at the end of "Springfield Road Race" is deleted.

You have finished formatting the first page of the newsletter.

4 Choose Type > Show Hidden Characters to turn off this option.

5 Save the file.

Threading text

When you autoflowed text in the document, InDesign created links between the frames so that text would flow from one frame to another. These links are called *threads*. You can break the threads between frames, add new frames between the threaded frames, and rearrange how frames are threaded.

1 In the Pages palette, double-click the numbers below the page 2–3 icons. Choose View > Fit Spread in Window to view the spread.

2 Select the selection tool ( ), and then click the text frame in the right column on page 2 to select it.

3 Choose View > Show Text Threads. Blue lines appear that represent the connections (threads) between text frames in the selected story. Each thread goes from the out port of one frame to the in port of the next frame in the sequence.

4 With the text frame in the right column of page 2 still selected, press Backspace or Delete. Select a different frame in the story to display the text threads.

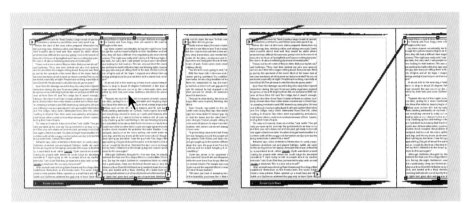

Before and after deleting a threaded frame

Notice that the text flows from the left column on page 2 to the left column on page 3. Although the text frame was deleted, no text in the story was deleted—it flowed into the next frame.

5 Make sure no frames are selected.

Now you'll import a picture. It's faster to open the Place dialog box using a keyboard shortcut.

6 Press Ctrl+D (Windows) or Command+D (Mac OS) to open the Place dialog box. Locate and double-click 05_e.tif in the ID_05 folder.

7 Click the loaded graphics icon in the upper left column just below the guide. If necessary, drag the graphic so that it snaps to the top of the column within the margins.

The graphic isn't as tall as anticipated. To avoid the extra white space at the bottom of the column, you will create a new text frame. To thread a new frame in the middle of a story, you can click the out port of the previous frame or the in port of the subsequent frame.

8 Drag a guide from the horizontal ruler to the 28p mark on page 2. To be precise, you can use the selection tool to select the guide, and then type **28p** in the Y box of the Transform palette.

9 Click the text frame in the left column of page 2 to select the frame, and then click the out port of the selected frame. Position the loaded text icon just below the 28p guide near the bottom of the right column, and click to create a frame that fills the rest of the column.

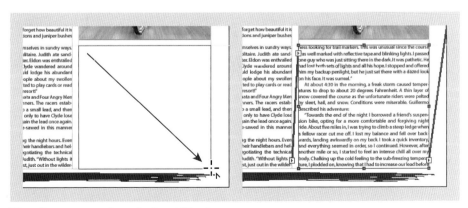

Threading a new text frame in the middle of a story

A text frame is created that is the width of the column. You have now completed page 2 of the newsletter.

10 Choose View > Hide Text Threads.

Now you'll use a keyboard shortcut for deselecting instead of using a menu.

11 Press Shift+Ctrl+A (Windows) or Shift+Command+A (Mac OS) to deselect everything. Then save the file.

Changing the number of columns on a page

You will now create a full-page sidebar on page 3 that provides three different bike routes for the newsletter readers. To simplify creating the three text frames for these routes, you will change the number of columns on page 3.

1 In the Pages palette, double-click the page 3 icon to center the page in the document window. Make sure only page 3 in the Pages palette is highlighted (if necessary, click another page icon, and then click the page 3 icon).

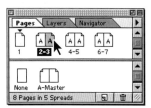

2 Choose Layout > Margins and Columns. Under Columns, type **3** for Number and click OK.

Even though the number of columns changed, the widths of the existing text frames did not change.

Notice that the text frames are independent of the number of columns. Column margins can determine how text frames are created, but the frame widths do not change when you redefine columns. One exception to this rule is when Layout Adjustment is turned on—you can learn more about Layout Adjustment in "On your own" at the end of this lesson.

3 Using the selection tool (↖), select a text frame on page 3 and press Backspace or Delete.

4 Select the other text frame on page 3 and press Backspace or Delete. Both text frames on page 3 should be deleted.

Once again, you have deleted text frames, but you did not delete any text; the text flowed into the text frames on page 4. Now you'll place an Adobe Illustrator file that has been sized to fit within the newsletter page.

5 Press Ctrl+D (Windows) or Command+D (Mac OS) to open the Place dialog box. Locate and double-click 05_f.ai in the ID_05 folder.

6 Click the loaded graphics icon in the upper left corner of page 3. If necessary, drag the illustration so that it snaps to the margin guides at the top, left, and right sides of the page.

Using semi-autoflow to place text frames

Now you will use semi-autoflow to place a text file into the three columns below the map illustration. Semi-autoflow lets you create text frames one at a time without having to reload the text icon.

1 Drag a guide from the horizontal ruler to the 28p location on page 3.

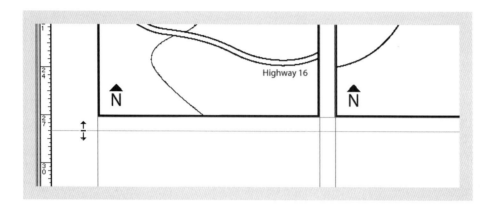

2 Press Shift+Ctrl+A (Windows) or Shift+Command+A (Mac OS) to make sure no objects are selected.

3 Open the Place dialog box, and then locate and double-click 05_g.doc in the ID_05 folder.

4 Holding down Alt (Windows) or Option (Mac OS), position the loaded text icon in the left column just below the 28p guide, and click.

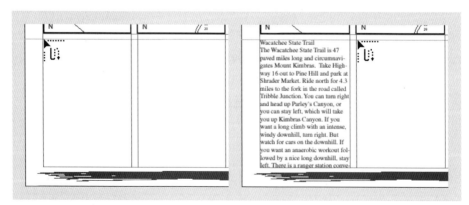

Flowing text semi-automatically

The text flows into the left column. Because you held down Alt/Option, the pointer is still a loaded text icon, ready for you to flow text into another frame.

5 Holding down Alt/Option, position the loaded text icon in the second column just below the guide, and click. Release the Alt/Option key.

Now you will create the final column. You won't hold down Alt/Option since there will only be three frames in this story.

6 Position the loaded text icon in the third column just below the guide, and click.

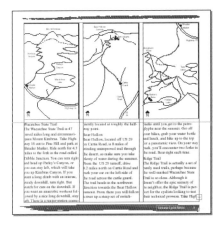

The text is overset in the third column, but after you format the text with styles, the text should fit within the frames.

Applying and editing the sidebar styles

To make the text consistent with the rest of the newsletter, you'll apply the sidebar styles to the text you just added. You will also edit the Sidebar Head style so that each heading starts at the top of the next column. You'll start by using the keyboard to select all the text in the story.

1 Using the type tool (T), click an insertion point in the sidebar. Then press Ctrl+A (Windows) or Command+A (Mac OS) to select all the text in the story.

2 Select the Sidebar Copy style in the Paragraph Styles palette.

3 Click an insertion point inside the "Wacatchee State Trail" heading, and then select the Sidebar Head style in the Paragraph Styles palette.

4 Apply the Sidebar Head style to the other two headings, "Bear Hollow" and "Ridge Trail."

Notice that the headings don't appear at the top of each frame. To make the headings appear at the top of each frame, you'll edit the sidebar heading.

5 Before you edit the style, deselect all text.

6 In the Paragraph Styles palette, double-click Sidebar Head to edit the style. Choose Keep Options from the menu.

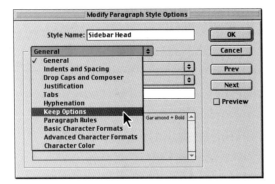

7 For Start Paragraph, choose In Next Column, and then click OK.

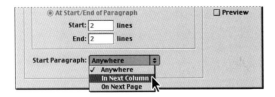

The sidebar headings on page 3 now appear at the top of each column. Now that you've finished placing text and graphics in the newsletter, you'll use some of InDesign's word-processing features to add finishing touches to the text throughout the newsletter.

8 Save the file.

Creating and applying a character style

In this lesson, you have applied and loaded styles. Now you'll learn how to create a character style. A *character style* can be applied to specified text within the body text. You can use the same methods to create character styles and paragraph styles: you can create a style based on formatted text, or you can create a style using the New Character Style dialog box.

Here you'll apply formatting to text and create a new character style based on that text. You'll then apply it to bicycle names in a text frame.

1 In the Pages palette, double-click the page 7 icon. Using the zoom tool ( ), zoom in to a level that allows you to read the type in the left column of page 7.

2 Using the type tool (T), select "Road Bikes—" (including the dash) at the beginning of the second paragraph below "New Series of Bicycles" on page 7.

First you will use the Character palette to format the text. Then you will use the Character Styles palette to create a style based on the formatted text.

3 Click the Character palette tab (or choose Type > Character) to make the palette visible. Select Cn Semibold for font style to format the text in Myriad® Condensed Semibold.

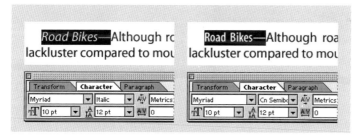

Before and after applying a character style to text within a paragraph

4 Click the Character Styles tab (or choose Type > Character Styles) to make the palette visible.

5 With the formatted text still selected, click the New Style icon ( ).

6 Double-click Character Style 1 (the default name for a new character style) to modify the style's options and name. For Style Name, type **Inline Head**, and then click OK.

7 With the type tool still selected, select "Mountain Bikes—" later in the same column on page 7. Select Inline Head in the Character Styles palette. Then deselect the words and view the new formatting.

The words automatically take on all the formatting attributes you selected for the Inline Head style. Notice that only the selected text was formatted with the style, not the entire paragraph.

8 Apply the Inline Head character style to "Specialty Bikes—" in the second column on page 7.

9 Save the file.

Finding and changing

Like most popular word processors, InDesign lets you find text and replace it. You can also search for and change formatting and special characters.

Finding text

You will search for occurrences of the word "Lincoln" in this document.

1 Choose Edit > Find/Change. For Find What, type **Lincoln**.

2 For Search, choose Document to search the entire document.

3 Click Find Next to display the next occurrence of the word.

4 Click Done to close the Find/Change dialog box.

Even when the Find/Change dialog box is closed, you can still search for the next occurrence of the most recent search.

5 Press Ctrl+Alt+F (Windows) or Command+Option+F (Mac OS) to find the next occurrence of "Lincoln."

6 Repeat the previous step several times. Notice that only some occurrences of "Lincoln" are underlined. Stop on an underlined occurrence of "Lincoln."

Finding and changing formatting

The author of the main article used underline instead of italics to indicate the title of the book, *Lincoln*. You want to remove the underlining and replace it with italics.

1 Choose Edit > Find/Change. Notice that the text from the previous search, "Lincoln," still appears in the Find What box.

2 Press Tab to move to the Change To box, and then type **Lincoln** in the Change To box. For Search, make sure Document is selected.

3 Click More to display additional formatting options in the dialog box.

4 Under Find Style Settings, click Format, and then choose Basic Character Formats from the menu.

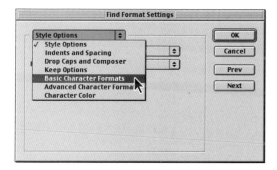

Notice that the check boxes next to the attributes at the bottom of the dialog box are grayed out check marks (Windows) or dashes (Mac OS), indicating that these attributes will not be included or excluded from the search.

5 Click Underline to select the check box, and click OK.

Notice the alert icon above the Find What box. This icon indicates that InDesign will search for text containing the specified formatting. In this case, InDesign will search for underlined occurrences of "Lincoln."

6 Under Change Style Settings, click Format, and then choose Basic Character Formats from the menu. Click Underline twice to deselect the check box. For Font, choose Adobe Garamond, and then choose Italic for font style. For Size, select 11 pt. For Leading, select 12 pt. Click OK.

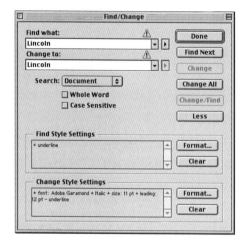

The Find/Change dialog box is now set up to search for underlined occurrences of "Lincoln" and remove the underlining, add italics, and increase the point size slightly. You're ready to change all the occurrences.

7 Click Change All to change the three occurrences of underlined "Lincoln."

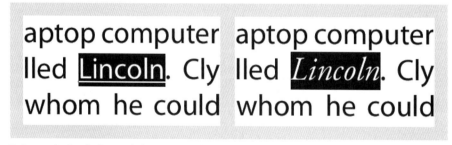

Before and after finding and changing attributes

8 Click OK, and then click Done to close the Find/Change dialog box. Save the file.

Finding and changing special characters

The text in the sidebar on page 1 uses hyphens between date numbers (such as August 8-9) instead of en dashes. You will replace these hyphens (-) with en dashes (–).

1 Turn to page 1, and use the zoom tool ( ) to magnify the "Upcoming Cycling Events" text frame.

2 Using the type tool (**T**), click inside the "Upcoming Cycling Events" sidebar.

3 Press Ctrl+F (Windows) or Command+F (Mac OS) to open the Find/Change dialog box.

In this case, you want InDesign to replace only the hyphens in the text frame on the first page, so you will limit the search range to only the *story,* which consists of only the sidebar frame.

4 For Search, choose Story to narrow the search to only the sidebar.

5 For Find What, select "Lincoln" and type - to replace the "Lincoln" text.

6 Press Tab to shift focus to the Change To box and select "Lincoln." Click the triangle ( ) to the right of the Change To box and choose En Dash from the pop-up menu (^= appears in the Change To box). Click Change All.

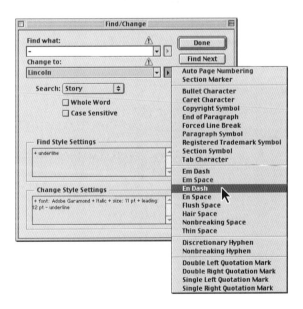

A message appears indicating that InDesign did not make any changes. The problem is that InDesign is looking for underlined hyphens because that is the formatting you specified in your last search, as indicated by the alert icons. Let's clear the formatting and try again.

7 Click OK to close the alert message. Under Find Style Settings, click Clear. Then click Clear under Change Style Settings. Click Change All.

The four hyphens (-) are replaced by en dashes (–) in the sidebar.

Note: If you are notified that considerably more than four changes were made, you may have forgotten to choose Story instead of Document for search, or you didn't click an insertion point inside the sidebar frame. Choose Edit > Undo Replace All Text and try again.

8 Click OK, and then click Done to close the Find/Change dialog box. Save the file.

Finding and changing a missing font

When you opened the document based on the template, the GracelessSans font was missing. You will search for text containing the GracelessSans font and replace it with the Myriad font.

1 In the Pages palette, double-click the page 8 icon (you may need to scroll in the Pages palette). Choose View > Fit Page in Window, and notice the text highlighted in pink.

2 Press Ctrl+F (Windows) or Command+F (Mac OS) to open the Find/Change dialog box.

3 For Search, choose Document.

4 Delete the hyphen in the Find What box, and then delete the en dash symbols (^=) in the Change To box so that the boxes are empty.

By leaving the boxes empty, you allow InDesign to find any text with the missing font, not just hyphens.

5 Under Find Style Settings, click Format, and then choose Basic Character Formats from the menu.

Missing fonts appear in brackets at the bottom of the Font list.

6 For Font, select [GracelessSans], and then click OK.

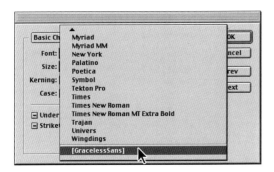

7 Under Change Style Settings, click Format, and then choose Basic Character Formats from the menu. For Font, select Myriad. For font style, select Bold, and then click OK.

8 Click Change All. Click OK, and then click Done to see the replaced font.

Note: For some projects, you may need to add the missing font to your system instead of replacing the missing font. You can fix missing fonts by installing the font on your system, by activating the font using ATM Deluxe or another font manager, or by adding the font files to the InDesign Fonts folder. For more information, see the InDesign User Guide.

Spell-checking a story

The text in the "Bad Clams" story on page 5 includes Spanish and Italian phrases. Before you spell-check the story, you will assign the appropriate language to each phrase.

1 In the document window, turn to page 5. Change your view so that you can see the paragraph below the image in the right column beginning with "William Johnson."

2 In the paragraph under the image in the right column, use the type tool (T) to select "¡Yo tengo un cuaderno rojo!" In the Character palette, choose Spanish: Castilian from the Language menu.

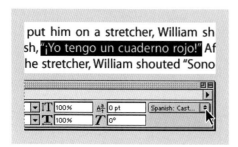

3 In the same paragraph, select "Sono il campione dell mondo" (misspelled). In the Character palette, choose Italian from the Language menu.

Notice that the text shifted when you applied the language attribute. This occurs because hyphenation rules are different for English and Italian.

4 Make sure the insertion point is in the same paragraph, and choose Edit > Check Spelling.

5 For Search, select Story so you don't have to spell-check the entire document.

6 Click Start. When "dell" is highlighted, select "del" under Suggested Corrections, and then click Change. When you finish spell-checking, click Done.

7 Save the file.

Congratulations. You have finished the lesson.

On your own

Follow these steps to learn more about layout adjustment and styles.

When you changed the number of columns in this lesson, the size of the text frames remained unchanged. However, if you need to change your document setup after you've begun laying out your document, you can turn on the Layout Adjustment option, which can save you time in reformatting your document. Try this:

1 Go to page 4 and choose Layout > Layout Adjustment. Select Enable Layout Adjustment and click OK. Now change the number of columns.

Notice that the photograph is resized and the two text frames shrink to fit the first two columns.

2 Resize the text frames and graphics frame to clean up the page. Add threaded text frames as necessary to finish the redesign.

Before column change (left), after column change with Layout Adjustment turned on (middle), and finished redesign (right)

In this lesson, we covered only the basics of creating and applying styles. If you do a lot of your writing in InDesign, you'll want to learn how Next Style works and how to apply styles using shortcut keystrokes.

Note: In Windows, Num Lock must be on for the following shortcut keystrokes to work.

3 With no text selected, double-click the Head 2 style in the Paragraph Styles palette. Click an insertion point in the Shortcut text box. Using numbers from only the keypad, press Ctrl+Alt+2 (Windows) or Command+Option+2 (Mac OS). For Next Style, select Body Copy. Click OK to close the dialog box. Now practice applying the Head 2 style using your keyboard shortcut. Notice that when you press Enter or Return at the end of a Head 2 paragraph, the next paragraph automatically has the Body Copy style.

Note: If text does not appear in the Shortcut text box, make sure you use the numbers from the numeric keypad. In Windows, make sure Num Lock is on.

4 Some designers prefer not to indent the first paragraph after a heading. Create a paragraph style called "Body Copy No Indent" that is based on Body Copy and does not have a first-line indent. For the Next Style option in Body Copy No Indent, select Body Copy. Edit the heading styles so that the Next Style option is set to Body Copy No Indent.

Review questions

1 How do you autoflow text? How do you flow text one frame at a time?

2 How can using styles save time?

3 When searching for text, you get a "Cannot find match" message. What are some reasons InDesign failed to find a match?

4 While spell-checking your document, InDesign flags words used in other languages. How can you fix this problem?

Review answers

1 When the loaded text icon appears after using the Place command or clicking an out port, hold down Shift and click. To flow text one frame at a time, you can hold down Alt (Windows) or Option (Mac OS) to reload the text icon after you click or drag to create a frame.

2 Styles save time by letting you keep a group of formatting attributes together that you can quickly apply to text. If you need to update the text, you don't have to change each paragraph formatted with the style individually. Instead, you can simply modify the style.

3 If you get a "Cannot find match" message, you may not have typed the text properly, you may have selected Whole Word or Case Sensitive, or you may not have cleared formatting used in a previous search. Another possibility is that you selected Story for Search while the text you're looking for is in a different story. Finally, you may be searching for text that does not exist in your document.

4 Before you spell-check your document, select any phrase from a different language and use the Character palette to specify the language for that text.

Hecho en Mexico

Exploring The
LIBRARY

Everyone knows that the Library has books. Lots and lots of books. But we also have fun displays and hands-on experiments that are just for kids. Here is a floor by floor guide!

...ng artists. Just ...for help and information.

Floor 2

Dinosaurs

Our new dinosaur exhibit is exciting for all ages. See real dinosaur eggs, learn about where to find local fossils, and get your own Prehistoric Passport!

Computers

Our growing computer lab is always fun. You can look for books in libraries all across the state! Andrea and Joe are glad to help guide you through the World Wide Web.

Bugs

See our new hands-on display of bugs and insects. Our collection of butterflies is always a treat. Our specialist Sonya can help get you up and running on school science projects. Just ask her!

...periodicals, video tapes, and more to help you pursue your future jobs. Ask for Emily and she will get you started!

Cafe

All this fun can work up an appetite. Come to the Cafe for a glass of lemonade, a slice of pizza, or one of Martin's chocolate chip cookies!

1-1: A document and its layers

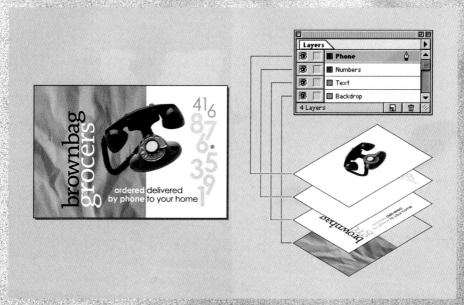

Think of layers as transparent sheets stacked on top of each other. Where objects don't exist on a layer, you can see through the layer to objects behind it.

1-2: Moving an object to another layer

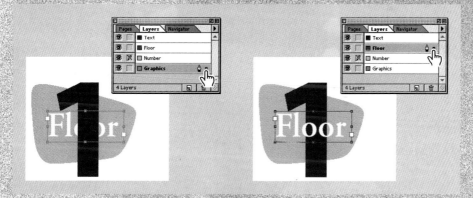

Drag the colored dot on the right side of the layer list to the layer where you want to move an object.

Lesson 2

The flight back from Oaxaca seemed to take forever, but I fear it was only Judith's disgust with me that made it seem interminable. Anyway, we got home and life returned to normal, or even better than normal, even supernormal, if there is such a word. I told Judith I was sorry about the comments I made about her parents and the *Day of the Dead* celebration, and she apologized for her brazen flirting with that good-for-nada bullfighter. Then, in an effort to cement our new-found bond, Judith enrolled us in an *origami* class. "Oh great, I thought, "my marriage has been reduced to folded paper." But now that I've been in the class for a few weeks, I must admit that I love it. Origami is amazing and beautiful.

The name origami was coined in 1880 for the words *oru* (to fold) and *kami* (paper). It started in the first century AD in China. (I thought it started in Japan, but Judith quickly pointed out the error in my thinking.) They say that's when paper

making started, and with paper making came paper folding. The Chinese developed some simple forms, some of which survive to this day. Buddhist monks brought Origami to Japan in the sixth century AD. It caught on quickly throughout the culture: paper was used in architecture and in many everyday rituals. Many of the earliest designs have been lost, since there was nothing written down about origami until 1797 with the publication of the *Senbadzuru Orikata* (How to Fold One Thousand Cranes). *The Ken no mado* (Window of Midwinter), a comprehensive collection of traditional Japanese figures, was published in 1845.

Origami flourished in other parts of the world, as well. Arabs brought the secrets of paper making to North Africa, and in the eighth century AD, the Moors brought the secrets of Spain. The Moors, devoutly religious, were forbidden to create representational figures. Their paper folding was a study in geometry. After the Moors were

Tsuru no On-gaeshi
(A Repaying Crane)

Once upon a time, there was a poor hunter. One day, he came across a trapped crane. He took pity on the crane and released it. A few days later, a lovely woman visited his house, and asked him to shelter for the night. Soon the two got married.

The bride was sweet in disposition as well as beautiful, so they lived happily. But the hunter couldn't afford to support his new wife. One day, she said she would weave cloth for him to sell at market, but she told him never to see her weaving.

She stayed in a weaving hut for three days. When she finished weaving, she emerged with a beautiful fabric.

He brought the fabric to town, where merchants were surprised and paid gold for it. The fabric was very rare and called *Tsuru-no-orabu-ori* (thousand feathers of crane).

Origami 3

Lesson 3

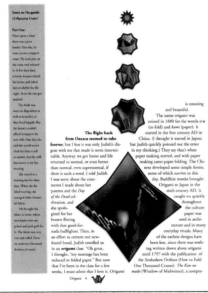

Tsuru no On-gaeshi
(A Repaying Crane)

Part One

Once upon a time, there was a poor hunter. One day, he came across a trapped crane. He took pity on the crane and released it. A few days later, a lovely woman visited his house, and asked him to shelter for the night. Soon the two got married.

The bride was sweet in disposition as well as beautiful, so they lived happily. But the hunter couldn't afford to support his new wife. One day, she said she would weave cloth for him to sell at market, but she told him never to see her weaving.

She stayed in a weaving hut for three days. When she finished weaving, she emerged with a beautiful fabric.

He brought the fabric to town, when merchants were surprised and paid gold for it. The fabric was very rare and called *Tsuru-no-orabu-ori* (thousand feathers of crane).

The flight back from Oaxaca seemed to take forever, but I fear it was only Judith's disgust with me that made it seem interminable. Anyway, we got home and life returned to normal, or even better than normal, even supernormal, if there is such a word. I told Judith I was sorry about the comments I made about her parents and the *Day of the Dead* celebration, and she apologized for her brazen flirting with that good-for-nada bullfighter. Then, in an effort to cement our new-found bond, Judith enrolled us in an *origami* class. "Oh great, I thought, "my marriage has been reduced to folded paper." But now that I've been in the class for a few weeks, I must admit I love it. Origami is amazing and beautiful.

The name origami was coined in 1880 for the words *oru* (to fold) and *kami* (paper). It started in the first century AD in China. (I thought it started in Japan, but Judith quickly pointed out the error in my thinking.) They say that's when paper making started, and with paper making came paper folding. The Chinese developed some simple forms, some of which survive to this day. Buddhist monks brought Origami to Japan in the sixth century AD. It caught on quickly throughout the culture: paper was used in architecture and in many everyday rituals. Many of the earliest designs have been lost, since there was nothing written down about origami until 1797 with the publication of the *Senbadzuru Orikata* (How to Fold One Thousand Cranes). *The Ken no mado* (Window of Midwinter), a compre-

Popular origami designs include animals, boxes, flowers, and mythical creatures. *From top to bottom:* fortune teller, fish, armadillo, swallow, crane. *This page* on four of the five designs shown here, the crane and fortune teller are most common; the armadillo is the most complex to create.

hensive collection of traditional Japanese figures, was published in 1845.

Origami flourished in other parts of the world, as well. Arabs brought the secrets of paper making to North Africa, and in the eighth century AD, the Moors brought the secrets of Spain. The Moors, devoutly religious, were forbidden to create representational figures. Their paper folding was a study in geometry. After the Moors were driven out of Spain during the Inquisition (Judith gave me a look, but then softened into a smile), the Spanish developed papiroflexia, which sounds to me like some sort of inflammation of the Pope's ligaments. Anyway, this technique is still popular in Spain and Argentina.

Modern origami owes its existence to a man named Akira Yoshizawa. In the 1930's, Yoshizawa designed thousand of models of various subjects. He is the originator of the system of lines and arrows used in modern paper folding. He exhibited his work throughout the west in the 1950's and 1960's and helped inspire many paperfolders in the west as well as Japan. As origami evolves, elaborate folding techniques produce amazing models.

Technology does not govern origami, however; true origami artists concentrate on the artistry and beauty of origami. Today's artists use new paper types and inventive compositions that will evolve into even more amazing creations in the future.

Speaking of the future, life with Judith gets better and better. The other day I heard her rustling around in her office. I knocked and heard more noise. Then a beaming Judith answered the door, attempting to block my view. She held something crumpled in her right hand. I looked over her shoulder and couldn't believe my eyes. Strung across the ceiling and walls were the most incredible cranes, looking as if they were holding hands (or wings, I guess). I looked at Judith for an explanation. She hugged me tightly and whispered in my ear, "Clyde, it's for you, to show my love." I've created one thousand cranes as a symbol of my love for you." She extended her palm and showed me a crumpled crane. "You frightened me when you banged on the

Part Two

The wife wove the material again and again. The hunter came to live in comfort. However, little by little, his wife got thinner. One day, she said that she could weave the fabric no longer. She was weak. Her husband had learned greed, and asked her to weave once more. At last she was persuaded and seemed to weave again.

She did not come out of the weaving hut to the third day. Three days passed. The hunter got worried, and finally broke their promise and peeked into the weaving hut. To his surprise, it was not a woman but a crane that was weaving fabric.

The bird was weaving his wife came out from the weaving hut with the last fabric in her hands. She said, "you have seen my true form, so I cannot stay with you any longer." And then, she turned into a crane and flew away, leaving the hunter crying.

Origami 4　　*Origami 5*

3-1: working with frames and their contents

Using the selection tool to select and modify frames containing objects

The selection tool activates a frame's bounding box.

With a frame's bounding box active, you can move a frame and its contents together, by dragging with the selection tool.

Resize a frame and its contents by selecting with the selection tool, then Ctrl-drag (Windows) or Command-drag (Mac OS) a bounding box handle.

Using the direct-selection tool to select and modify objects in frames

The direct-selection tool lets you select content independent of its frame.

When you drag contents with the direct-selection tool, you reposition contents within the frame, masking any areas that extend beyond the frame edge.

When you use the direct-selection tool to re-size selected contents, the frame isn't affected.

Using the direct-selection tool to select and modify frames

   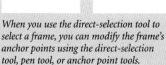

The direct-selection tool lets you select a frame independent of its contents.

When you drag a frame with the direct-selection tool, you reposition the frame around the contents, masking any areas that extend beyond the frame edge.

When you use the direct-selection tool to select a frame, you can modify the frame's anchor points using the direct-selection tool, pen tool, or anchor point tools.

Lesson 4

O R I G A M I

a short story by
CLYDE BELL

The ART of
PAPER FOLDING

The flight back from Oaxaca seemed to take forever, but I fear it was only Judith's disgust with me that made it seem interminable. Anyway, we got home and life returned to normal, or even better than normal, even supernormal, if there is such a word. I told Judith I was sorry about the comments I made about her parents and the *Day of the Dead* celebration, and she apologized for her brazen flirting with that good-for-nada bullfighter. Then, in an effort to cement our new-found bond, Judith enrolled us in an ***origami*** class. "Oh great, I thought, "my marriage has been reduced to folded paper." But now that I've been in the class for a few weeks, I must admit that I love it. Origami is amazing and beautiful.

The name origami was coined in 1880 for the words *oru* (to fold) and *kami* (paper). It started in the first century AD in China. (I thought it started in Japan, but Judith quickly pointed out the error in my thinking.) They say that's when paper making started, and with paper making came paper folding. The Chinese developed some simple forms, some of which survive to this day. Buddhist monks brought Origami to Japan in the sixth century AD. It caught on quickly throughout the culture: paper was used in architecture and in many everyday rituals. Many of the earliest designs have been lost, since there was nothing written down about origami until 1797 with the publication of the *Senbazuru Orihata* (How to Fold One Thousand Cranes). *The Kan no mado* (Window of Midwinter), a comprehensive collection of traditional Japanese figures, was published in 1845.

Origami flourished in other parts of the world, as well. Arabs brought the secrets of paper making to North Africa, and in the eighth century AD, the Moors brought the secrets of Spain. The Moors, devoutly religious, were forbidden to create representational figures. Their paper folding was a study in geometry. After the Moors were

Origami   3

Tsuru no On-gaeshi
(A Repaying Crane)

Once upon a time, there was a poor hunter. One day, he came across a trapped crane. He took pity on the crane and released it. A few days later, a lovely woman visited his home, and asked him to shelter for the night, from the two got married.

The bride was sweet in disposition as well as beautiful, so they lived happily. But the hunter couldn't afford to support his new wife. One day, she said she would weave cloth for him to sell at market, but she told him never to see her weaving.

She stayed in a weaving hut for three days. When she finished weaving, she emerged with a beautiful fabric.

He brought the fabric to town, where merchants were surprised and paid gold for it. The fabric was very rare and called *Tsuru no oriki-ori* (thousand feathers of crane).

4-1: Additive and subtractive color models

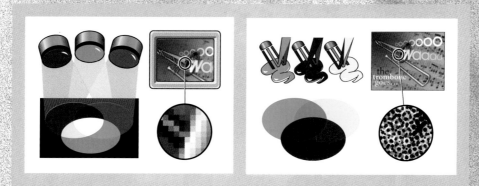

Additive color (RGB), left, and Subtractive color (CMYK), right

4-2: L*a*b color model

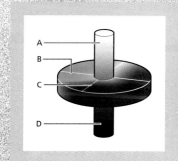

A. *Luminance=100 (white)* **B.** *Green to red component*
C. *Blue to yellow component* **D.** *Luminence=0 (black)*

Lesson 5

5-1: Hidden characters

.... Springfield·Days·(MTB)

.... Tuesday·Nite·Cyclocross

.... Springfield·Road·Race

Before and after showing hidden characters

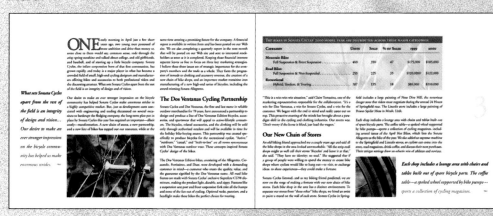

6-1: Viewing the baseline grid

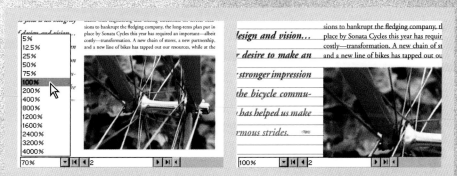

If the baseline grid does not appear, its threshold value is set higher than the current document view—in this case 100%. Set the document magnification to match or exceed the grid threshold value.

6-2: Gradient filled text

> *What sets Sonata Cycles apart from the rest of the field is an integrity of design and vision... Our desire to make an ever stronger impression on the bicycle commu-nity has helped us make enormous strides.*

> *What sets Sonata Cycles apart from the rest of the field is an integrity of design and vision... Our desire to make an ever stronger impression on the bicycle commu-nity has helped us make enormous strides.*

Applying a gradient swatch to selected text creates a left-to-right gradient fill.

6-3: Setting the direction of a gradient fill in text

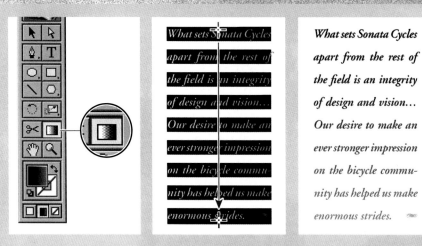

The gradient tool (left) lets you set the direction of the gradient fill.

6-4: Adding fill and stroke to text

Original drop cap (left), drop cap with color fill (middle), and drop cap with fill and stroke (right)

6-5: Composition methods

Each shop includes a lounge area with chairs and tables built out of spare bicycle parts. The coffee table—a spoked wheel supported by bike pumps—sports a collection of cycling magazines.

Each shop includes a lounge area with chairs and tables built out of spare bicycle parts. The coffee table—a spoked wheel supported by bike pumps—sports a collection of cycling magazines.

Pull quote formatted using the single-line composer (left), and the multi-line composer (right)

6-6: Completed table

THE BIKES IN SONATA CYCLES' 2000 MODEL YEAR ARE DISTRIBUTED ACROSS THESE MAJOR CATEGORIES:					
CATEGORY	UNITS	SOLD	% OF SALES	1999	2000
Mountain Bikes					
Full Suspension & Front Suspension	400	350	47	$175,000	$185,000
Road Bikes					
Full Suspension & Non-Suspended	250	225	35	$120,0000	$122,000
Recreational					
Hybrid, Tandem, & Touring	187	135	18	$81,000	$110,000

Use tabs to create tables and position text in specific horizontal locations in a frame.

Lesson 7

7-1: Setting clipping path options

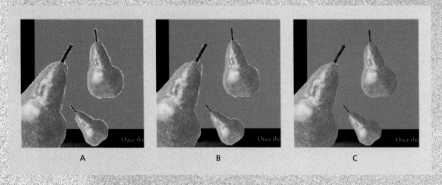

A. Threshold value of 10 and Tolerance value of 1 B. Threshold = 65 and Tolerance = 5
C. Threshold = 10 and Tolerance = 10

8-1: Dragging a new curved segment

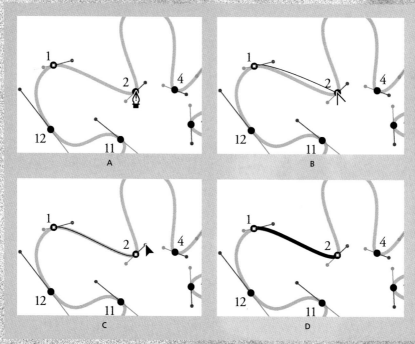

A. Position the pen tool B. Pen tool when mouse button is down C. Drag up to the red dot
D. Result

8-2: Colorizing and masking a bitmap image

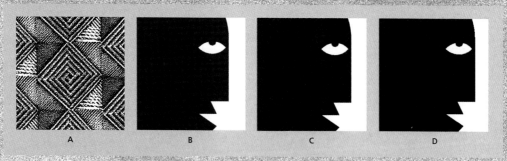

A. Original bitmap B. Compound path drawn using InDesign C. bitmap placed inside path D. Bitmap with brown color applied

8-3: Colorizing a bitmap image

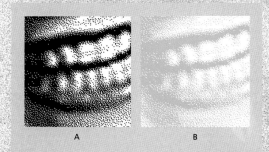

A. *Original bitmap* **B.** *Bitmap colorized in InDesign*

Lesson 9

9-1: **Creating a clipping path**

Select an object (left), and select threshold and tolerance levels to remove an object's background.

9-2: **Nested objects**

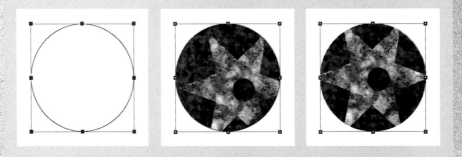

Multiple, grouped objects can be pasted into another object, and then moved or transformed within the object.

9-3: Completing the flower

Use the selection tool to move and otherwise transform objects and their nested elements.

9-4: Transforming objects

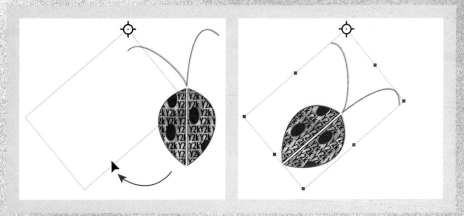

Nested objects can be grouped with other objects, and then rotated or otherwise transformed as one element.

Lesson 10

10-1: Color gamuts

Visible spectrum containing millions of colors (far left) compared with color gamuts of various devices and document

10-2: The CMS process

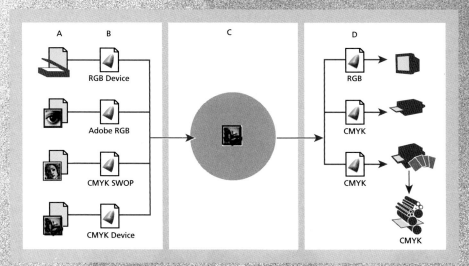

A. *Scanners and software applications create color documents* **B.** *ICC source profiles describe document color spaces.* **C.** *A color management engine uses ICC source profiles to map document colors to a device-independent color space through supporting applications.* **D.** *The color management engine maps document colors from the device-independent color space to output device color spaces using destination profiles.*

10-3: White point adjustments

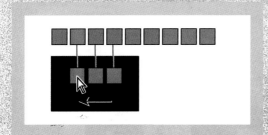

Clicking the left square will reset all the squares a shade cooler.

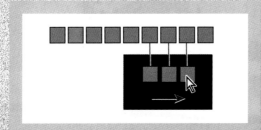

Clicking the right square will reset all the squares a shade warmer.

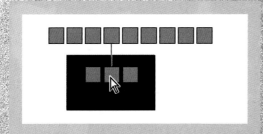

Clicking the center square will commit the settings.

Lesson 11

11-1: Destination and source profiles

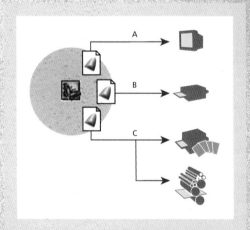

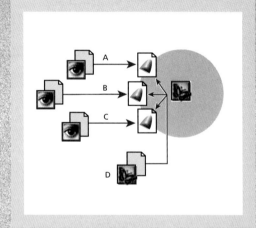

Destination profiles *A. Monitor profile* **B.** *Composite profile* **C.** *Separations profile (which can be an output device or press standard, such as SWOP)*

Source profiles *A. LAB profile* **B.** *RGB profile* **C.** *CMYK separations profile* **D.** *InDesign document using appropriate profiles from sources used to create graphic*

Lesson 12

12-1: Trapping

Gap created by misregistration (left); gap hidden by trapping (right)

12-2: Chokes and spreads

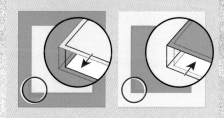

Spread: Object overlaps background (left);
Choke: Background overlaps object (right)

12-3: Knocking out vs. overprinting

Spot-colored type set to knock out, misregistered (left); spot-colored type set to over-print, hiding misregistration (right)

12-4: Overprinting a stroke

The stroke will overprint ink into the black background, and the fill will knock out.

12-5: Results of overprinting

On-screen appearance (left) and printed result (right)

12-6: Rich black

Without cyan support screen (left) and with cyan support screen (right)

12-7: Misregistered rich black

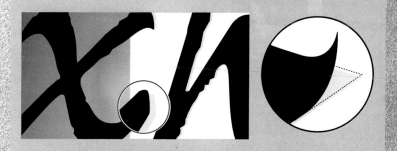

A fringe of cyan appears (left) when the cyan separation is misregistered (right).

12-8: Overprinting strokes in a rich black

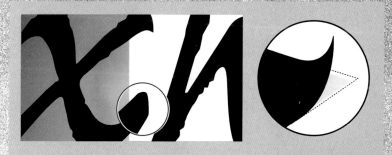

Overprinting a black stroke (left) chokes back the support screen from the edge (right).

12-9: Overprinting a varnish

Pink colored objects represent areas where the spot varnish will be applied.

12-10: Color separations

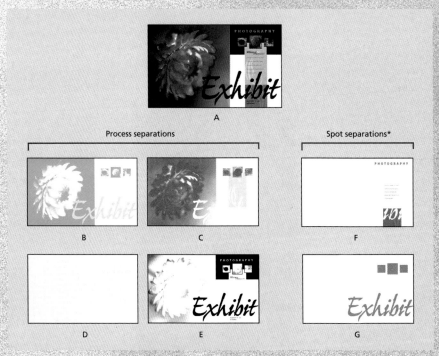

A. Composite *B.* Cyan separation *C.* Magenta separation *D.* Yellow separation *E.* Black separation *F.* Spot color separation *G.* Spot varnish separation

*Pantone 165CVC is simulated in these examples. This book was printed using the four process colors only.

Lesson 6

6 | Working with Typography

Using InDesign tools, you can precisely control the type and formatting of your document. Palettes make it easy to change fonts and type styles, modify the alignment, add tabs and indents, and apply gradients and strokes to text.

In this lesson, you'll learn how to do the following:

- Prepare and use a baseline grid.

- Change type spacing and appearance.

- Create special characters.

- Create a tabbed table with tab leaders and hanging indents.

- Export a file to Portable Document Format (PDF).

Note: *To view the exported PDF file, you will need to have Adobe Acrobat Reader installed. You can install Acrobat Reader from the Adobe InDesign CD, or download it from the Adobe Web site (www.adobe.com).*

Getting started

In this lesson, you'll create an annual report for the Sonata Cycles company. Before you begin, you'll need to restore the default preferences for Adobe InDesign.

1 To ensure that the tools and palettes function exactly as described in this lesson, delete or deactivate (by renaming) the InDesign Defaults file and the InDesign SavedData file. See "Restoring default preferences" on page 2.

2 Start Adobe InDesign.

To begin working, you'll open an existing InDesign document.

3 Choose File > Open, and open the 06_a.indd file in the ID_06 folder, located inside the Lessons folder within the IDCIB folder on your hard disk.

4 Choose File > Save As, rename the file **06_report.indd**, and save it in the ID_06 folder.

5 If you want to see what the finished document will look like, open the 06_b.indd file in the same folder. You can leave this document open to act as a guide as you work. When you're ready to resume working on the lesson document, choose its name from the Window menu.

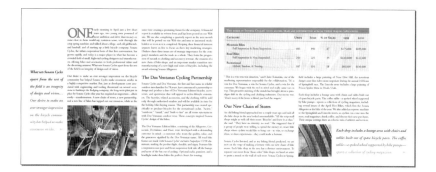

 For a color version of the finished document, see the color section.

Adjusting vertical spacing

InDesign provides several options for customizing and adjusting the vertical spacing in your document. You can automatically set the space between all lines of text using a baseline grid, or you can set the space between each line or each paragraph separately using the Leading option or the Space Above/Space Below options in the Character palette.

Using a baseline grid to align text

One of the first things you may want to do, once you've decided on the font size and leading for your document's body text, is set up a baseline grid (also called a leading grid) for the entire document. Baseline grids represent the leading for your document's body text and are used to align the baselines of one column of text with the baselines of neighboring columns.

Before you set the baseline grid, you'll want to check the margin value for the top of your document and the leading value for the body text so that these elements work with the grid in a cohesive design.

1 To view the top margin value for the document, choose Layout > Margins and Columns. The top margin is set to 6p0 (6 picas, 0 points). Click Cancel to close the dialog box.

2 To determine the leading value, select the type tool (T) in the toolbox and click in a body text paragraph. Then click the Character palette tab (or choose Type > Character) to make the palette visible. Check the leading value (⒜) in the Character palette. The leading is set to 14 pt (14 points).

3 Choose File > Preferences > Grids to set your grid options. In the Baseline Grid section, type **6** for Start to match your top margin setting of 6p0. This option sets the location of the first grid line for the document. If you use InDesign's default value of 3p0, the first grid line would appear above the top margin.

4 For Increment every, type **14pt** to match your leading. When you select another option, InDesign automatically converts the points value to picas, or 1p2.

5 Choose 100% for View Threshold. This option sets the document view value at which you can see the grid on-screen.

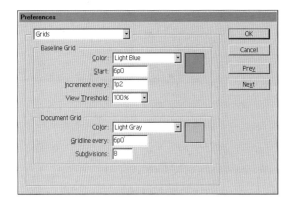

6 Click OK to close the dialog box.

Viewing the baseline grid

Now you'll make the grid you just set up visible on-screen.

1 To view the grid in the document window, choose View > Show Baseline Grid. The grid does not appear because the document view is lower than the grid's View Threshold value. Choose 100% from the magnification menu at the lower left corner of the document window—the grid now appears on-screen.

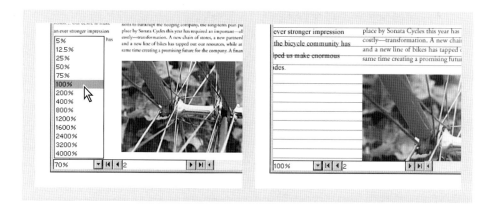

Now you'll use the Paragraph palette to align all the text to the grid. You can align multiple stories independently of one another or all at once. You'll align all the stories in this spread simultaneously.

2 Click the Paragraph tab (or choose Type > Paragraph) to make the palette visible.

3 With the type tool still selected, click an insertion point anywhere in the first paragraph on the spread, and then choose Edit > Select All to select all the text in the main story.

When applying paragraph attributes, it is not necessary to select an entire paragraph with the type tool. Just select a portion of the paragraph or paragraphs you want to format. If you are formatting only one paragraph, you can simply click in the paragraph to make an insertion point.

4 In the Paragraph palette, click the Align to Baseline Grid button (≣). The text shifts so that the baselines of the characters rest on the grid lines.

Before and after aligning the text to the baseline grid

5 If necessary, scroll to the left side of the spread so you can see the pull quote on the side of the page; then click an insertion point in the pull quote.

6 In the Paragraph palette, click the Align to Baseline Grid button. Because this text is formatted using 18 point leading, not the baseline grid leading value of 14pt or 1p2, aligning to the grid causes the text to expand to every other grid line (using 28 point leading).

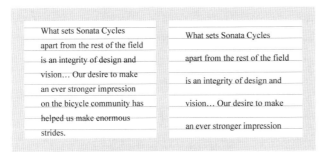

Before and after aligning the text to the baseline grid

7 Save the file.

Changing the spacing above and below paragraphs

When you apply a space before or after a paragraph that you have previously aligned to grid, the space automatically adjusts to the next highest multiple of the grid value. For example, if your grid is set to 14 points (1p2) and you specify a space after to any value under 14, InDesign automatically increases the space value to 14; if you specify a space to a value over 14, such as 16, InDesign increases it to the next higher multiple—28. You can use the Space Before or After value instead of the baseline grid value, by deselecting the Align to Grid option for the affected paragraph.

No space (left), space adjusted to fit grid at 28 pt (middle), and actual space value at 16 pt (right)

Here you'll increase the space after the second paragraph of the main story. All other paragraphs in the spread have already been formatted with a 1p2 space after value.

1 Make sure the type tool (**T**) is still selected, and click anywhere in the second paragraph on the page on the left (page 2).

2 In the Paragraph palette, type **1p2** for Space After (⬛) and press Enter or Return. The text in the next heading shifts automatically to the next grid line.

Before and after applying a Space After value to the paragraph

Now you'll increase the space before the heading "The Dos Ventanas Cycling Partnership" to give it even more space.

3 Click an insertion point in the heading "The Dos Ventanas Cycling Partnership." In the Paragraph palette, type **0p6** for Space Before (⬚) and then press Enter or Return. Because you previously aligned the heading to the baseline grid, the space before jumps to 14 points instead of 6.

To use the 0p6 value instead of 14, and to add more space between the heading and the following paragraph, you'll unalign the heading from the grid.

4 With an insertion point still in the heading "The Dos Ventanas Cycling Partnership," click the Do Not Align to Baseline Grid button (⬚) in the Paragraph palette. The heading shifts upward a bit, away from the body text below.

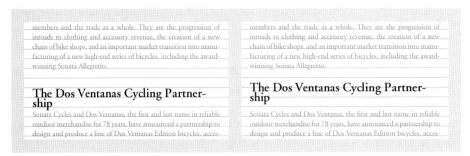

Before and after unaligning the heading from the baseline grid

This heading and the heading on the page on the right (page 3) are formatted using the Head 1 style. To automatically update the second heading so that it uses the same spacing values as the heading you just edited, you'll redefine the style.

5 Click the Paragraph Styles palette tab (or choose Type > Paragraph Styles) to make the palette visible.

6 Click an insertion point in the heading "The Dos Ventanas Cycling Partnership." Notice that a plus sign (+) appears after the Head 1 style name in the palette. This sign indicates the formatting for the selected text is different from the original formatting for the style.

7 Position the pointer on the black triangle to the right of the Paragraph Styles tab, and choose Redefine Style from the Paragraph Styles palette menu.

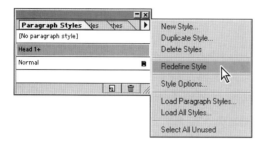

Notice that the plus sign disappears and the space before is added to the heading on page 3.

8 To unalign the heading on page 3 from the grid, click in the heading and then select the Head 1 style in the Paragraph Styles palette to reapply the style.

9 Save the file.

Changing fonts and type style

Changing the fonts and type styles of text can make a dramatic difference to the appearance of your document. Here you'll change the font family, type style, and size for the text in one of the pull quotes along the border of the spread. You'll make these changes using the Character palette.

About Fonts

A font, also known as a face or typeface, is a complete set of characters: letters, numbers, and symbols that share a common weight, width, and style, such as the bold style of Utopia, Minion, or Adobe Garamond.

A font family (or type family) is a collection of fonts sharing an overall appearance and designed to be used together, such as Adobe Garamond. A type style is a variant version of an individual font in a font family. Typically, the Roman or Plain member of a font family is the base font, which includes styles such as regular, bold, italic, and bold italic.

–From the Adobe InDesign User Guide, Chapter 5

1 Click the Character palette tab (or choose Type > Character).

2 Using the type tool (**T**), triple-click in any word in the pull quote along the left side of page 2 to select the entire paragraph.

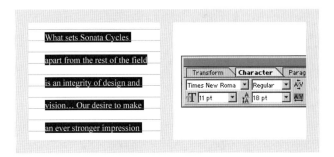

3 In the Character palette, select Adobe Garamond from the Font Family menu and Semibold Italic from the Type Style menu.

4 In the Font Size text box, type **15** and press Enter or Return.

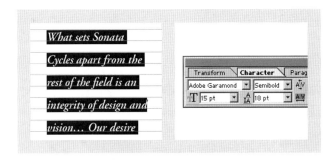

5 Choose Edit > Deselect All to deselect the text. Notice how the text stays aligned to the grid even after changing these attributes.

6 You won't be using the baseline grid for the remainder of the lesson, so you can hide it from view. To hide it, choose View > Hide Baseline Grid.

7 Save the file.

Changing paragraph alignment

You can easily manipulate how a paragraph fits in its text frame by changing the alignment. You can align text with one or both edges of a text frame or text frame inset. Justifying text aligns both edges. In this section, you'll justify the pull quote.

1 Using the type tool (T), click an insertion point in the pull quote on page 2.

2 Click the Paragraph palette tab (or choose Type > Paragraph), and then click the Justify All Lines button (≣).

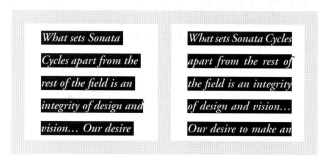

Before and after justifying text

Adding a decorative font and special character

Now you'll add a decorative font character and a flush space (special character) to the end of the pull quote. Used together, a decorative font and flush space can make a dramatic difference to the look of a justified paragraph.

1 Using the type tool (T), click an insertion point in the pull quote, just after the final period.

2 Choose Type > Insert Character. In the Insert Character dialog box, you can select a specific font family and type style from the menu at the bottom of the dialog box and then select a character from the scrollable list.

3 Select Adobe Wood Type° for the font family and Ornaments Two for the type style.

4 From the scrollable list select the first character in the first row and click Insert. The character appears at the insertion point in the document.

5 Click Done.

Notice how the word spacing in the last line of the pull quote has an overly large space in the center. You can address this by adding a flush space to the end of the paragraph. A flush space adds a variable amount of space to the last line of a fully justified paragraph. You'll insert the flush space between the period and the decorative end-of-story character you just added.

Now you'll create a flush space using the context menu.

6 Using the type tool, click an insertion point in the pull quote after the last period and before the decorative character.

7 Right-click (Windows) or Control-click (Mac OS) and choose Insert Special Character > Flush Space.

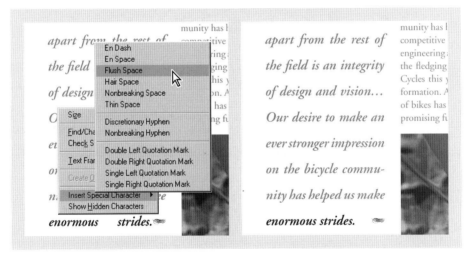

Before and after applying a flush space

Applying special font features

You can add creative touches to your document using InDesign's special font features. For example, you can make the first character or word in a paragraph a drop cap, or apply a gradient or color fill to text. Other features include superscript and subscript characters, ligatures, and old style numerals.

Applying a gradient to text

InDesign makes it easy to apply gradients to the fill and stroke of text characters. You can apply gradients to an entire text frame or to different character ranges within a frame. Here you'll apply a gradient to the pull quote on page 2. You'll use a gradient swatch that was previously created and added to the Swatches palette.

1 Click the Swatches palette tab (or choose Window > Swatches) to make the palette visible. Then drag the lower right corner of the palette until all the swatches are visible.

2 Make sure the type tool (**T**) is still selected, and then triple-click anywhere in the pull quote on page 2 to select all of the text in the paragraph.

3 Select the Fill box (▬) in the toolbox, and then select the Text Gradient swatch in the Swatches palette. To see the gradient, choose Edit > Deselect All.

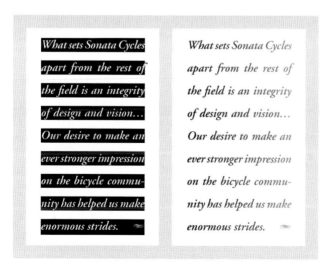

Applying a gradient swatch to selected text creates a left-to-right gradient fill.

Notice how the gradient flows from the left to right. If you want to change the direction of the gradient, you can use the gradient tool. You'll do that now to make the gradient flow from top to bottom, like the pull quote on page 3.

4 Using the type tool, triple-click anywhere in the pull quote to select all of the text.

5 Select the gradient tool (not the Gradient button) in the toolbox (▭), and drag a line from the top to the bottom of the highlighted text. To ensure that you draw a straight line, hold down the Shift key as you drag.

To view the gradient fill, you'll use a keyboard shortcut to deselect all the text.

6 Press Shift+Ctrl+A (Windows) or Shift+Command+A (Mac OS) to deselect the text.

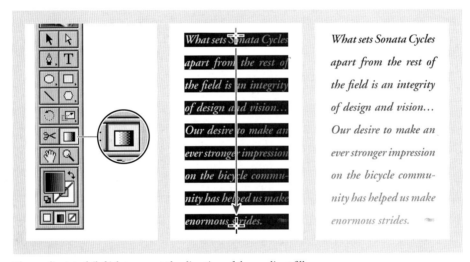

The gradient tool (left) lets you set the direction of the gradient fill.

Creating a drop cap

Here you'll create a three-letter drop cap in the first paragraph of the document.

1 Using the type tool (T), click an insertion point in the first paragraph on page 2.

> ### About text gradients
>
> *A gradient's endpoints are always anchored in relation to the bounding box of the gradient's path or text frame. Individual text characters display the part of the gradient over which they are positioned. If you resize the text frame or otherwise cause text characters to reflow, the characters are redistributed across the gradient, and the colors of individual characters change accordingly.*
>
> *If you want to adjust a gradient so that its complete color range spans a specific range of text characters, you have two options:*
>
> *• Use the gradient tool to reset the gradient's endpoints so that they span only the characters you selected when you applied the gradient.*
>
> *• Select the text and convert it to outlines (editable paths), and then apply a gradient to the resulting outlines.*
>
> –From the Adobe InDesign User Guide, Chapter 9

2 In the Paragraph palette, type **3** for Drop Cap Number of Lines (⊞) to make the letters drop down three lines. Then type **3** for Drop Cap One or More Characters (⊞) to enlarge the first three letters. Press Enter or Return.

ONE early morning in April just a fe
men possessed of more ambition and
close to them would say, common s
spring sunshine and talked about col
baseball, and of starting up a little bic
the infant corporation born of that
rapidly, and today is a major player in
field of small, high-end cycling designe

ONE early morni
years ago, t
more ambiti
some close to them would say, comr
crisp spring sunshine and talked abou
and baseball, and of starting up a li
Cycles, the infant corporation born c
grown rapidly, and today is a major

Before and after applying the drop cap

Applying a fill and stroke to text

Next, you'll add a fill and stroke to the drop cap letters you just created.

1 With the type tool (**T**) still selected, select the drop cap characters on page 2.

2 If necessary, select the Fill box in the toolbox (▣).

3 In the Swatches palette, select Sonata Red. InDesign fills the letters with red, though you can't see it yet because the text is still selected.

Note: *If you don't see Sonata Red in the palette, click the Show All Swatches button (▣).*

4 Select the Stroke box in the toolbox ().

5 In the Swatches palette, select Black. A stroke appears around each of the letters.

The default size of the stroke is 1 point, which is a little heavy for the letters. You'll change it to a half point.

6 Choose Window > Stroke to open the Stroke palette.

7 In the Stroke palette, choose 0.5 pt for Weight. Then, press Shift+Ctrl+A (Windows) or Shift+Command+A (Mac OS) to deselect the text to view the fill and stroke effect.

Original drop cap (left), drop cap with color fill (middle), and drop cap with fill and stroke (right)

8 Close the Stroke palette, and then save the file.

Adjusting letter and word spacing

You can change the spacing between words and letters using InDesign's kerning and tracking features. You can also control the overall spacing of text in a paragraph using the single-line or multi-line composers.

Metrics, optical, and manual kerning

Metrics kerning uses kern pairs, which are included with most fonts. Kern pairs contain information about the spacing of specific pairs of characters. A sample of these are: LA, P., To, Tr, Ta, Tu, Te, Ty, Wa, WA, We, Wo, Ya, Yo, and yo. InDesign uses metrics kerning by default so kern pairs are automatically honored when you import or type text.

Optical kerning adjusts the spacing between adjacent characters based on their appearance. You can also use manual kerning, which is ideal for adjusting the space between two letters.

If you click an insertion point between two letters, InDesign displays the kerning values in the Character palette. Metrics and Optical kerning values (kern pairs) appear in parentheses.

–From the Adobe InDesign User Guide, Chapter 5

Adjusting the kerning and tracking

In InDesign you can control the space between letters by using the kerning and tracking features. *Kerning* is the process of adding or subtracting space between specific letter pairs. *Tracking* is the process of creating an equal amount of spacing across a range of letters. You can use both features on the same text.

Here you'll manually kern some letters in the heading "The Dos Ventanas Cycling Partnership" to close up noticeable gaps. Then you'll track the heading to bring it all onto one line.

1 To distinguish the amount of space between letters more easily and to see the results of the kerning more clearly, select the zoom tool (🔍) in the toolbox and drag a marquee around the heading "The Dos Ventanas Cycling Partnership."

2 If necessary, move palettes or the toolbox out of the way or adjust the zoom level in the magnification menu in the lower left corner of the document window.

3 Select the type tool (**T**) and click an insertion point between the "V" and the "e" in the word "Ventanas."

4 Press Alt+Left Arrow (Windows) or Option+Left Arrow (Mac OS) to move the letter "e" to the left. Press this key combination repeatedly until the two adjacent letters look visually pleasing to you. We pressed it four times.

Note: *The kerning value changes in the Character palette as you press the key combination.*

Before and after kerning

5 If you've moved the letter too far, press Alt+Right Arrow (Windows) or Option+Right Arrow (Mac OS) to move the letter to the right.

6 Click an insertion point between the "P" and the "a" in the word "Partnership."

7 Press Alt/Option+Left Arrow to move the letter "a" to the left. Press this key combination repeatedly until the two adjacent letters look visually pleasing to you. We pressed it four times.

Before and after kerning

Now you'll set a tracking value for the entire heading "The Dos Ventanas Cycling Partnership" to condense the overall spacing and bring it all onto one line. To set tracking you must first select the entire range of characters you want to track.

8 Choose 200% from the magnification menu at the lower left corner of the document window to view more of the page on-screen.

9 Triple-click "The Dos Ventanas Cycling Partnership" to select the entire heading.

10 Click the Character palette tab (or choose Type > Character). Then select -5 for Tracking (A̲V̲) and press Enter or Return.

Before and after tracking

Now you'll use a keyboard shortcut to deselect the text.

11 Press Shift+Ctrl+A (Windows) or Shift+Command+A (Mac OS).

12 Press Ctrl+1 (Windows) or Command+1 (Mac OS) to return to a 100% view.

13 Save the file.

Applying the multi-line and single-line composers

The density of a paragraph (sometimes called its *color*) is determined by the composition method used. When composing text, InDesign considers the word spacing, letter spacing, glyph scaling, and hyphenation options you've selected, and then evaluates and chooses the best line breaks. InDesign provides two options for composing text: the multi-line composer, which looks at multiple lines at once, or the single-line composer, which looks separately at each individual line.

When you use the multi-line composer, InDesign composes a line by considering the impact on the other lines in the paragraph; in the end, the best overall arrangement of the paragraph is established. As you change type in a given line, previous and subsequent lines in the same paragraph may break differently, making the overall paragraph appear more evenly spaced. When you use the single-line composer, which is the standard for other desktop layout and word processing programs, only the lines following the edited text are recomposed.

The text in this lesson was composed using the default multi-line composer. Here you'll edit the text in the pull quote on page 3 and recompose it using both composers to compare the differences. First you'll recompose the text using the single-line composer.

1 Move the scroll bar at the bottom of the page to the right to bring page 3 into view.

2 With the type tool (**T**) still selected, click an insertion point in the pull quote in the lower right corner. Then click the Paragraph tab (or choose Type > Paragraph). Choose Adobe Single-line Composer from the Paragraph palette menu.

3 Click an insertion point immediately after the word "spare" in the pull quote. Then insert a space and type "**bicycle**". Notice that the text no longer fits in the text frame and each line has a different density.

The single-line composer looks at each line individually and, consequently, can make some lines in a paragraph appear more dense or sparse than others, as is the case here. Because the multi-line composer looks at multiple lines at once, the density of the lines in a paragraph are more consistent.

4 Choose Adobe Multi-line Composer from the Paragraph palette menu. Notice how the lines of text have a consistent density and all the text fits neatly in the text frame.

Each shop includes a lounge area with chairs and tables built out of spare bicycle parts. The coffee table—a spoked wheel supported by bike pumps—sports a collection of cycling magazines.

Each shop includes a lounge area with chairs and tables built out of spare bicycle parts. The coffee table—a spoked wheel supported by bike pumps—sports a collection of cycling magazines.

Pull quote formatted using the single-line composer (left), and the multi-line composer (right)

Creating a table using tabs

You can use tabs to create tables and position text in specific horizontal locations in a frame. Using the Tabs palette, you can organize text and create tab leaders, indents, and hanging indents. Here you'll format the table at the top of page 3 using the Tabs palette. The tab markers have already been entered in the text, so all you will be doing is setting the final location of the text.

1 If necessary, scroll to the top of page 3 until the table appears on-screen. Then, if you want to view the tab markers in the table, choose Type > Show Hidden Characters. Choose Type > Show Hidden Characters again to hide them.

2 Using the type tool (**T**), click in the word "Category" at the top of the table.

3 Choose Type > Tabs to open the Tabs palette. When an insertion point is in a text frame, the Tabs palette snaps to the border of the frame so that the measurements in the palette's ruler exactly match the text.

4 To center the page on your screen, double-click the page 3 icon in the Pages palette. Because the Tabs palette moves independently of the table, the two are no longer aligned.

5 Click the magnet icon (⌂) in the Tabs palette to realign the palette with the text.

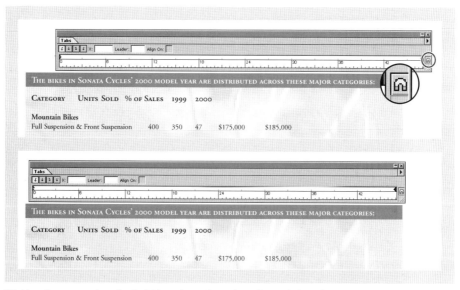

Clicking the magnet icon in the Tabs palette aligns the ruler with the selected text.

6 Using the type tool, select all of the text in the table's text frame, from the word "Category" to the number "$110,000."

7 In the Tabs palette, click the Center-Justified Tab button (↓) so that when you set the new tab positions, they will align from the center.

8 In the Tabs palette, position the pointer in the top third of the ruler, just above the numbers, and then click to set tab markers at the following locations: **24, 29, 34, 40,** and **45.** You can view the location of the pointer on the ruler in the X: text box. To precisely set the value, drag in the ruler while watching the X value before releasing the mouse button.

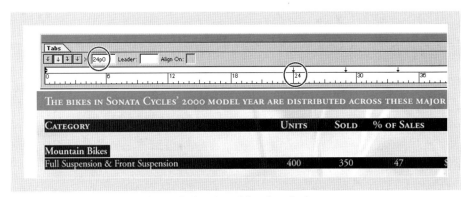

The value in the X: text box indicates the location of the selected tab.

Note: *If you don't get the tab locations correct the first time, you can select the tab in the ruler and type the location in the text box.*

9 Press Shift+Ctrl+A (Windows) or Shift+Command+A (Mac OS) to deselect the text and view the new tab settings.

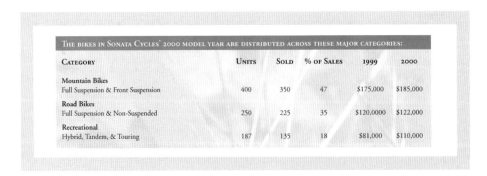

Category	Units	Sold	% of Sales	1999	2000
Mountain Bikes Full Suspension & Front Suspension	400	350	47	$175,000	$185,000
Road Bikes Full Suspension & Non-Suspended	250	225	35	$120,0000	$122,000
Recreational Hybrid, Tandem, & Touring	187	135	18	$81,000	$110,000

(THE BIKES IN SONATA CYCLES' 2000 MODEL YEAR ARE DISTRIBUTED ACROSS THESE MAJOR CATEGORIES:)

Now you'll set a tab leader for some of the tabs.

10 Select all the text in the table from "Mountain" to "$110,000."

11 In the Tabs palette, click the first tab arrow along the ruler to select it. Now, the leader you create will affect any selected tabs at that tab marker.

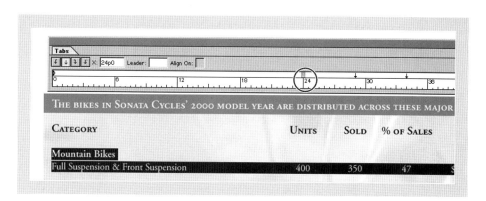

12 In the Leader text box, type ._ (period, space) and press Enter or Return. You can use any character as a tab leader. We used a space between periods to create a more open dot sequence.

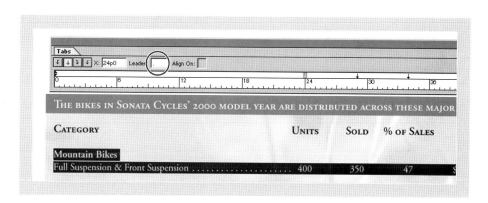

13 Deselect the table text and view the leaders.

Creating a hanging indent

Now you'll use the Tabs palette to create hanging indents. The text frame for this table has an inset value of 6 points at the top and 9 points on the sides and bottom. (To see the inset values, choose Object > Text Frame Options.) An *inset* sets the text apart from the frame; now you'll set it apart even more by indenting the three categories in the table.

You can set an indent in the Tabs palette or the Paragraph palette. You'll keep the Paragraph palette visible so you can see how the values change there too.

1 Make sure the Paragraph palette is visible.

2 In the table, use the type tool (**T**) to select all the text from "Mountain" to "$110,000."

3 Make sure the Tabs palette is still aligned directly above the table. If it has moved, click the magnet icon (⌂).

4 In the Tabs palette, drag the indent markers (▶) on the left side of the ruler to the right until the X value is 2p0. Dragging the bottom marker moves both at once. Notice how all the text shifts to the right and the indent option in the Paragraph palette changes to 2p0. Don't deselect the text yet.

Now you'll bring just the category headings back to their original location in the table to create a hanging indent.

5 In the Tabs palette, drag the top index marker back to the left until the X: value is -2p0. Deselect the text and view the hanging indent.

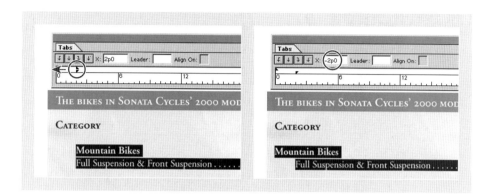

6 Close the Tabs palette and save the file.

Adding a rule below a paragraph

You can also add a rule, or line, above or below a paragraph. Rules change in size in relation to changes to the paragraph's text frame. For example, if you make the text frame wider, the rule also becomes wider. Here you'll add a rule under the table headings.

1 Using the type tool (T), click an insertion point in the word "Category" in the table.

2 From the Paragraph palette menu, choose Paragraph Rules.

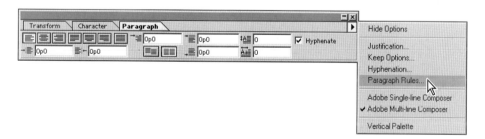

3 In the Paragraph Rules dialog box, choose Rule Below from the menu at the top of the dialog box, and then select Rule On to activate the rule.

4 To view the rule as you select your options, select Preview and move the dialog box so that it is not obstructing your view of the heading.

5 For Weight, choose 1 pt; for Color, choose Sonata Red; for Width, choose Column; and for Offset, type **0p9**. Then click OK.

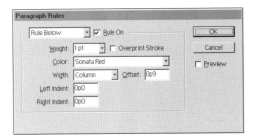

6 Save the file.

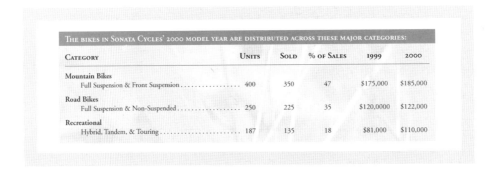

THE BIKES IN SONATA CYCLES' 2000 MODEL YEAR ARE DISTRIBUTED ACROSS THESE MAJOR CATEGORIES:					
CATEGORY	UNITS	SOLD	% OF SALES	1999	2000
Mountain Bikes					
Full Suspension & Front Suspension	400	350	47	$175,000	$185,000
Road Bikes					
Full Suspension & Non-Suspended	250	225	35	$120,0000	$122,000
Recreational					
Hybrid, Tandem, & Touring	187	135	18	$81,000	$110,000

Exporting a document to PDF

Now you'll export the document to Portable Document Format (PDF) so you can distribute it electronically or link it to your Web site. When you export a document to PDF, all of the formatting remains intact, including all fonts and images, as well as all of the spacing settings, special characters, tabs, and other special formatting you applied in this lesson. If you link it to a Web site, everyone who views it through their browser will see it exactly as you do.

1 Choose File > Export. In the dialog box choose Adobe PDF for Save as Type (Windows) or Format (Mac OS). Then name the file Report.pdf, and save it in the ID_06 folder.

2 If desired, in the Export PDF dialog box, select View PDF after Exporting. Leave all of the settings at their defaults and click Export.

InDesign saves the copy of the report as a PDF that can be viewed electronically using Adobe Acrobat Reader. It can also be linked to your Web page to be viewed in a browser. Acrobat Reader is provided on the Adobe InDesign CD and is available on the Adobe Web site (http://www.adobe.com) for free distribution.

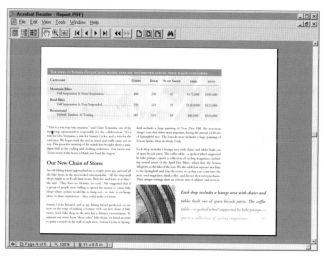

Your InDesign document exported as PDF

On your own

Now that you have learned the basics of formatting text in an InDesign document, you're ready to apply these skills on your own. Try the following tasks to improve your typography skills.

1 Create a one-letter, three-line raised cap (as opposed to a drop cap) for the word "The" that appears at the beginning of the last paragraph on page 2 of the final 06_report.indd file. The basic steps to achieving this effect are: (A.) Create a three-line drop cap for the paragraph. (B.) Click an insertion point after the first letter in the paragraph, and then press Enter/Return once to move the text down three lines. Another drop cap is created. (C.) Set the new Drop Cap values to 0.

2 Refine the text in the raised cap by kerning the first and second letter so it appears as shown:

Original drop cap (left), second drop cap, created to make raised cap (middle), raised cap (right)

3 Use the context menu to add a copyright symbol to the end of the company name "Sonata Cycles" in the first paragraph on page 2.

4 Apply Optical Margin Alignment to each paragraph in the main story (everything except the pull quotes and table). You can access the Optical Margin Alignment feature from Story command in the Type menu. Make sure to set the font size correctly.

Review questions

1 How do you view a baseline grid?

2 When and where do you use a flush space?

3 How do you apply a gradient to only a few words or characters in a paragraph?

4 What is the difference between the multi-line composer and the single-line composer?

Review answers

1 To view a baseline grid, choose View > Show Baseline Grid. The current document view must be at or above the View Threshold set in the Baseline Grid preferences. By default, that value is 75%.

2 You use a flush space on justified text. For example, if used with a special character or decorative font at the end of a paragraph, it absorbs any extra space in the last line.

3 To apply a gradient to a specific range of characters, you first select the text with the type tool. Next, you apply the gradient to the text. If the entire range of colors does not appear, select the gradient tool and drag from one end of the selected text to the other in the direction you want the gradient to flow.

4 The multi-line composer evaluates multiple lines at once when determining the best possible line break. The single-line composer looks at only one line at a time when determining a line break.

Lesson 7

7 Importing and Linking Graphics

You can easily enhance your document
with photographs and artwork created
in Adobe Photoshop, Adobe Illustrator,
or other graphics programs. InDesign can
tell you when a newer version of a graphic
is available, and you can update
or replace any graphic at any time.

In this lesson, you'll learn how to do the following:

- Distinguish between vector and bitmap graphics.

- Place Adobe Photoshop and Adobe Illustrator graphics into an Adobe InDesign layout.

- Import clipping paths with graphics, and create clipping paths using InDesign and Photoshop.

- Place Adobe PDF files.

- Manage placed files using the Links palette.

- Use and create libraries for objects.

Getting started

In this lesson, you'll assemble a booklet for a compact disc by importing and managing graphics from Adobe Photoshop and Adobe Illustrator. After printing and trimming, the insert will be folded so that it fits into a CD box. Before you begin, you'll need to restore the default preferences for Adobe InDesign. You'll also make sure your color management settings are consistent for InDesign and Photoshop, so that the colors you use appear consistently across both programs.

Note: The topic "Creating a clipping path using Photoshop" on page 256 requires a full version of Adobe Photoshop 4.0 or later, and enough RAM to run both InDesign and Photoshop at the same time.

1 To ensure that the tools and palettes function exactly as described in this lesson, delete or deactivate (by renaming) the InDesign Defaults file and the InDesign SavedData file. See "Restoring default preferences" on page 2.

2 To set up the InDesign color management settings, see Chapter 11, "Ensuring Consistent Color."

3 To make sure Photoshop's color management settings match InDesign, see "Embedding a profile in a Photoshop TIFF image" on page 375.

4 Start Adobe InDesign.

5 Choose File > Open, and open the 07_a.indd file in the ID_07 folder, located inside the Lessons folder within the IDCIB folder on your hard disk. A message box appears, saying that the publication contains missing or modified links. Click OK; you will fix this later in the lesson when you learn how to resolve links to imported graphics which are missing or modified.

6 Move the Links palette out of the way so it doesn't obscure your view of the document.

7 If you want to see what the finished document will look like, open the 07_b.indd file in the same folder. If you prefer, you can leave the document open as you work to act as a guide. When you're ready to resume working on the lesson document, choose its name from the Window menu.

For a color version of the finished document, see the color section.

8 Choose File > Save As, rename the file **07_cdbook.indd**, and save it in the ID_07 folder.

Note: As you work through the lesson, feel free to move palettes around or change the magnification to a level that works best for you. For more information, see "Changing the magnification of your document" on page 50 and "Using the Navigator palette" on page 57.

Adding graphics from other programs

InDesign supports many common graphics file formats. While this allows you to use graphics created using a wide range of graphics programs, InDesign works most smoothly with other Adobe professional graphics programs such as Photoshop and Illustrator.

By default, imported graphics larger than 48K on disk are *linked,* which means that InDesign displays a graphics file on your layout without actually copying the entire graphics file into the InDesign document. This saves disk space, especially if you reuse the same graphic in many InDesign documents. All linked graphics and text files are listed in the Links palette, which provides buttons and commands for managing links. When you create final output using PostScript® or PDF, InDesign uses the links to produce the highest level of quality available from the original, externally stored versions of placed graphics.

Comparing vector and bitmap graphics

Adobe InDesign and Adobe Illustrator create *vector graphics,* also called draw graphics, which are made up of shapes based on mathematical expressions. Vector graphics consist of smooth lines that retain their clarity when scaled. They are appropriate for illustrations, type, and graphics such as logos that are typically scaled to different sizes.

Bitmap images are based on a grid of pixels and are created by image-editing applications such as Adobe Photoshop. In working with bitmap images, you edit individual pixels rather than objects or shapes. Because bitmap graphics can represent subtle gradations of shade and color, they are appropriate for continuous-tone images such as photographs or artwork created in painting programs. A disadvantage of bitmap graphics is that they lose definition and appear "jagged" when enlarged.

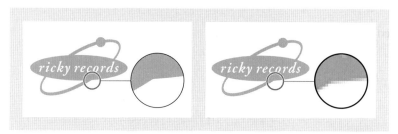

Logo drawn as vector art (left), and rasterized as bitmap art (right)

In general, use vector drawing tools to create art or type with clean lines that look good at any size. You can create vector artwork using InDesign's drawing tools, or you might prefer to take advantage of the wider range of vector drawing tools available in Illustrator. You can use Photoshop to create bitmap images that have the soft lines of painted or photographic art and for applying special effects to line art.

Managing links to imported files

When you opened the document, you saw an alert message about problems with linked files. You'll resolve those issues using the Links palette, which provides complete information about the status of any linked text or graphics file in your document.

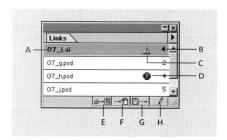

A. Link B. Page containing linked graphic
C. Modified-link icon D. Missing-link icon
E. Relink button F. Go To Link button
G. Update Link button H. Edit Original button

Identifying imported images

You'll use the Links palette to identify some of the images that have already been imported into the document. Later in this lesson, you'll use the Links palette to edit and update imported graphics.

1 If necessary, zoom or scroll the document window so that you can see both of the document's spreads.

2 If the Links palette is not visible, choose File > Links.

3 Using the selection tool, select the Orchard of Kings logotype on page 4, the far right page of the first spread. Notice that the graphic's filename, 07_i.ai, becomes selected in the Links palette when you select it on the layout.

 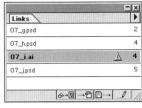

4 Using the selection tool, select the large hand graphic that spans all pages of the second spread. In the Links palette, this graphic's filename, 07_j.psd, becomes selected.

Now you'll use the Links palette to locate a graphic on the layout.

5 In the Links palette, select 07_h.psd, and then click the Go To Link button (⇥🗐). The graphic becomes selected and centered on the screen. This is a quick way to find a graphic with a known filename.

6 If the Links palette is still in the center of the document window, you may want to move or close it so that it doesn't block your view of the page as you work through the rest of the lesson. The Links palette opens automatically whenever you open an InDesign document that contains missing or modified links.

These techniques for identifying and locating linked graphics are useful throughout this lesson and whenever you work with a large number of imported files. Later in this lesson, you'll also use the Links palette to inspect, modify, and update linked graphics.

Viewing information about linked files

You can use the Links palette to manage placed graphics or text files in many other ways, such as updating or replacing text or graphics. All of the techniques you learn in this lesson about managing linked files apply equally to graphics files and text files you place into your document.

1 If the Links palette is not visible, choose File > Links to display it. Drag the lower right corner of the Links palette to enlarge the Links palette so that you can see as many filenames as possible.

2 Double-click the link 07_g.psd. The Link Information dialog box appears, describing the file that the link refers to.

3 Click Next to view information about the next file. You can quickly examine all of the document's links this way. One or more links may display an alert icon; they indicate a linking problem that you'll address in the next topic. After you've examined some link information, click OK.

By default, files are sorted in the Links palette so that files that are not up to date are listed first. You can use commands in the Links palette menu to sort the file list in different ways.

4 In the Links palette, choose Sort by Page from the Links palette menu. This lists files on the first page at the top of the Links palette, and files on other pages are listed accordingly.

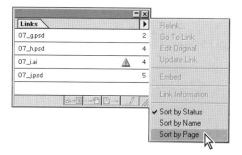

Updating a graphic with a newer version

As you use other programs to update text and graphics placed in your document, the Links palette indicates which files have been modified outside of InDesign, and gives you the choice of updating your document to represent the latest versions of those files.

Viewing link status in the Links palette

A linked graphic can appear in the Links palette in any of the following ways:

• *An up-to-date graphic displays only the graphic's filename and its page in the document.*

• *A modified graphic displays a yellow triangle with an exclamation point (⚠). This icon means that the version of the graphic on disk is more recent than the version in your document. For example, this icon will appear if you import a Photoshop graphic into InDesign, and then another artist edits and saves the original graphic using Photoshop.*

• *A missing graphic displays a red circle with a question mark (⊘). This icon means that the graphic isn't at the location from which it was originally imported, though the graphic may still exist somewhere. This can happen if someone moves an original file to a different folder or server after it's been imported into an InDesign document. You can't know whether a missing graphic is up to date until its original is located. If you print or export a document when this icon is displayed, the graphic may not print or export at full resolution.*

–From the Adobe InDesign User Guide, chapter 7

In the Links palette, the file 07_i.ai has an icon (⚠) that marks it as out of date. This is the file that caused the alert message when you opened this document. You'll update its link so that the InDesign document uses the current version.

1 In the Links palette, select the file 07_i.ai, and click the Go To Link button (⋯⊕). You don't have to do this step to update a link, but it's a quick way to double-check which imported file you are about to update.

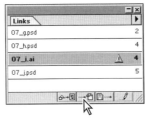

2 Click the Update Link button ( ). The appearance of the image in the document changes to represent its newer version.

 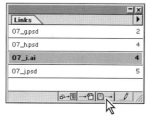

You'll replace the large, wide image of the hand that spans the second spread (pages 5–7) with a modified image. You can use the Relink button to reassign the link to that graphic.

3 Go to pages 5–7 (the second spread) and choose View > Fit Spread in Window.

4 Select the 07_j.psd image on pages 5–7. The filename of the image becomes selected in the Links palette.

5 Click the Relink button ( ) in the Links palette.

6 Click Browse, locate the file 07_h.psd in the ID_07 folder, and then click Open (Windows) or Choose (Mac OS). The old image is replaced by the one you just selected, and the Links palette is updated accordingly.

7 Choose File > Save to save the file.

💡 *All of the buttons at the bottom of the Links palette are also available as commands on the Links palette menu.*

Placing a Photoshop file

Now that you've resolved all of the file's links, you're ready to start adding more graphics. You'll place a Photoshop file in the InDesign document. InDesign imports Photoshop files directly; there is no need to save them in other file formats.

1 Go to page 7. If necessary, zoom or scroll the document window so that you can see the entire page. In the Layers palette, click the Photos layer to target it.

2 Choose File > Place, and double-click the file 07_c.psd in the ID_07 folder.

3 Position the loaded graphics icon to the left and slightly below the top edge of the green square, and click.

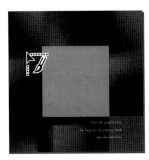 

Don't be concerned about the white rectangular background behind the image. You'll remove it in the next section. Now you'll zoom in using a high magnification so that you can learn about options for display quality.

4 Click the Navigator palette tab (or choose Window > Navigator) to make the palette visible. Use the palette to zoom to 400%, keeping the image you placed in the center of the view.

As you place the image, InDesign automatically creates a proxy (low-resolution) version of it. This and any other images in this document are currently displaying their low-resolution proxies, which is why the image appears to have jagged edges. You'll control the degree of detail InDesign displays for placed graphics. Reducing the on-screen quality of placed graphics displays pages faster, and doesn't affect the quality of final output.

5 Choose File > Preferences > General. For Display, choose Full Resolution Images, and click OK.

On-screen display using proxy images (left) and full resolution images (right)

Now InDesign displays the image using all available detail. Images now look their best, but they will also take longer to appear.

6 Zoom out until you can see all three pears.

7 Choose File > Save.

Working with clipping paths

The image has a solid rectangular background that is blocking your view of the area behind it. You can hide unwanted parts of an image using a *clipping path*—a drawn vector outline that acts as a mask.

Creating a clipping path using InDesign

You can use the Clipping Path command to remove a solid white background from an image. This command hides areas of an image by changing the shape of the frame containing the image, adding anchor points as necessary. For more information about frames and anchor points, see "About paths and frames" on page 101.

1 Using the direct-selection tool ( ), select the pear image 07_c.psd by clicking the image's frame (its edge). You'll know that the image's default rectangular frame is selected when you see four hollow anchor points. (Six solid anchor points means that the image itself is selected, and six solid handles with a dot inside each handle means that the image's bounding box is selected.)

Note: If you have trouble selecting the image's frame, choose Edit > Deselect All and try again.

Clicking the image's frame with the direct-selection tool makes the frame's anchor points visible during this procedure, so that you can see exactly how InDesign changes the frame into a clipping path. The procedure will still work if you select the image instead of the frame, or if you use the selection tool, but you won't get as much visual feedback.

2 Choose Object > Clipping Path. If necessary, drag the Clipping Path dialog box so you can see the pear image.

3 Make sure Preview is selected, and then for Threshold, drag the slider to hide as much of the white background as possible without hiding parts of the subject (darker areas). We used a Threshold value of **6**.

Note: If you can't find a setting that removes all of the background without affecting the subject, specify a value that leaves the entire subject visible along with small bits of the white background. You'll eliminate the remaining white background by fine-tuning the clipping path in the following steps.

The Threshold option works by hiding light areas of the image, starting with white. As you drag to the right, increasingly darker tones are included within the range of tones that becomes hidden.

4 For Tolerance, drag the slider to the left until the Tolerance value is 0.

The Tolerance option determines how many points define the frame that's automatically generated. As you drag to the right, InDesign uses fewer points so that the clipping path fits the image more loosely (higher tolerance). Using fewer points on the path may speed up document printing, but may be less accurate.

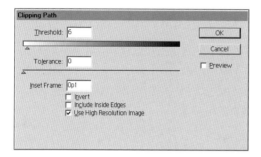

5 For Inset Frame, specify a value that closes up any remaining background areas, and click OK. We specified a value of 0p1 (zero picas, one point). This option shrinks the current shape of the clipping path uniformly, and is not affected by the lightness values in the image.

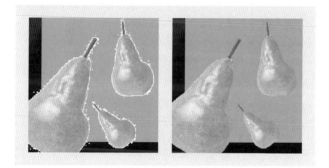

Before and after applying an inset of 1 point

Now that you've completed the clipping path for this image, it's a good time to speed up screen redraw by switching image display back to low-resolution proxy images.

6 Choose File > Preferences > General. For Display, choose Proxy Images, and click OK.

7 Save the file.

Creating a clipping path using Photoshop

When an image has a background that isn't solid white, the InDesign Clipping Path command may not be able to remove the background effectively. With such images, hiding the background's lightness values will hide any parts of the subject that use the same lightness values. Instead, you can prepare a clipping path using Photoshop's advanced background removal tools, and let InDesign use that clipping path.

You imported the previous image using the Place command. This time you'll simply drag a Photoshop image directly onto an InDesign spread. You'll then open Photoshop directly from that image, add a clipping path, and replace the old version with the new one. InDesign can import the clipping path directly—you don't need to save the Photoshop file in a different file format.

Note: *This section requires a full version of Photoshop 4.0 or later and enough available RAM to run both InDesign and Photoshop at the same time. If your configuration doesn't meet these requirements, skip to step 11, and in that step choose the file 07_dt.psd instead of 07_d.psd. The 07_dt.psd file already has the Photoshop clipping path you would have prepared in steps 1 through 5.*

1 In Explorer (Windows) or the Finder (Mac OS), open the ID_07 folder so that the file 07_d.psd is visible. Arrange the InDesign document window and the ID_07 folder window so that you can see both of them side by side.

2 In InDesign, make sure you can see the lower left quarter of page 2 in the document window.

3 Drag the file 07_d.psd to the lower left corner of page 2 in the InDesign document. If necessary, use the selection tool (↖) to reposition the graphic within the page boundaries.

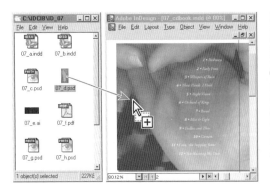

In this image, the hand and the background share many of the same lightness values. Therefore, InDesign's Clipping Path command isn't likely to isolate the background reliably. Instead, you'll use the Links palette to open the image directly in Photoshop.

Note: A CMS Profile Mismatch dialog box may appear as the image opens in Photoshop. If you've properly configured all Photoshop and InDesign color management settings for your workflow using accurate ICC profiles, click Convert to reproduce the image properly in Photoshop. If you are not using color management, you may click Don't Convert.

4 If necessary, use the selection tool to select the 07_d.psd image in InDesign.

5 If you want, maximize the InDesign window now that you've finished importing the file.

6 Choose File > Links. The image's filename is selected automatically in the Links palette.

 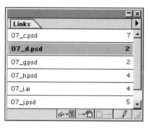

7 In the Links palette, click the Edit Original button (..✐). This opens the image in a program that can view or edit it. This image was saved from Photoshop, so if Photoshop is installed on your computer, InDesign starts Photoshop with the selected file.

Note: *Sometimes the Edit Original button opens an image in a program other than Photoshop or the program that created it. The Edit Original button uses your operating system's settings for associating files with programs. You can change those settings; see the documentation for your operating system. Also, some installer utilities change those settings.*

 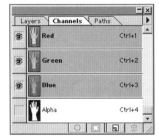

Photoshop file saved with an alpha channel

💡 *The Edit Original button also exists as a command on the context menu that appears when you right-click (Windows) or Control-click (Mac OS) an image selected with the direct-selection tool (▸). If the image was selected with the selection tool, the Edit Original command appears on the Graphic submenu on the context menu.*

The image was saved with an *alpha channel* which carries information about transparent and opaque areas. An alpha channel is commonly saved with images used for photo or video compositing. InDesign does not recognize alpha channels, so the alpha channel has been converted into a path in Photoshop, the program in which the image was originally prepared. You'll set up the path as a clipping path that InDesign can use.

8 In Photoshop, choose Window > Show Paths to display the Paths palette. More than one path is currently stored with this image.

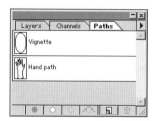

9 Position the pointer over the black triangle to the right of the Paths tab, and choose Clipping Path from the Paths palette menu. For Path, choose Hand Path, leave the Flatness value blank, and then click OK. Because an image can be saved with multiple paths, choosing a path from the Path menu tells other programs which path to use as the clipping path.

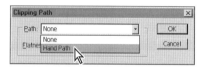

10 In Photoshop, choose File > Save, and then choose File > Exit (Windows) or File > Quit (Mac OS) to close Photoshop.

For InDesign to read the new clipping path, you must place the graphic again. It usually isn't necessary to place a graphic again after you've used Edit Original command to edit the file; you can usually use the Relink or Update Link buttons on the Links palette. However, when you edit a clipping path—or perform any other action that affects options in the Image Settings section of the Import Image Options dialog box—you must use the Place command. (The Import Image Options dialog box appears when you select Show Import Options in the Place dialog box.) First you'll delete the instance of the file that didn't have a clipping path.

11 Switch to InDesign. Using the selection tool (⬆), make sure the 07_d.psd Photoshop file is still selected on the page, and press Delete.

12 Choose File > Place and double-click 07_d.psd. This is the version of the file that you saved with a clipping path.

13 Position the loaded graphics icon so that the graphic will appear in the lower left corner of page 2, and click. If necessary, use the selection tool (⬆) to reposition the graphic.

The graphic appears on the page, masked by the clipping path you added in Photoshop.

14 Save the file.

Adding an Illustrator file

InDesign takes full advantage of the smooth lines provided by EPS vector graphics such as those from Adobe Illustrator. When you turn on InDesign's full-resolution screen display, EPS vector graphics and type are displayed smoothly at any size or magnification. Most EPS vector graphics don't require a clipping path because most programs save them with transparent backgrounds. You'll drag an Illustrator graphic from a folder to the InDesign document.

1 Make sure that the ID_07 folder and the InDesign document window are both visible simultaneously. In InDesign, zoom or scroll if necessary so that pages 5 and 6 are both visible.

2 In InDesign, choose View > Show Guides. In the Layers palette, target the Text layer.

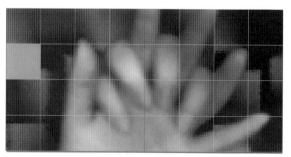 

3 Drag the Illustrator file 07_e.ai to the InDesign document. Position it so that its left edge snaps to the first grid guide on the left, and center it between the top and bottom of the page.

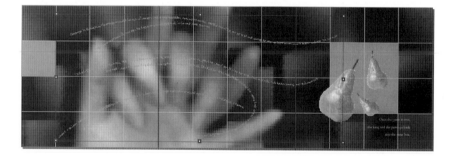

4 If you want, maximize the InDesign window now that you've finished importing the file.

Now you'll see how InDesign's high-resolution display affects EPS vector graphics.

5 Display the Navigator palette. With the Illustrator graphic selected, type **1000** in the magnification text box, and press Enter or Return.

6 If necessary, drag the view box in the Navigator palette so that you can see some of the text in the Illustrator graphic.

The type appears jagged because of two things: You are viewing the EPS file at 1000% magnification, and earlier in the lesson you chose the Proxy Images (low-resolution) option for graphics display. You'll switch to high-resolution display and observe the difference.

7 Choose File > Preferences > General. For Display, choose Full Resolution Images, and click OK.

On-screen image resolution before and after changing display resolution setting

At the Full Resolution Images setting, you can see the Illustrator graphic at its highest level of detail and accuracy. At this setting you can often position and align Illustrator and EPS graphics precisely by sight alone, particularly when you zoom in. You'll switch back to proxy images to speed up image display for the rest of the lesson. For faster access to the Preferences dialog box, you'll use a keyboard shortcut this time.

8 Press Ctrl+K (Windows) or Command+K (Mac OS). For Display, choose Proxy Resolution Images, and click OK.

9 Save the file.

Placing a PDF file

You can include Portable Document Format (PDF) files in your InDesign layout. PDF is a popular format for exchanging graphics such as advertisements, because it preserves professional-quality color, vector graphics, bitmap images, and text among a wide range of programs and computing platforms. You can use PDF to publish the same document on paper and on the Internet while maintaining quality for both media. You'll import a PDF file that contains a company logo created and saved directly from Adobe Illustrator.

1 Go to page 3, and make sure that all of page 3 is visible. In the Layers palette, target the Graphics layer.

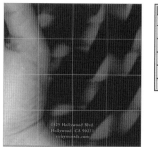 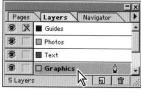

Now you'll use a keyboard shortcut to open the Place dialog box.

2 Press Ctrl+D (Windows) or Command+D (Mac OS). Select Show Import Options, and in the ID_07 folder, locate and double-click the file 07_f.pdf.

The import options for PDF files let you customize how a PDF file is placed into your document. For example, this PDF file contains only one page, but when you place a multiple-page PDF file, you can choose which page to place.

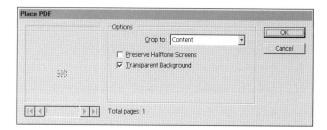

3 Make sure Content is selected in the Crop To menu. This sets the size of the placed PDF file to the smallest rectangle that encloses all of the objects in the file. For example, in this case the logo is much smaller than the page size, so it makes sense for the imported file to be the size of the logo, not the page. Leave the other settings as they are.

4 Click OK, and then click the loaded graphics icon above the address on page 3.

 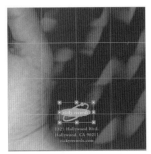

5 Save the file.

Using a library to manage objects

Object libraries let you store and organize graphics, text, and pages you frequently use. You can also add ruler guides, grids, drawn shapes, and grouped images to a library. Each library appears as a separate palette which you can group with other palettes any way you like. You can create as many libraries as you need—for example, different libraries for each of your projects or clients. You'll import a graphic currently stored in a library, and then you'll create your own library.

1 Choose Window > Libraries > Open, select the file 07_k.indl in the ID_07 folder, and click Open. Drag the lower right corner of the palette to reveal more of the items in it.

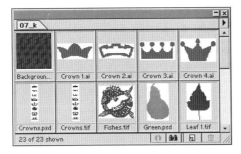

2 In the 07_k.indl library palette, click the Show Library Subset button (🔍). In the last box for the Parameters option, type **Tree**, and click OK.

3 Type **5** into the page navigation box at the bottom of the InDesign document window to go to that page, and then press Enter or Return.

4 Make sure that the Links palette is visible. In the Layers palette, target the Graphics layer.

5 Out of the 2 objects visible in the 07_k.indl library palette, drag Tree.tif to page 5. The file is added to the page, and the filename appears in the Links palette.

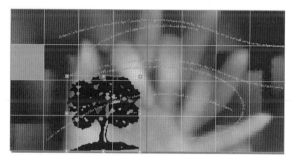

6 Using the selection tool, position Tree.tif against the bottom of page 5, with its left edge aligned approximately with the left edge of the large hand image behind it.

Now you'll create your own library.

7 Choose Window > Libraries > New. Type **CD Projects** as the library filename, navigate to the ID_07 folder, and click Save. The library appears in its own floating palette, labeled with the filename you specified.

8 Go to page 3 and, using the selection tool, drag the ricky records logo to the library you just created. The logo is now saved in the library for use in other InDesign documents.

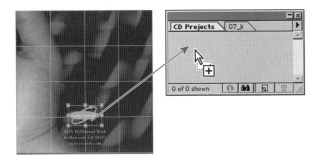

9 In the CD Projects library, double-click the ricky records logo. For Item Name, type **Logo,** and then click OK.

10 Using the selection tool, drag the address text block to the library you created. It appears in the CD Projects library palette.

In the CD Projects library, double-click the address text block. For Item Name, type **Address,** and then click OK. Now your library contains both text and graphics. As soon as you make changes to the library, InDesign saves the changes.

11 Save the file.

Congratulations! You've created a CD booklet by importing, updating, and managing graphics from many different graphics file formats.

On your own

Now that you've had some practice working with imported graphics, here are some exercises to try on your own.

1 Place different file formats with the Show Import Options turned on in the Place dialog box, and see what options appear for each format. For a full description of all the options available for each format, see Chapter 7, "Importing, Exporting, and Managing Graphics" in the InDesign User Guide.

2 Place a multiple-page PDF file with Show Import Options turned on, and import different pages from it.

3 Create libraries of text and graphics for your work.

Review questions

1 How can you determine the filename of an imported graphic in your document?

2 What kind of image works best with InDesign's Clipping Path command?

3 What is the difference between updating a file's link and replacing the file?

4 When an updated version of a graphic becomes available, how do you make sure it's up to date in your InDesign document?

Review answers

1 Select the graphic and then choose File > Links to see if the graphic's filename is highlighted in the Links palette. The graphic will appear in the Links palette if it takes up more than 48KB on disk and was placed or dragged in from the desktop.

2 An image with a solid white background works best with the Clipping Path command, such as clip art. For colored or patterned backgrounds, use Photoshop.

3 Updating a file's link simply uses the Links palette to update the on-screen representation of a graphic so that it represents the most recent version of the original. Replacing a selected graphic uses the Place command to insert another graphic in place of the selected graphic. If you want to change any of a placed graphic's import options, you must replace the graphic.

4 Check the Links palette and make sure that no alert icon is displayed for the file. If an alert icon appears, you can simply select the link and click the Update Link button as long as the file has not been moved. If the file has been moved you can locate it again using the Relink button.

Lesson 8

8 | Drawing

You can use the pen tool to draw straight lines and smooth, flowing curves with great precision. The pen tool will be familiar to you if you've used the pen tools in Adobe Illustrator and Photoshop. Shapes you draw with the pen tool can enhance your page designs in combination with text and imported graphics.

In this lesson, you'll learn how to do the following:

- Draw and edit straight and curved path segments, and open and closed paths.

- Create a hole in a filled shape by combining paths into a compound path.

- Apply a shape (like an arrowhead) to the end of a path.

- Slice paths into smaller pieces.

- Paste an image inside a drawn path.

- Scale, reflect, and duplicate objects.

- Add a graphic so that it becomes part of a text story and flows with it.

Getting started

In this lesson, you'll create the front and back of a direct-mail piece. You'll use InDesign's drawing tools to draw some of the vector objects, or *paths*, in the design. Before you begin, you'll need to restore the default preferences for Adobe InDesign.

1 To ensure that the tools and palettes function exactly as described in this lesson, delete or deactivate (by renaming) the InDesign Defaults file and the InDesign SavedData file. See "Restoring default preferences" on page 2.

2 Start Adobe InDesign.

To begin working, you'll open an existing InDesign document.

3 Choose File > Open, and open the 08_a.indd file in the ID_08 folder, located inside the Lessons folder on your hard disk.

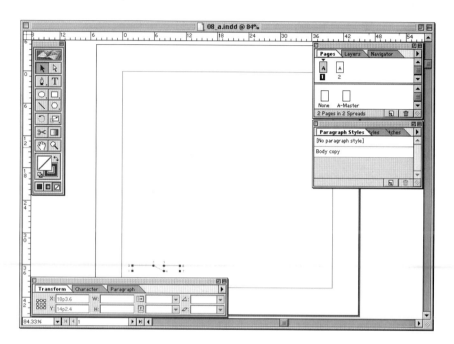

4 Choose File > Save As, rename the file **08_Mailer.indd**, and click Save.

You'll notice that the page is blank except for a shape near the bottom left corner of the page. This document contains everything you need to create the completed version of the document, but to keep things simple, it uses layers to hide everything except the tracing template for the shape you're currently drawing. Right now you see the tracing template for the first shape you'll draw. As you progress through the lesson, you'll use the Layers palette to show and hide other parts of the document. When you're finished, you'll display all layers except the layers containing the tracing templates. For more information about using layers, see "Working with Layers" on page 99 in the User Guide.

5 If you want to see what the finished document will look like, open the 08_b.indd file in the same folder. You can leave this document open to act as a guide as you work. When you're ready to resume working on the lesson document, choose its name from the Window menu.

For a color version of the finished document, see the color section.

Note: Because you'll be using the Layers palette and Swatches palette throughout this lesson, you may want to enlarge those palettes so that you can easily see all of their items. In addition, feel free to move palettes around or change the magnification to a level that works best for you. For more information, see "Changing the magnification of your document" on page 50 and "Using the Navigator palette" on page 57.

Setting up the document grid

Many of the paths you draw in this lesson will be straight lines, precise corners, and symmetrical curves. It's easier to draw these kinds of paths if you set up the document grid in a convenient way.

1 Choose File > Preferences > Grids.

2 In the Document Grid section, for Gridline Every make sure **10p0** (10 picas, 0 points) and **10** subdivisions are entered. Then click OK.

Now you'll display the grid and constrain drawing to it.

3 Choose View > Show Document Grid.

4 Choose View > Snap To Document Grid, and select the command if it isn't already on.

Note: The grid is drawn starting at the ruler origin (zero point).

Drawing straight segments

You draw straight lines by using the pen tool to click two *anchor points*, which define a segment. You can create straight lines that are vertical, horizontal, or diagonal by holding down Shift as you click with the pen tool. This is called *constraining* the line.

Drawing an open path of straight segments

You'll begin by drawing a simple open path, tracing over the template at the bottom left corner of page 1. (If you can't see the template, it may be obscured by a palette at the bottom left corner of the document window; if so, you can move or close the palette.)

1 Click the Layers palette tab (or choose Window > Layers) to make the palette visible.

The tracing template for the shirt collar top exists on the Template 1 layer. The eye icon (👁) indicates that the layer is visible, and the crossed-out pencil icon (✗) for that layer indicates that the layer is locked. All of the template layers are locked so that you don't draw on them by accident.

2 In the Layers palette, select the Collar layer. The path you'll draw will appear on the Collar layer because it is the target layer, as indicated by the pen icon (✒) to the far right of the layer name.

3 Using the zoom tool (🔍), zoom in so that you can read the numbers on the shirt collar template.

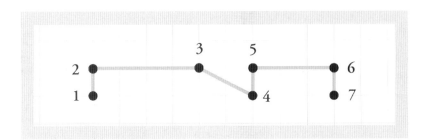

4 Select the pen tool (✒), and position the pointer on point 1 on the template for the top edge of the shirt collar.

Notice that the pointer has a small hollow arrowhead (✒.) next to it. This indicates that the pointer will snap to the closest guide or grid intersection when you click. Because you turned on the document grid, the pointer will always snap to the closest grid intersection, so the hollow arrow will always be on when you use the pen tool, unless another icon takes precedence over the hollow arrow.

5 Using the pen tool, click point 1.

6 With the pen tool still selected, click point 2 on the collar top template.

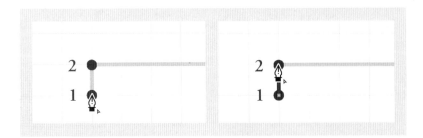

When you click the second point, a caret (^) appears next to the pointer as long as the tip of the pen tool icon is on the new endpoint. The caret indicates that you can split the anchor point to create a curve by dragging the pen tool from that anchor point. You'll create curves later in this lesson.

Also notice that the path and anchor points you've drawn appear in lavender. This is because the Collar layer uses lavender as its layer color, indicated by the colored square immediately to the left of the Collar layer name in the Layers palette. The layer color identifies the layers that contain the currently selected objects.

💡 *When the Snap To Document Grid command is not on, you can still position points at 45-degree angles by holding down Shift as you click.*

7 Click points 3 and 4. Because you're clicking at positions that fall on the grid, the shape is perfect.

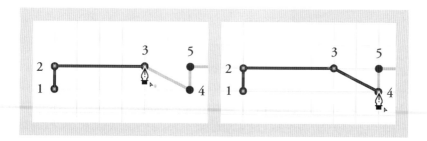

8 Click points 5, 6, and 7.

You must end the path before you can draw any other segments that aren't connected to this path.

9 End the path using one of the following methods:

• Choose Edit > Deselect All.

• Click the pen tool in the toolbox.

• Hold down Ctrl (Windows) or Command (Mac OS) to temporarily activate the most recently used selection tool, and then click in an empty area to deselect the path. If you use this method, make sure you're not selecting any white objects.

Now you'll hide the Template 1 layer to more clearly see the path you just drew.

10 In the Layers palette, click the eye icon for the Template 1 layer to hide that layer.

The default fill and stroke colors are still applied to the path, so now you'll apply the correct colors for the design. The colors for this illustration have already been stored in the Swatches palette for you.

11 Using the selection tool ( ), select the path.

12 Click the Swatches palette tab (or choose Window > Swatches) to make the palette visible.

13 In the toolbox, select the Stroke box (▣), and then in the Swatches palette select TRUMATCH 25-c1 (You may need to enlarge the palette or scroll through it). Then select the Fill box and make sure that [None] is selected in the Swatches palette.

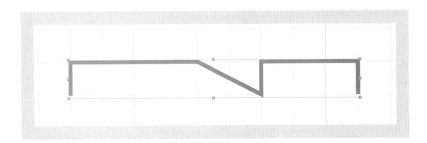

14 Choose Edit > Deselect All, and then choose File > Save to save the file.

Drawing a closed path of straight segments

You'll continue by drawing a closed shape below the open shape you just drew. First you'll show the Template 2 layer, which you will use for this section.

1 In the Layers palette, click the square to the far left of the Template 2 layer to display the eye icon (👁). This contains the template for the bottom of the shirt collar. In the document window, change the view if necessary so that you can see the entire closed collar shape and the numbers next to it.

2 Make sure the Collar layer is targeted in the Layers palette.

Notice that the top edge of the template you just displayed is the same as the collar top you've already drawn. You can save time by duplicating and editing the collar top.

3 Select the direct-selection tool ( ), and then hold down Shift+Alt (Windows) or Shift+Option (Mac OS) as you drag a copy of the top collar path down until it lines up with the top edge of the template for the collar bottom.

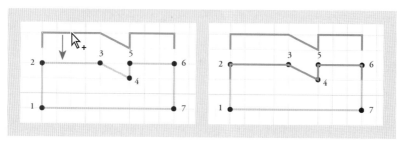

Dragging a copy of upper path (left), and the new copy in position (right)

You used the direct-selection tool to align the path itself—if you had used the selection tool, the path would have aligned with the outer edge of its stroke width instead.

When you drag any object, holding down Alt/Option drags a copy of the object; holding down Shift constrains movement to multiples of 45-degree angles.

Note: If you find yourself dragging one point instead of the entire shape, choose Edit > Undo and try again, making sure you drag the path from a segment (as shown in the above illustration), not from an individual point.

Now you'll extend the sides of the collar by moving individual points.

4 Using the direct-selection tool, click the lower copy of the collar shape. The path and its anchor points become visible. Position the pointer on the lower left endpoint of the collar path. Then drag the lower left endpoint down to point number 1 on the template.

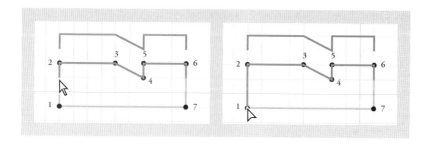

5 Position the pointer on the lower right endpoint of the collar path. Then drag it down to the point number 7 on the template.

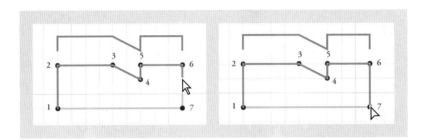

Now you'll switch back to the pen tool, using a convenient keyboard shortcut.

6 Press the P key to select the pen tool, and position the pointer on the endpoint by the number 1. Notice that a slash ( ) appears next to the pointer when its tip is directly on an endpoint. The slash indicates that clicking will continue that endpoint's path rather than starting a new path.

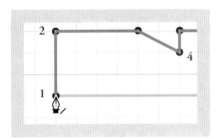

7 Click the endpoint. The slash next to the pointer changes to the caret ( ).

8 Position the pointer on the lower right endpoint until a loop appears next to the pointer ( ). Then click to close the collar shape.

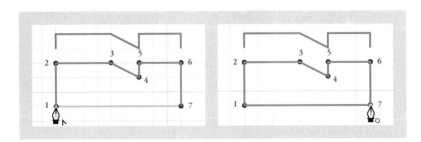

The loop indicates that clicking the endpoint will close the path.

9 In the Layers palette, click the eye icon for the Template 2 layer to hide that layer. The default fill and stroke colors are still applied to the path, so now you'll apply the correct colors for the design.

10 With the path still selected, in the toolbox select the Fill box (■), and then in the Swatches palette select TRUMATCH 25-c1 50% (the second instance of the color).

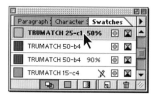

11 Press the X key.

This shortcut is the same as clicking the Swap Fill and Stroke icon (↳) in the toolbox. This doesn't change the fill and stroke that are applied, only whether the fill or stroke of an object is active. Because the fill was active, pressing X activates the stroke.

12 In the Swatches palette, select [None] to remove the stroke.

13 Press Shift+Control+A (Windows) or Shift+Command+A (Mac OS).

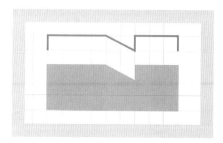

The keyboard shortcut corresponds to the Edit > Deselect All command, and is the fastest way to make sure you've deselected all objects.

14 Choose View > Fit Page in Window, and then save the file.

Drawing curved segments

In this part of the lesson, you'll learn how to draw smooth curved lines using the pen tool. With the pen tool, you draw a curve by setting anchor points and dragging to define the shape of the curve. Although drawing curves this way takes some getting used to, it gives you the most control and flexibility in computer graphics.

You'll examine a single curve, and then draw a closed shape that's completely made up of curves, using template guidelines to help you. First you'll turn off the document grid because you won't need to use it for a while.

1 Choose View > Snap to Document Grid to deselect it.

2 Choose View > Hide Document Grid.

Selecting a point on a curve

When you select a point that's part of a curved segment, the segment displays additional controls you can use to adjust a curve precisely. Before you begin drawing curves, it's helpful to recognize these controls.

1 In the Layers palette, click the square to the far left of the Hair layer to display the eye icon (👁). This contains the wavy lines you'll use in this section.

2 Using the zoom tool, zoom in on the set of wavy lines.

💡 *Pressing the Z key selects the zoom tool in the toolbox.*

3 Press the A key to switch to the direct-selection tool (▸), and then click any of the wavy lines. In the Layers palette, the Hair layer becomes selected, and the path and its anchor points appear in the Hair layer color of magenta.

4 With the direct-selection tool still selected, select the second anchor point from the left of any of the wavy lines. When selected, the anchor point becomes solid and displays two direction lines.

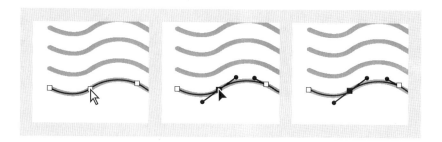

The direction lines cause the anchor point to connect the two adjacent path segments as a continuous curve shaped by the direction lines. The angular collar path you drew in the previous section only has corners because its anchor points don't have any direction lines.

As their names imply, the anchor points anchor the curved segments, and the direction lines control the direction of the curves. You can drag the direction lines or their endpoints, called *direction points,* to adjust the shape of the curve.

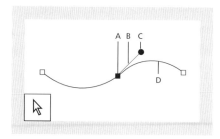

A. Anchor point B. Direction line
C. Direction point D. Path segment

Anchor points, direction points, and direction lines are aids to help you draw. Anchor points are square and, when selected, appear solid. When unselected, anchor points appear hollow. Direction points are always round and solid. Direction lines and points do not appear in print or in any other output; they exist only to help you draw precisely.

Drawing curves

Now you'll use the pen tool to draw a shape completely made up of curves. As with the straight line segments you drew, drawing curves with the pen tool involves positioning points that anchor the path. However, instead of simply clicking the pen tool, you'll drag to extend the two direction lines that precisely influence curve direction. When you release the mouse, a curve's starting point is created with its direction lines. Then you drag the pen tool to end the curve and to set the starting point and direction of the next curve.

1 Choose View > Fit Page in Window.

2 In the Layers palette, click the eye icons (👁) for the Hair and Collar layers to hide each. Click the square to the far left of the Template 3 layer to display the eye icon. The Template 3 layer contains the template for the flower you'll draw, which will appear in front of the collar you drew.

3 In the Layers palette, make sure the Flower layer is targeted and set to be visible. In the document window, scroll or zoom if necessary so that you can easily see all of the numbers and colored direction line guidelines on the flower template.

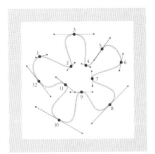

4 Choose Window > Stroke to display the Stroke palette.

5 Press Shift+Control+A (Windows) or Shift+Command+A (Mac OS) to make sure no objects are selected. In the Stroke palette, make sure the Weight is 1 point.

When you adjust any option while no objects are selected, you adjust the default setting for that option. For this lesson, you want the default stroke weight to be 1 point so that the paths you draw don't obscure the lines on the template layer.

6 If the Stroke palette is in the way, drag it to a different position.

7 Press P to select the pen tool ( ).

Notice that the pen tool has a small *x* ( ) next to it. This indicates that the pen tool will start a new path when you click. You didn't see the *x* before because the snap-to cursor ( ) took precedence.

8 Position the pointer on point 1 on the template. Press the mouse button and drag to the right from point 1 to the red dot at the end of the red guideline, then release the mouse. Don't be concerned about the direction line that appears over the blue guideline; you'll correct it later in this section.

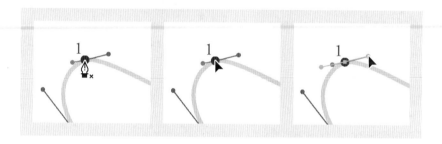

By learning the keyboard shortcuts for drawing, you don't have to move the mouse back to the toolbox. This makes it possible to draw more naturally. Keep the mouse in one hand, and keep the other hand over the keyboard to press tool shortcut and modifier keys.

Next, you'll create the second anchor point and its direction lines, which will complete the first curved segment. As you do the next step, notice how you control the shape of the curve by changing the length and angle of the direction lines you drag out of the anchor point.

9 Drag from point 2 to its red dot, and then release the mouse button. Anchor points 1 and 2 are now connected by a curve shaped by the direction lines you dragged.

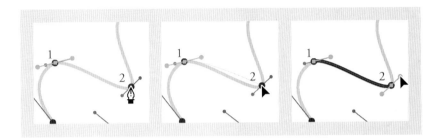

10 For points 3 through 12, drag from each numbered dot to its corresponding red dot. If you make a mistake, simply choose Edit > Undo and try again.

Notice how both direction lines extend to the same length and angle, so that dragging to the red dot automatically makes the opposite direction line extend to the corresponding blue dot. Later in this lesson, you'll learn how to manipulate the direction lines separately.

💡 *To reposition an anchor point while drawing, hold down the spacebar as you drag.*

11 After you draw point 12, end the path by positioning the pointer on point 1 until you see the small loop next to the pointer, and then drag left (backwards) to point 1's blue dot (not the red dot).

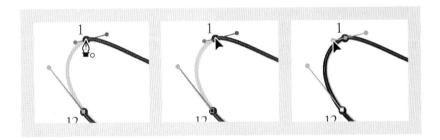

12 In the Layers palette, click the eye icon for the Template 3 layer to hide it.

The default fill and stroke colors are still applied to the path, so now you'll apply the correct colors for the design.

13 In the toolbox, select the Fill box (■), and then in the Swatches palette select TRUMATCH 25-c1.

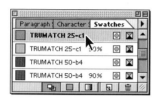

This shape is one solid color that doesn't require a separate stroke. You'll remove the stroke color and weight from the path.

14 Press X to select the Stroke box (▣) in the toolbox, and then in the Swatches palette select [None].

15 Press Shift+Control+A (Windows) or Shift+Command+A (Mac OS) to deselect everything.

Now you'll use a keyboard shortcut to see the entire page.

16 Press Ctrl+0 (Windows) or Command +0 (Mac OS) to fit the page in the window. Then save the file.

Note: *If the keyboard shortcut for Fit Page in Window doesn't work, make sure you pressed the numeral zero above the letter keys, not the letter O or the zero on the numeric keypad.*

Drawing combinations of curved and straight segments

When you drew curves for the previous shape, two direction lines pivoted together around each anchor point. Those anchor points are called *smooth points* because they connect segments as a continuous curve. You can use the pen tool with a modifier key to drag each of the two direction lines at different angles, which converts a smooth point into a *corner point* with two direction lines that move independently. The only difference between the corner points you first created in this lesson and the corner points you'll create in this section is that these corner points will have direction lines.

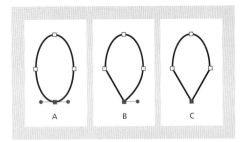

A. *Smooth point* **B.** *Corner point with direction line*
C. *Corner point without direction lines*

Drawing the head shape

The final head shape includes a mix of curves and straight segments joined by corner points. You'll draw the entire outline using the pen tool only.

1 In the Layers palette, click the eye icon ( ) to the far left of the Flower layer to hide it. Then click the squares to the far left of the Template 4 layer to display the eye icon. The Template 4 layer contains a tracing template for the head.

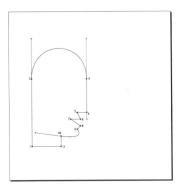

You may have noticed that the finished artwork uses curved segments for the mouth. Don't be concerned that this template contains only straight lines for the mouth—after you draw the outline, you'll return to the mouth segments and change them from straight to curved segments.

2 In the Layers palette, make sure the Head / Eye layer is both targeted and set to be visible. In the document window, scroll or zoom if necessary so that you can easily see all of the numbers and direction lines on the Template 4 layer.

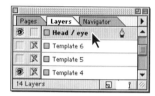

Now you'll use keyboard shortcuts to make the grid visible and make objects snap to it.

3 Press Ctrl+' (Windows) or Command+' (Mac OS) to show the document grid.

4 Press Shift+Ctrl+' (Windows) or Shift+Command+' (Mac OS) to make objects snap to the document grid.

5 Select the pen tool ( ). Position the pointer on point 1 on the template, and then click.

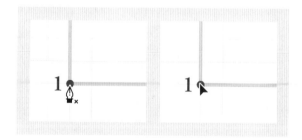

The next segment is a semicircular curve connected to the existing straight segment. You can draw the entire curve simply by strategically placing points 2 and 3 and dragging their direction lines.

6 Position the pointer on point 2. Drag from point 2 up to the red dot at the end of the red guideline. Then release the mouse.

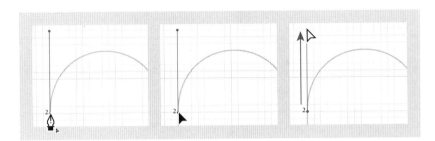

When the document grid is off, you can maintain an existing vertical segment, such as the one connecting points 1 and 2, by pressing Shift as you drag.

7 Position the pointer on point 3. Drag from point 3 down to the red dot; this should create a curve that matches the curve on the template.

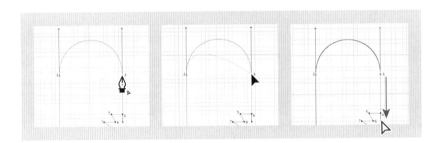

8 Position the pointer on point 3 until the caret appears, and click. This retracts the lower direction line. Because a direction line can create a curve, retracting it ensures that the next segment will be perfectly straight.

9 Position the pointer on point 4, and click. This creates a vertical straight segment connecting points 3 and 4.

10 Click point 5.

Now you'll quickly block out the shape of the mouth using straight segments. These are the straight segments you will later change into curves.

11 Click points 6, 7, 8, and 9.

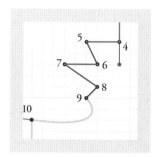

You'll draw the chin by drawing a curved segment in between two straight segments.

12 Position the pointer on point 10. Drag left from point 10 to the red dot.

13 Click point 10 to remove the left direction line. Removing it allows the next segment to be perfectly straight.

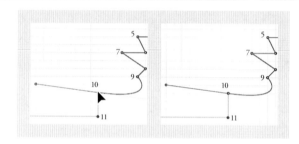

14 Click points 11 and 1 to draw the right angle at the bottom of the neck and to close the path.

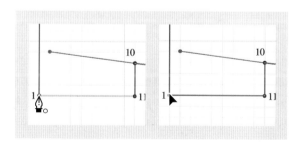

15 In the Layers palette, click the eye icon for the Template 4 layer to hide it, and then save the file.

You'll adjust the fill and stroke of this path later, after you've edited the mouth and drawn the eye.

Changing the shape of existing segments

Now you'll create a more expressive mouth by changing some of the straight segments to curves. It's easy to change the shape of existing segments at any time.

1 Click the square to the far left of the Template 5 layer to display the eye icon (👁). The Template 5 layer contains a template for the finished mouth.

2 In the document window, zoom in so that you can see the nose, mouth, and chin.

3 Press A to select the direct-selection tool (▷), and make sure the head path is still selected and that you can see the path's anchor points. You must use the direct-selection tool because the selection tool displays the path's bounding box, not its anchor points.

4 Press P to select the pen tool (✒), and position it on point 6. You'll know it's positioned on the point when you see a minus sign next to the pointer (✒⁻).

5 With the pen tool still positioned, hold down Alt (Windows) or Option (Mac OS). Notice that the pointer changes to the icon for the convert-direction-point tool (⌄)—this switches to the actual tool, not the pen with a caret. Continue holding down Alt or Option as you drag down from point 6 to the red dot. Direction lines appear, converting the corner point to a smooth point.

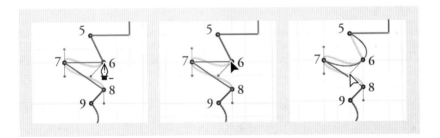

Don't be concerned that the segments between points 5, 6, and 7 don't match the template. You'll fine-tune the segments in the following steps. First you'll retract the upper direction line to restore the straight segment between points 5 and 6.

💡 *If you Alt/Option-click a smooth point, you convert it to a corner point, removing its direction lines.*

6 Position the pen tool on point 6's upper direction point. Then hold down Alt or Option as you drag the upper direction point down into point 6.

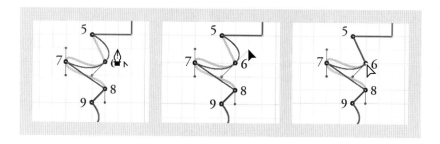

7 Position the pen tool on point 7, and then hold down Alt or Option as you drag from point 7 down to the red dot. You've converted point 7 from a corner point to a smooth point. Extending the direction lines also shapes the left half of the segment between points 6 and 7 so that it now matches the template.

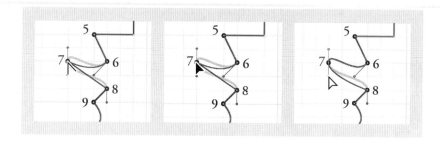

8 Position the pen tool on point 8, and then hold down Alt or Option as you drag from point 8 down to the red dot so that the segment between points 8 and 9 becomes straight. Now all of the mouth curves match the template; the only thing left to do is straighten the path between points 8 and 9.

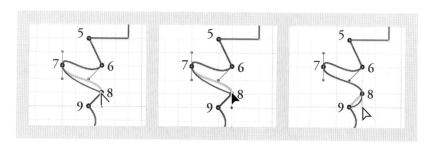

9 Position the pen tool on point 8's lower direction point. Then hold down Alt or Option as you drag the lower direction point up into point 8.

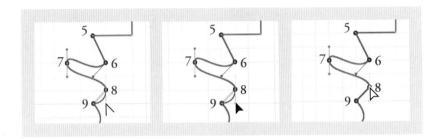

10 Press Ctrl+0 (Windows) or Command+0 (Mac OS) to fit the page in the window.

11 In the Layers palette, click the eye icon for the Template 5 layer to hide it, and then save the file.

Different artists use various drawing styles. Some prefer to lay down all corners and curves correctly the first time, and others prefer to rough out a shape by clicking corner points, and then returning later to create and refine the curves as you did in this section. With practice, you'll realize which way you prefer to draw.

Drawing the eye

To draw the eye for the head, you'll practice more techniques for interactively controlling corner angles and curve shapes as you draw. First you'll turn off and hide the document grid, which you don't need for this section.

1 Press Ctrl+' (Windows) or Command+' (Mac OS) to hide the document grid.

2 Press Shift+Ctrl+' (Windows) or Shift+Command+' (Mac OS) to turn off snapping to the document grid.

3 Click the square to the far left of the Template 6 layer to display the eye icon (☻). This layer contains the template for the eye. In the document window, zoom in on the eye template.

4 Make sure the Head / Eye layer is targeted in the Layers palette.

5 Using the pen tool ( ), position the pointer on point 1 on the template, and then click.

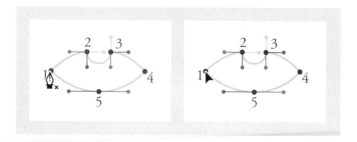

6 Position the pointer on point 2, and then hold down Shift as you drag right to the gray dot.

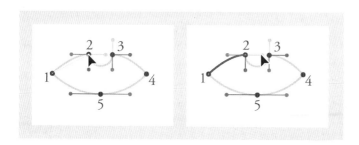

The next curved segment requires a direction line pointing down, but neither direction line does that. In one motion, you'll convert the smooth point to a corner point and reposition the second direction line only.

7 Position the pointer on point 2's right direction point (on the gray dot). Hold down Alt (Windows) or Option (Mac OS) as you drag the direction point down to the red dot. Point 2's left direction line remains intact.

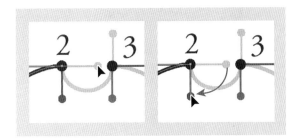

8 Hold down Shift as you drag from point 3 up to the gray dot.

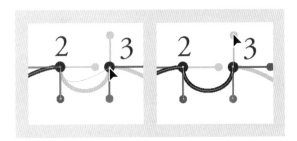

9 Hold down Alt/Option as you drag point 3's upper direction line down and right to the red dot. This will shape the left half of the next segment.

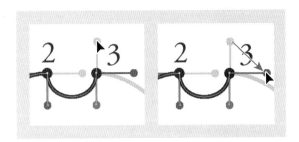

10 Click the pen tool at point 4.

11 Hold down Shift as you drag from point 5 to the red dot.

Holding down Shift constrains your dragging to a perfectly horizontal line.

Note: *If you have trouble with this step, choose Edit > Undo and make sure you start dragging before you press Shift.*

12 Click point 1 to close the path, and then press Shift+Control+A (Windows) or Shift+Command+A (Mac OS) to make sure the path is deselected.

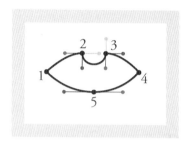

13 In the Layers palette, click the eye icon for the Template 6 layer to hide it.

Notice that as you clicked new segments, the pen tool preserved any existing smooth and corner points, and that pressing Alt/Option changed the default behavior of the pen tool.

Creating a compound path

Now you'll combine the eye with the head as a *compound path*. When you make a compound path, overlapping areas become holes. In this illustration, the eye will become a hole in the head through which you will be able to see the background behind the head.

A compound path isn't the same as a group, where different objects in the group retain their own attributes. All parts of a compound path have to be paths, and they will all share the same set of attributes such as color and stroke weight.

1 In the document window, scroll or zoom if necessary so that you can easily see the entire head.

You'll fill the head with a color first. This will make it easier to see the effect of creating a compound path.

2 Using the selection tool (◤), click the head path to select it.

3 In the toolbox, make sure the Fill box (◼) is selected. In the Swatches palette, select TRUMATCH 50-b4 90%. Then press X and set the stroke to [None].

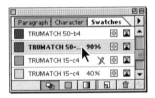

4 With the head still selected, hold down Shift as you click the eye to select both paths.

5 Choose Object > Compound Paths > Make.

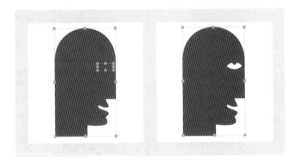

The head and the eye are now two *subpaths* of the same compound path. The compound path uses the eye shape as a hole.

6 Deselect everything, and then save the file.

Note: When you use the selection tool to select a compound path, it selects the entire compound path. To select one of the subpaths, use the direct-selection tool to click a point on a subpath.

Creating a perfect semicircle

The finished document contains a semicircle outside another circle, both located inside the head shape. Although you could draw the semicircle using the pen tool, it's easier to slice an arc out of a circle.

Duplicating as you scale

The semicircle you'll create must be larger than and concentric with an existing circle. In a single action, you can scale the existing circle from the center and make a copy of the result.

1 In the Layers palette, click the eye icon for the Head / Eye layer to hide it.

2 Click the square to the far left of the Circles layer to display the eye icon. This layer contains the circle shape you'll duplicate.

3 Make sure the Circles layer is targeted in the Layers palette. In the document window, zoom in on the circles, leaving some room for the larger circle you'll create.

4 Using the selection tool ( ), select the blue circle.

5 Click the Transform palette tab (or choose Window > Transform) to make the palette visible.

6 In the Transform palette, click the center proxy point (⊞).

This ensures that the next action you take in the Transform palette will be measured from the center of the selection.

7 In the Scale X Percentage option (▯⫐) in the Transform palette, enter **120** and then press Ctrl+Alt+Enter (Windows) or Command+Option+Return (Mac OS). A larger duplicate of the circle appears.

Note: The larger duplicate of the circle also has a heavier stroke weight. When you scale a path, its stroke weight is scaled as well.

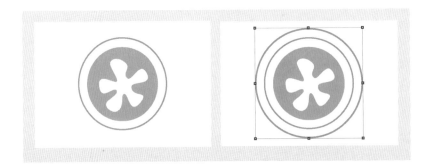

If you simply wanted to scale the horizontal (X) dimension of the circle, you'd press only Enter or Return after typing in the value. In this case, you pressed Ctrl (Windows) or Command (Mac OS) to also make the other (W) dimension scale proportionally, and you pressed Alt or Option to duplicate the original circle using the new scale value.

Slicing a path with the scissors tool

Now you can simply slice off the part of the circle that you don't need.

1 Choose the direct-selection tool (▶), and make sure the larger circle is selected so that you can see its anchor points.

Note: If the larger circle still displays a bounding box after you switch to the direct-selection tool, deselect it and then use the direct-selection tool to select it again.

2 Select the scissors tool (✂) from the toolbox.

3 Using the scissors tool, click the new circle at the anchor point on its left side. Then click the anchor point on its right side. Then deselect everything. Now that you've made two cuts, the path has become two separate paths.

Clicking left anchor point, and right anchor point

Note: *You don't have to click the scissors tool on a point, but because you're creating a perfect semicircle here, the circle's anchor points are convenient places to slice.*

4 Switch to the selection tool (↖), and make sure the bottom of the larger circle is selected. Notice that the bounding box surrounds the bottom half only because it is no longer connected to the top half.

5 Press the Delete key.

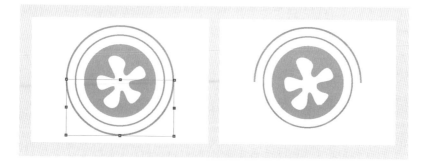

Adding an end shape to an open path

You can instantly add an end shape, such as an arrowhead, to either end of a path by using the Stroke palette. Here, you'll add a loop to the end of the semicircle you just created.

1 With the selection tool, select the semicircle.

2 Click the Stroke palette tab (or choose Window > Stroke) to make the palette visible. If the Stroke palette is displaying the Weight option only, position the pointer on the black triangle to the right of the Stroke tab, and choose Show Options from the Stroke palette menu.

3 In the Stroke palette, choose Circle from the Start menu. This adds a circle shape to the start of the path—the first point drawn when the path was created.

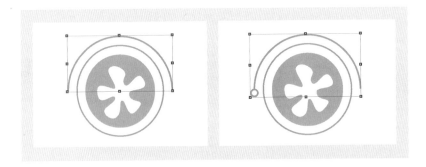

💡 *To reverse the start and end of a path, use the direct-selection tool to select a point on the path and then choose Object > Reverse Path.*

4 Deselect everything, zoom out to see the entire page, and then save the file.

Creating a texture effect using a colorized image

In the final version of this file, you can see that the head is filled with a texture, which is actually a colorized image placed directly inside the compound path. You'll add the image to the compound path now.

1 In the Layers palette, click the square to the far left of the Head / Eye layer to display the eye icon (👁), and make sure the Head / Eye layer is targeted.

2 Using the selection tool (↖), select the head. Using the selection tool selects the entire compound path you created from the head path and eye path earlier in this lesson.

Now you'll use a keyboard shortcut for placing a file.

3 Press Ctrl+D (Windows) or Command+D (Mac OS). Double-click the file 08_c.psd in the ID_08 folder.

The image appears inside the head automatically, because the head was selected when you placed the image. Notice that you can still see through the eye. The brown pattern you see is actually the path's brown fill showing through the pixels of the black 1-bit image. In InDesign, empty areas of a 1-bit image are transparent.

Now you'll use InDesign to colorize the image, which you can do only if the image was saved as a 1-bit or grayscale image.

4 Using the direct-selection tool (↖), click the image inside the head. Select the Fill box in the toolbox, and then in the Swatches palette select TRUMATCH 50-b4. The pattern is still visible but more subtle now, because the image and the path are each filled with different tints of the same color.

5 Deselect everything, and save the file.

Adding an inline graphic

You can add a graphic between any text characters or spaces so that the graphic flows with the text as you add or remove text. Such a graphic is called an *inline graphic*. The invitation text uses an ornamental inline graphic at the end of the text, often called a *dingbat*.

1 In the Layers palette, click the square to the far left of the Text layer to display the eye icon (👁), and make sure the Text layer is targeted.

2 In the document window, zoom in so that you can more clearly see the bottom half of the paragraph of text at the lower right corner of page 1.

3 Select the text tool (T), and then click an insertion point after the period at the end of the sentence at the bottom of the text that reads "…we have a class for you."

4 Press Ctrl+D (Windows) or Command+D (Mac OS). Double-click the file 08_e.eps in the ID_08 folder. The graphic is placed directly into the text where you clicked the insertion point.

Depending on where the insertion point was flashing when you placed the inline graphic, the graphic might be right up against a character in the text. You can add space around the graphic by typing a space character, because the inline graphic behaves as if it were simply another text character.

5 With the text tool still selected, click an insertion point just before the dingbat and press the spacebar to add a little more space as needed before or after the dingbat.

6 Using the selection tool ( ), drag the dingbat down so that it sits nicely between the lines above and below it.

7 Deselect everything, zoom out to see the entire page, and then save the file.

Reflecting objects

The back of the completed invitation (page 2) will use duplicates of objects from the front. The duplicates will be reflected so that you see them as if from behind. You will quickly duplicate the objects on page 1 and then use the Transform palette to flip them.

1 In the Layers palette, make the Hair, Circles, Head / Eye, Squares, Flower, and Collar layers visible in the document. If necessary, hide any currently visible Template layers. Make sure all visible layers are also unlocked, that is, they do not display the crossed-out pencil icons ($\cancel{\mathbb{R}}$).

You can't select objects on hidden layers, so don't be concerned about the lock status of hidden layers.

2 In the document window, zoom out so that you can see both pages of the document.

3 Choose Edit > Select All.

4 Hold down Alt (Windows) or Option (Mac OS) as you drag all of the selected objects down to Page 2, positioning them on the page within the margins like the originals on page 1.

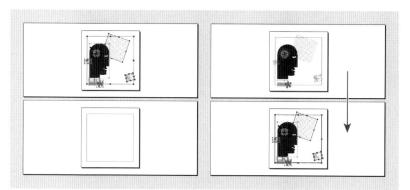

All objects selected on first spread (left), and duplicate objects dragged to the second spread (right)

Note: *If you make a mistake, be sure to activate the page 1 spread (click the first spread in the document window, not in the Pages palette) before you choose Select All again. Otherwise, the Select All command will try to select objects on page 2, the last page you worked on.*

5 Make sure all of the objects on page 2 are still selected. In the Transform palette, click the center point on the proxy (⊞), and then choose Flip Horizontal from the Transform palette menu.

6 Deselect everything and save the file.

7 In the Layers palette, make the Headline and Text layers visible. You can now see the entire document you've created.

Congratulations! You've completed a design using a wide variety of drawn shapes, imported graphics, and layout effects.

On your own

Now that you've had a chance to create your own drawings, here are some additional exercises to try on your own.

1 Use the path-editing skills you learned in this lesson to change the shapes of frames. For example, change the shape of an image's frame so that the image is masked by a star shape, or use the direct-selection tool to change a rectangular text frame to a trapezoid-shaped text frame by dragging the text frame's anchor points.

2 Scan shapes you'd like to draw, and practice using the pen tool to trace the shapes. To make them easy to trace, save the scans as 1-bit or grayscale images, place them into an InDesign document, apply a light tint to them if necessary, and put them on a separate locked layer. On another layer in front of the shapes, trace the shapes using the pen tool.

3 Use the pen tool to draw shapes from life. You may find it easier to draw objects as collections of planes. For example, instead of drawing a cube starting with the outline of the cube's silhouette, draw each face of the cube as a separate closed path. Another way to determine which paths to draw is to think of how you would re-create the same scene using shapes cut out of colored paper, and draw a closed path for each paper shape you'd need.

4 Use the step-and-repeat feature to create the tilted square area on page 1 that's drawn with green circles. First draw one green circle that's 7.325 points in diameter. With the circle selected, Choose Edit > Step and Repeat, enter 14 for the Repeat Count, enter 1p3 for the Horizontal Offset, and click OK. Then select the entire row, choose Edit > Step and Repeat, enter 14 for the Repeat Count, 0 for the Horizontal Offset, and 1p3 for the Vertical Offset. Finally, select all of the circles, select the Rotate tool, and rotate them -19 degrees.

Review questions

1 Why is the direct-selection tool more useful than the selection tool when drawing or editing paths?

2 What is the key difference between smooth and corner points?

3 Which tool can change an anchor point from a corner point to a smooth point or vice versa?

4 How do you make sure a transformation (rotating, scaling, etc.) occurs in relation to the center of an object?

Review answers

1 The selection tool displays only the path's bounding box. The direct-selection tool displays the path itself, and the exact location of the anchor points on it.

2 The two direction lines of a smooth point always exist at the same angle. The direction lines of a corner point (if present) usually exist at different angles, creating a corner at the anchor point.

3 You can switch between smooth and corner points using the convert-direction-point tool (⌐). It's grouped with the pen tool in the toolbox.

4 With the object selected, click the center of the proxy (⊞) in the Transform palette.

Lesson 9

9 Using Advanced Frame Techniques

One of the most powerful features in InDesign is the ability to nest frames within other frames. In this lesson, you will create a calendar page based on a template, and then you will create several images by nesting frames within shapes.

In this lesson you'll learn how to do the following:

- Create a calendar based on a template

- Nest frames within other frames

- Make a compound path

- Add a gradient to text

- Create inline frames

- Export the document to PDF

Getting started

In this lesson, you'll create a calendar page based on a template, and then you'll complete the calendar page design by nesting frames within frames. A template makes it easy to create documents that all have the same basic layout. For this lesson, we have already created a template for a calendar month. You will start a new document based on this template. Before you begin, you'll need to restore the default preferences for Adobe InDesign.

1 To ensure that the tools and palettes function exactly as described in this lesson, delete or deactivate (by renaming) the InDesign Defaults file and the InDesign SavedData file. See "Restoring default preferences" on page 2.

2 Start Adobe InDesign.

Filenames for InDesign documents include .indd extensions. Filenames for InDesign templates include .indt extensions.

3 Choose File > Open, and open the 09_a.indt file in the ID_09 folder, located inside the Lessons folder within the IDCIB folder on your hard disk.

Notice that the document has the name "Untitled." When you open a document based on the template, the file is unnamed.

4 Choose File > Save As, name the file **09_Cal**, and save it in the ID_09 folder.

5 If you want to see what the finished document will look like, ope...
the same folder. You can leave this document open to act as a gui...
you're ready to resume working on the lesson document, choose...
Window menu.

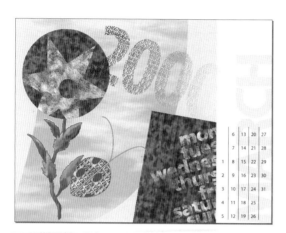

For a color version of the finished document, see the color section.

Creating and opening document templates

Templates are useful starting points for standard documents because you can preset them with layout, graphics, and text. For example, if you prepare a monthly magazine, you can create a template that contains the layout of a typical issue, including ruler guides, grids, master pages, placeholder frames, layers, and any standard swatch colors, graphics, or text. That way you can simply open the template each month and import new content.

You create a template the same way you create a regular document; the only difference occurs when you save the document. To save the document as a template, you can choose File > Save As and then select InDesign Template from the Save as Type menu (Windows) or select Stationery Option from the Format menu (Mac OS).

To edit a template, choose File > Open, select Original in the Open a File dialog box, and then double-click the template document.

—From the Adobe InDesign User Guide, Chapter 2

Updating the calendar

The calendar document includes background objects that were placed on the master page. You will turn to the master page so that you can edit the name of the month and position the first day of the month next to the appropriate day of the week.

1 In the Pages palette, double-click the A-Master page icon.

2 If necessary, scroll in the document window or move palettes so you can see the word "MONTH" on the right side of the page.

This word appears in a text frame that has been rotated 90 degrees. You will replace this placeholder text with the name of a month.

3 Using the type tool (T), position the pointer on the top half of the word "MONTH" on the right side of the page, and double-click the word to select it.

4 Type **MARCH** to replace the selected text.

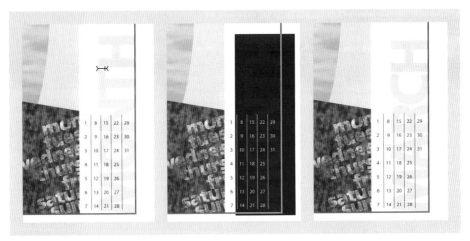

Selecting and replacing the vertical text

Next, you'll align the first day of the month next to the appropriate day of the week. The text frame on the right side of the page includes five columns.

5 Using the type tool, click just before the number 1 in the text frame on the right side of the page to place an insertion point. Press Enter twice so that the number 1 is aligned with Wednesday.

Moving the first day of the month to Wednesday

6 In the Pages palette, double-click the page 1 icon to return to page 1.

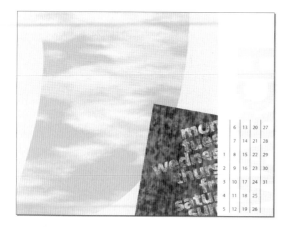

7 Choose File > Save.

Creating the flower image

To complete the calendar page, you'll create three objects: the flower image, the text frame containing "2000," and the ladybug object. For all three of these images, you will nest frames within other frames.

First you'll create the flower, which consists of a stem image and a set of nested shapes.

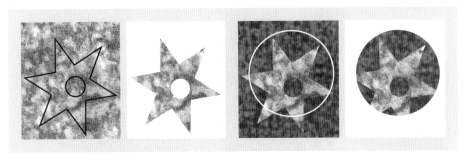

The brown background image is placed inside a star with a compound path. The star is then grouped with a red background image and pasted into a circle.

Placing the stem image

You'll place the stem image on the calendar page and then create a clipping path to remove the image's white background.

1 Select the selection tool ( ). Choose Edit > Deselect All to make sure no text or objects are selected.

2 Click the Layers palette tab (or choose Window > Layers) to make the palette visible. Then click the Graphics layer to target it.

3 Choose File > Place, and then double-click 09_c.tif in the ID_09 folder.

4 Click the loaded graphics icon anywhere on the page. Using the selection tool, drag the stem image so the bottom of the image snaps to the bottom of the page. Position the left edge of the stem frame approximately two picas from the left edge of the page.

5 To view the stem image in full resolution, choose File > Preferences > General. Under Images, select Full Resolution Images for Display, and then click OK.

Note: *If InDesign takes too long to display images as you step through this lesson, you may want to reset this preferences option to Proxy Images. For more information, see "Creating a clipping path using Photoshop" on page 256.*

Notice the white background of the stem image. To remove this white background, you need to add a clipping path to the stem. As you may have learned in Lesson 7, you can create a clipping path in Adobe Photoshop or in InDesign. The stem is a relatively dark object against a light background, so it will be easy to create a clipping path in InDesign.

6 With the object still selected, choose Object > Clipping Path. Move the dialog box so that you can see the stem image. Make sure Use High Resolution is selected. Select Preview, and then drag the Threshold slider if necessary until the stem loses its white background. We set the Threshold at 25. Click OK.

For a color version of creating a clipping path, see figure 9-1 in the color section.

When you create a clipping path, the frame is resized to conform to the object's shape. You can reshape this clipping path frame like any other frame. Use the direct-selection tool ( ) to move points, and use the pen tool ( ) to add or remove points.

Creating the star image

You'll complete the flower effect by creating a shape in the pasteboard that consists of a circle within a star. To allow a background image to show through the circle, you'll make a compound path.

1 Scroll to the left so that you can view a large area of the pasteboard.

2 Double-click the polygon tool (⬠). For Number of Sides, type **6**. For Star Inset, type **50**. Then click OK.

3 In the pasteboard, drag to create a star. The star we created is approximately 25p0 (25 picas and zero points) wide by 23p0 tall as indicated in the W and H boxes of the Transform palette.

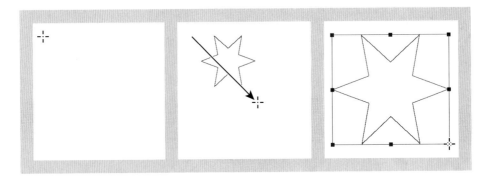

4 Select the ellipse tool (○). Holding down Shift, drag to create a small circle inside the star that is slightly off-center. Our circle is 5p by 5p. Release the Shift key.

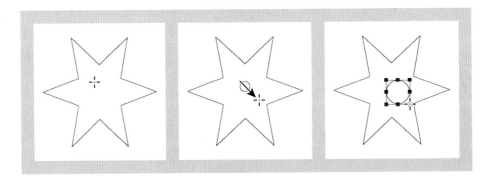

5 Select the selection tool (▶). Shift-click to select both the star and the circle, and then choose Object > Compound Paths > Make. The two shapes are combined.

6 With the star shape still selected, choose File > Place, and then double-click 09_d.tif in the ID_09 folder.

Placing the background image inside the star shape

A brown texture image is now nested within the star. Notice that the compound path allows for a hole to appear in the star.

7 To center the background within the star, make sure the star frame is still selected and choose Object > Fitting > Center Content.

8 To remove the stroke from the star, make sure the star frame is still selected, select the Stroke box (⬚) in the toolbox, and then click the None button (☑) .

9 Save the file.

Nesting the star within a circle

To complete the flower, you will combine the star shape with a red texture image, and then you will paste this grouped image into a circle. You can use the Paste Into command to nest a frame and its image inside another frame.

1 Choose Edit > Deselect All to make sure no objects are selected.

You'll find it's faster to open the Place dialog box if you use a keyboard shortcut.

2 Press Ctrl+D (Windows) or Command+D (Mac OS) to open the Place dialog box. Then double-click 09_e.tif in the ID_09 folder. Click the loaded graphics icon anywhere in the pasteboard to place the background image.

3 Drag the star shape you created over the center of the background image.

The star is hidden behind the background image because the star was created before the background image was placed. You'll move the star in front of the background image.

4 With the star still selected, choose Object > Arrange > Bring to Front.

💡 *When you need to select an image that is behind another image, you can hold down Ctrl (Windows) or Command (Mac OS) and click to select through the images in the stack.*

You need to paste both the star image and the background image into a third frame; however, you can paste only one image into a frame. (After you paste an image into a frame, you may notice that the Paste Into command on the Edit menu is dimmed when the frame is selected.) To nest both images inside a frame, you will group them.

5 Using the selection tool (↖), Shift-click to select both the star and the background image, and then choose Object > Group.

6 Select the ellipse tool (○). On a blank area of the pasteboard, hold down Shift and drag a circle that is slightly smaller than the star. Our circle is 22p6 by 22p6. Release the Shift key.

7 Using the selection tool, select the star/background object group, and then choose Edit > Cut.

8 Click the border of the circle to select it, and then choose Edit > Paste Into (not Paste).

9 Choose Object > Fitting > Center Content.

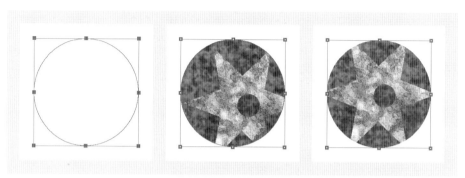

Pasting the grouped objects into the circle and centering the circle's contents

For a color version of nested objects, see figure 9-2 in the color section.

10 To remove the circle's stroke, select the Stroke box ( ) in the toolbox, and then click the None button ( ).

Finishing the flower image

After you nest a frame within another frame, you can still modify, move, and transform the nested frames and images. Now you will rotate and move the star within the circle to make the star slightly offset.

1 Select the direct-selection ( ) tool, and then click the border of the star to select it.

2 In the Transform palette, click the center point in the Proxy icon ( ) to set the point of origin for the rotation. Type **-10.6** for rotation angle ( ) and press Enter or Return.

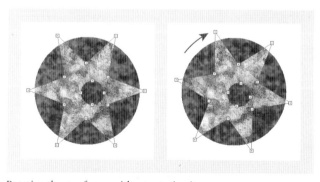

Rotating the star frame without rotating its contents

Notice that the frame of the star rotated, but the brown background image did not rotate along with the frame (you may want to choose Edit > Undo Rotate Item and then Edit > Redo Item to see the shape rotate without its contents).

When using the direct-selection tool to move or rotate an image, you can hold down Ctrl (Windows) or Command (Mac OS) to move or rotate a frame and its contents.

3 Holding down Ctrl (Windows) or Command (Mac OS), drag the star's border down and to the left so that it is slightly off-center within the circle. Do not drag a point, or you'll reshape the star.

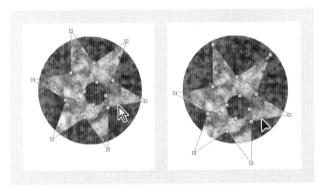

Moving the star frame and its contents

💡 *Another way to move both the star frame and its contents is to select the star using the direct-selection tool (▷), press **v** to select the selection tool (▶), and then use the arrow keys to move the star object. Hold down Shift to move the object in larger increments.*

4 Select the selection tool ( ), click anywhere within the circle to select it, and then drag it to the top of the stem to create a flower effect.

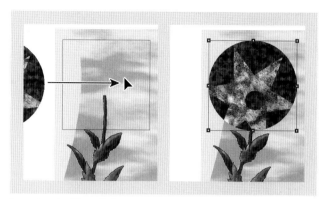

Dragging the "flower" from the pasteboard to the document page

For a color version of completing the flower, see figure 9-3 in the color section.

5 Save the file.

Creating the year 2000 frame

To create the frame containing the year, you will work with two text frames. The first frame, which will contain the year "2000," will be converted to a graphic. The second frame will contain gradient text that you will paste into the first frame. You'll use the pasteboard again to assemble the image.

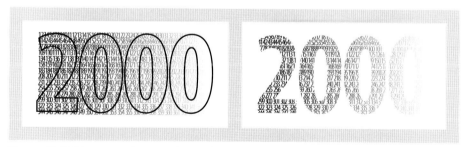

The text "2000" is converted to a graphic so that the background text can be pasted into the year name.

1 Make sure you can see a large area of your pasteboard.

2 Using the type tool (T), drag to create a large text frame (approximately 37p by 20p), and then type **2000**.

3 Double-click the year to select it.

4 Click the Character palette tab (or choose Type > Character) to make the palette visible. Use the palette options to change the font to Myriad, the font style to Cn Bold, and the point size to 260.

Note: If the text disappears, use the selection tool (▸) to drag one of the corner handles until the frame is large enough to display all the text.

To move the characters closer together, you'll change the tracking.

5 Using the type tool, make sure "2000" is still selected. In the Character palette, type **-25** for Tracking (⁗). Then press Enter or Return.

There is too much space between the "2" and "0" in the year, so you'll kern the characters manually.

6 With the type tool still selected, click an insertion point between the 2 and the 0, and then type **-25** for kerning (⁗). Then press Enter or Return.

As you have learned, you can paste an image into a selected frame or graphic; however, you cannot paste an image into text. To paste an image into the characters, you must convert the text to a graphic.

7 Select the selection tool (↖), make sure the text frame is selected, and then choose Type > Create Outlines.

You're now finished with the first frame.

8 Save the file.

Adding a gradient to text

Now you'll import a text file containing numbers and apply a gradient fill to the text. You will then paste this numbered text into the "2000" frame you just created. To begin, you'll use a keyboard shortcut to make sure no frames are selected.

1 Press Shift+Ctrl+A (Windows) or Shift+Command+A (Mac OS) to make sure nothing is selected.

2 Press Ctrl+D (Windows) or Command+D (Mac OS) to open the Place dialog box. Then double-click 09_f.doc in the ID_09 folder.

3 Using the loaded text icon, drag to create a text frame approximately 34p by 16p on the pasteboard. If necessary, use the selection tool (↖) to select the text frame, and then click the Transform palette tab (or choose Window > Transform) and type the height and width in the H and W boxes of the palette.

4 Using the type tool (T), click inside the text frame. Click the Paragraph palette tab (or choose Type > Paragraph) to make the palette visible. Then click Justify All Lines (≡).

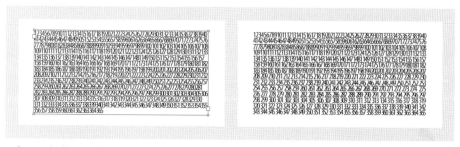

Before and after justifying all lines

5 With the insertion point still in the text frame, choose Edit > Select All.

6 Select the Fill box (▮) in the toolbox. Then click the gradient button (▱) at the bottom of the toolbox to apply a gradient fill to the text.

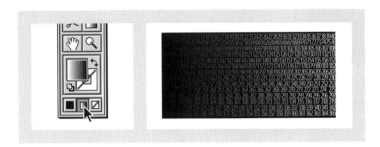

7 To reverse the direction of the gradient, select the gradient tool (▱), and then drag from the right side of the frame to the left side.

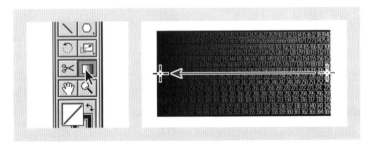

Using the gradient tool to change the direction of the gradient

8 Press Shift+Ctrl+A (Windows) or Shift+Command+A (Mac OS) to deselect everything so you can view the gradient.

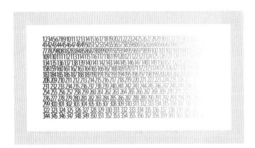

9 Save the file.

Pasting the text frame into the text outline

Now you'll nest the gradient-filled numbers within the "2000" frame.

1 Select the selection tool (↖), select the text frame containing the small numbers, and choose Edit > Cut.

2 Select the frame containing "2000." Make sure the Fill box (⬛) is selected in the toolbox, and then click the None button (⊘) to remove the fill.

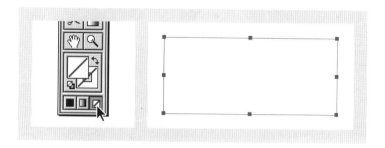

You should remove the fill so that the gradient will not appear too dark when pasted into the "2000" frame.

3 Choose Edit > Paste Into (not Paste).

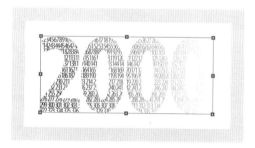

4 Using the selection tool, drag the "2000" frame to the upper right side of the calendar page. We positioned the left side of the frame at 23p6 and the top of the frame at 1p.

5 Click the Transform palette tab (or choose Window > Transform) to make the palette visible. Type **-20** for Rotation Angle (⊿), and then press Enter or Return.

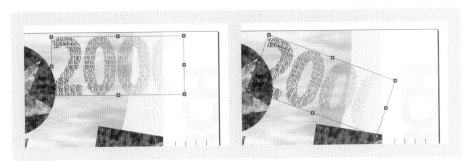

Positioning and rotating the year 2000 object

6 Save the file.

Creating the ladybug image

To complete the calendar page, you'll create the ladybug image, which consists of a text frame and background pattern nested within a drawn shape.

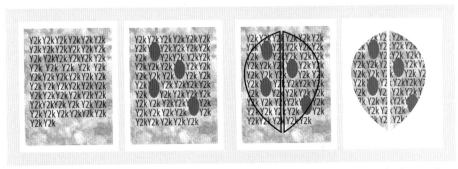

Ovals are pasted into a text frame as inline images. This text frame is grouped with a background image and pasted into the ladybug shell.

Using the pen tool to draw the ladybug's shell

You will use the pen tool to draw the shell of the ladybug. We've created a template layer in this file so you can practice using the pen tool by tracing over the lines on the template.

1 In the Layers palette, click the square to the far left of the Template layer to display the eye icon (👁). Make sure that the Graphics layer is still selected.

2 Change the view so that you can see the bug template in the pasteboard to the left of the document. It may be helpful to zoom in on the bug template.

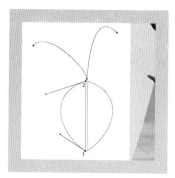

3 Select the pen tool (✒), move the tip of the pen tool to point 1 on the template, and click.

4 With the pen tool still selected, hold down Shift as you click point 2 on the bug template to draw a straight line.

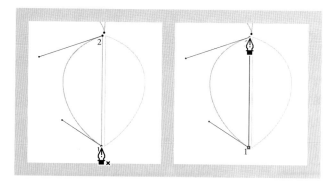

5 Position the pen tool over point 2 on the template so that the pen tool includes a caret ( ). Hold down the mouse button and drag from point 2 to the red dot. Then release the mouse button.

Note: If you don't hold the pen tool exactly over point 2 when you drag, you may create an unwanted point. If this occurs, choose Edit > Undo Add Path Points and try again.

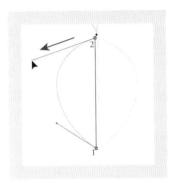

6 Complete the shape by positioning the pointer on point 1 until you see the small loop next to the pointer ( ). Drag from point 1 to the red dot. Then release the mouse button.

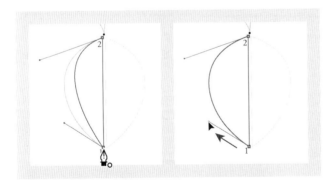

7 Deselect everything, and then save the file.

Duplicating and grouping the ladybug shape

Here you'll duplicate the ladybug shape, flip it horizontally, align the two sides, and then group them by making a compound path.

1 Using the selection tool ( ), select the edge of the drawn image, and then choose Edit > Duplicate.

2 In the Transform palette, position the pointer on the black triangle to the right of the Transform tab, and select Flip Horizontal from the Transform palette menu.

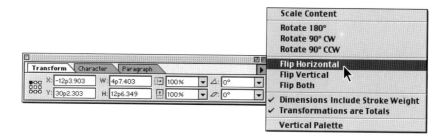

3 Drag the duplicated object next to the original so that it covers the right side of the ladybug shell shown in the template.

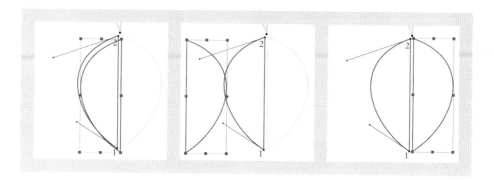

4 To make sure the two objects are vertically aligned, Shift-click to select both sides of the shell. Release the Shift key, and then choose Window > Align. Click the Vertical Align Top (💠) button, and then close the Align palette.

5 With the two sides still selected, choose Object > Compound Paths > Make.

You may wonder why you made a compound path instead of simply grouping the objects. Creating a compound path lets you paste an object into the shape; you cannot paste an object into a grouped set of objects.

6 In the Layers palette, click the eye icon for the Template layer to hide it (you'll show it again later to help you draw the antennae). Make sure the Graphics layer is still selected.

7 Save the file.

Creating the background for the ladybug

Now you'll create the background to paste into the ladybug shape. As part of the design, you will create an ellipse and then paste it into the text. These inline frames will act as dots on the ladybug's shell.

1 Zoom out and scroll to make sure you can see a large area of the pasteboard.

2 Make sure nothing is selected. Open the Place dialog box and double-click 09_g.tif, and then click anywhere in the pasteboard to place the light brown texture image.

Now you'll place a text frame over the light brown image.

3 Make sure nothing is selected. Open the Place dialog box and double-click 09_h.doc, and then drag the loaded text icon to create a text frame that will fit inside the light brown image (our text frame is 11p6 wide and 15p high).

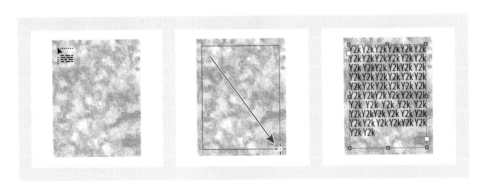

Now you will create an ellipse that you will cut and paste several times into the text frame.

4 Select the ellipse tool (○), and then drag to create an oval shape that is approximately 1p8 wide and 2p10 high.

5 Using the selection tool (▶), make sure the oval shape is selected, select the Fill box (■), and then select Deep Red in the Swatches palette. Select the Stroke box (▣), and then click the None button (☑).

6 With the oval still selected, choose Edit > Cut.

7 Select the type tool (T). Click an insertion point on the second line of the text frame containing "Y2k," and then choose Edit > Paste to create an inline image. Click a different area of the text frame, and then choose Edit > Paste again. Continue to paste the image until you complete a pattern—don't worry about spacing the dots evenly.

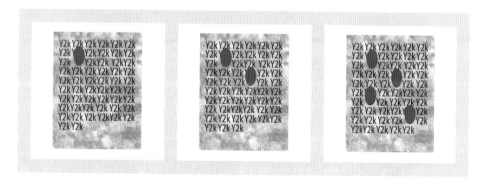

8 Select the selection tool (▶). Shift-click to select both the text frame and the light brown background image, and then choose Object > Group. Then choose Edit > Cut.

9 Select the ladybug object and choose Edit > Paste Into (not Paste).

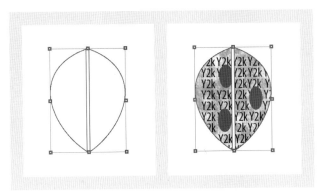

Pasting the grouped objects into the ladybug shell

10 Using the direct-selection tool (⇗), click the "Y2k" text to select the text frame, and then drag the text frame to position it where you want it within the ladybug shell.

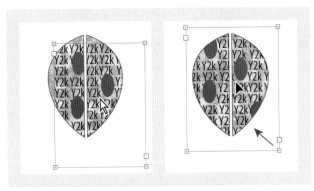

Moving the nested frame within the ladybug shell

11 Select the selection tool (⬆), and then click the ladybug image to select it. Select the Stroke box (⬚) in the toolbox, and then select Deep Red in the Swatches palette.

Completing the ladybug image

You will finish the ladybug by drawing a pair of antennae, grouping and rotating the ladybug image, and moving the image onto the page. Before you draw, you'll set the default stroke and fill colors.

1 Make sure nothing is selected. Select the Fill box (■) in the toolbox, and then click the None button (☑). Select the Stroke box (▣), and then select Deep Red 60% in the Swatches palette.

2 Choose Window > Stroke to display the Stroke palette. Type **2** for Weight, and then close the Stroke palette.

Now that you've defined the stroke and fill colors, you're ready to draw the antennae.

3 Using the pen tool (✒), draw the antennae. If necessary, view the Template layer.

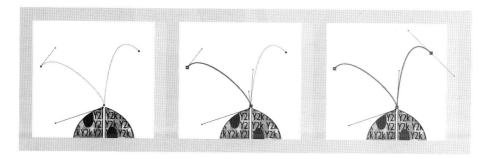

4 When you're done drawing, select the selection tool (▶). If necessary, hide the Template layer.

5 Using the selection tool, drag a marquee around the bug and the antennae to select the objects, and then choose Object > Group.

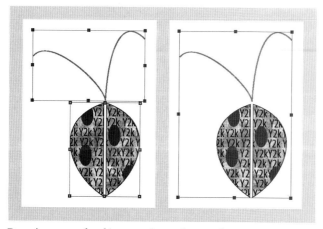

Dragging across the objects to select and group them

6 Select the rotate tool (⟳). Drag to rotate the image approximately 50 degrees clockwise (you should see -50 for rotation angle (△) in the Transform palette).

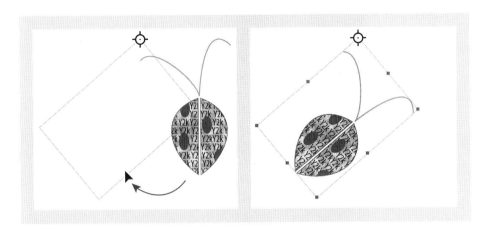

🔵 For a color version of transforming objects, see figure 9-4 in the color section.

💡 *When you drag a frame to rotate it, only the frame rotates until you release the mouse button. To see the contents of the frame rotate while you drag, click and hold the mouse over the image until the pointer becomes a triangle arrow (▶), and then drag to rotate. You can also use this technique when transforming a frame in other ways, such as sizing or scaling.*

7 Using the selection tool (▶), drag the ladybug image onto the page so that the shell covers the part of the lowest stem leaf.

8 To view the final design, choose View > Fit Page in Window. Press Tab to hide the toolbox and palettes. Press Tab again when you're ready to view the palettes.

9 Save the file.

Exporting the document to PDF

If you need to send out a copy of your calendar, the PDF format is the most convenient way. You'll create a PDF so that people in your group can open the calendar using Adobe Acrobat Reader.

Note: To complete this procedure, you must have the free Acrobat Reader on your system. You can install Acrobat Reader from the Classroom in a Book CD.

1 Choose File > Export.

2 For Save as Type (Windows) or Format (Mac OS), select Adobe PDF.

3 For File Name, type **09_Cal.pdf**, and then click Save.

4 Select View PDF after Exporting, and then click Export.

5 After viewing the exported file, exit Acrobat Reader.

Congratulations! You have finished the lesson.

Review questions

1 What are the advantages of using a template?

2 When cutting or copying an image, what is the difference between using the Paste Into and Paste commands?

3 What are the advantages of creating a compound path instead of grouping two objects?

4 How do you move or rotate a frame that is nested within another frame? How do you move or rotate the nested frame and its contents?

Review answers

1 Using a template lets you create a group of documents that have the same basic formatting. You can also create a common set of tools for your documents such as styles and swatches.

2 When you choose Edit > Paste, the copied image is placed on the page into a new frame; when you choose Edit > Paste Into, the copied image is nested within the selected frame.

3 Creating a compound path lets you nest another frame within the compound path. You cannot paste a copied object into a grouped set of objects.

4 Using the direct-selection tool (⬚), click the frame to select it and then drag or rotate it. Hold down Ctrl (Windows) or Command (Mac OS) to move or rotate the frame and its contents together.

Lesson 10

10 | Setting Up Your Monitor for Color Management

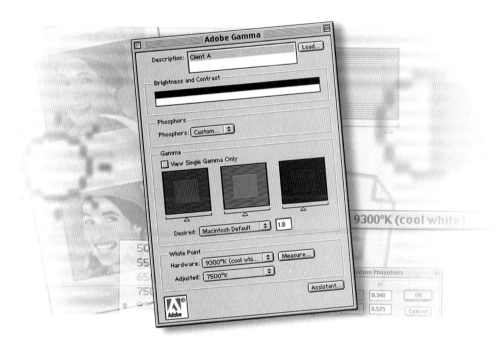

The most basic requirement for color management is to calibrate your monitor and create an ICC profile for it. Applications that support color management will use your monitor's ICC profile to display color graphics consistently. If you don't have a hardware-based calibration and profiling utility, you can get reasonably accurate results using Adobe Gamma.

In this lesson, you'll learn how to do the following:

- Examine the principles associated with color management.

- Calibrate your monitor using Adobe Gamma.

- Create an ICC profile for your monitor using Adobe Gamma.

Note: You can skip this lesson if you have already calibrated your monitor using a hardware-based tool or an ICC-compliant calibration tool such as the Adobe Gamma utility included with InDesign 1.0 and later, Photoshop 5.0 and later, or Illustrator 8.0 and later and if you haven't changed your video card or monitor settings. However, you might want to review the basic color management principles in the first main section of this lesson.

Getting started

In this lesson, you'll learn some basic color management concepts and terminology. In addition, you'll calibrate your monitor to a known color standard, and then create an ICC profile that describes your monitor's specific color characteristics. Before you begin, you'll need to restore the default preferences for Adobe InDesign.

To ensure that the tools and palettes function exactly as described in this lesson, delete or deactivate (by renaming) the InDesign Defaults file and the InDesign SavedData file. See "Restoring default preferences" on page 2.

Color management: An overview

Devices and graphics have different color gamuts. Although all color gamuts overlap, they don't match exactly, which is why some colors on your monitor can't be reproduced in print or online. The colors that can't be reproduced in print are called *out-of-gamut* colors because they are outside the spectrum of printable colors. For example, you can create a large percentage of colors in the visible spectrum using programs such as InDesign, Photoshop, and Illustrator, but you can reproduce only a subset of those colors on a desktop printer. The printer has a smaller *color space* or *gamut* (the range of colors that can be displayed or printed) than the application that created the color.

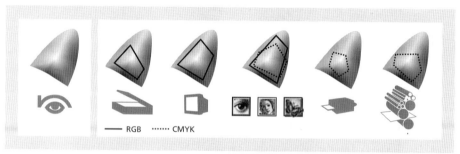

Visible spectrum containing millions of colors (far left) compared with color gamuts of various devices and graphics

For a color version of color gamuts, see figure 10-1 in the color section.

To compensate for these differences and to ensure the closest match between on-screen colors and printed colors, applications use a color management system (CMS). Using a color management engine, the CMS translates colors from the color space of one device into a device-independent color space, such as CIE (Commission Internationale d'Éclairage) LAB. From the device-independent color space, the CMS fits that color information to another device's color space by a process called *color mapping*, or *gamut mapping*. The CMS makes any adjustments necessary to represent the color consistently among devices.

A CMS uses three components to map colors across devices:

• A device-independent (or reference) color space.

• ICC profiles that define the color characteristics of different devices and graphics.

• A color management engine that translates colors from one device's color space to another.

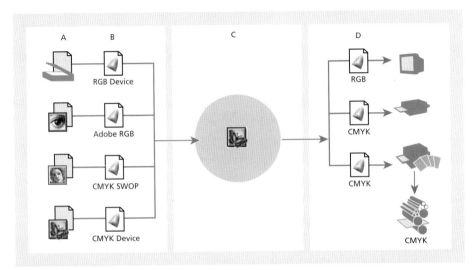

*A. Scanners and software applications create color documents **B.** ICC source profiles describe document color spaces. **C.** A color management engine uses ICC source profiles to map document colors to a device-independent color space through supporting applications. **D.** The color management engine maps document colors from the device-independent color space to output device color spaces using destination profiles.*

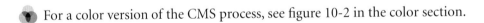 For a color version of the CMS process, see figure 10-2 in the color section.

About the device-independent color space

To successfully compare gamuts and make adjustments, a color management system must use a reference color space—an objective way of defining color. Most CMSs use the CIE (Commission Internationale d'Éclairage) LAB color model, which exists independently of any device and is big enough to reproduce any color visible to the human eye. For this reason, CIE LAB is considered *device-independent*.

About ICC profiles

An *ICC profile* describes how a particular device or standard reproduces color using a cross-platform standard defined by the International Color Consortium (ICC). ICC profiles ensure that images appear correctly in any ICC-compliant applications and on color devices. This is accomplished by embedding the profile information in the original file or assigning the profile in your application.

At a minimum, you must have one *source profile* for the device (scanner or digital camera, for example) or standard (SWOP or Adobe RGB, for example) used to create the color, and one *destination profile* for the device (monitor or contract proofing, for example) or standard (SWOP or TOYO, for example) that you will use to reproduce the color.

About color management engines

Sometimes called the color matching module (CMM), the color management engine interprets ICC profiles. Acting as a translator, the color management engine converts the out-of-gamut colors from the source device to the range of colors that can be produced by the destination device. The color management engine may be included with the CMS or may be a separate part of the operating system.

Translating to a gamut—particularly a smaller gamut—usually involves a compromise, so multiple translation methods are available. For example, a color translation method that preserves correct relationships among colors in a photograph will usually alter the colors in a logo. Color management engines provide a choice of translation methods, known as *rendering intents*, so that you can apply a method appropriate to the intended use of a color graphic. Examples of common rendering intents include *Perceptual (Images)* for preserving color relationships the way the eye does, *Saturation (Graphics)* for preserving vivid colors at the expense of color accuracy, and *Relative* and *Absolute Colorimetric* for preserving color accuracy at the expense of color relationships.

Color management resources

You can find additional information on color management on the Web and in print. Here are a few resources:

• At the Adobe Web site (www.adobe.com), search for **color management**.

• At the Apple Web site (www.apple.com), search for **ColorSync**.

• At the LinoColor Web site (www.linocolor.com), open the "Color Manager Manual."

• At the Agfa Web site (www.agfa.com), search for the publication, "The Secrets of Color Management."

• At the ColorBlind Web site (www.color.com), click Color Resources.

• At your local library or bookstore, look for *GATF Practical Guide to Color Management*, by Richard Adams and Joshua Weisberg (May 1998); ISBN 0883622025.

Calibrating and characterizing your monitor using Adobe Gamma

The first requirement for color management is to calibrate your monitor and create an accurate ICC profile for it. Although this doesn't address your entire workflow, at least it ensures that your monitor displays colors as precisely as it can. *Calibration* is the process of setting your monitor, or any device, to known color conditions. *Characterization*, or profiling, is the process of creating an ICC profile that describes the unique color characteristics of your device or standard. Always calibrate your monitor, or any device, before creating a profile for it.

Although monitor calibration and characterization are best done with specialized software and hardware, you can get reasonably accurate results with the newest version of the Adobe Gamma utility included with your Adobe product. If you are satisfied with your existing monitor profile, you do not need to use Adobe Gamma, as Adobe Gamma will overwrite those settings.

💡 *You may find it helpful to have your monitor's user guide handy while using Adobe Gamma.*

1 If you have the Mac OS Gamma control panel (included with Adobe Photoshop 4.0 and earlier) or the Monitor Setup utility (included with PageMaker® 6.0) for Windows, remove it because it is obsolete. Use the latest Adobe Gamma utility instead.

2 Make sure your monitor has been turned on for at least a half hour. This gives it sufficient time to warm up for a more accurate color reading.

3 Make sure your monitor is displaying thousands of colors or more.

4 Set the room lighting to the level you plan to maintain consistently.

5 Remove colorful background patterns on your monitor desktop. Busy or bright patterns surrounding a document interfere with accurate color perception. Set your desktop to display neutral grays only, using RGB values of 128. For more information, see the manual for your operating system.

6 If your monitor has digital controls for choosing the white point of your monitor from a range of preset values, set those controls before starting Adobe Gamma. Later, in Adobe Gamma, you'll set the white point to match your monitor's current setting. Be sure to set the digital controls before you start Adobe Gamma. If you set them after you begin the calibration process in Adobe Gamma, you'll need to begin the process again.

For more information on controlling the colors and light in your work environment, see "Creating a viewing environment for color management" in the Adobe InDesign online Help.

Starting Adobe Gamma

You'll use the Adobe Gamma utility to calibrate and characterize your monitor. The resulting ICC profile uses the calibration settings to precisely describe how your monitor reproduces color. Depending on your workflow scenario, an ICC monitor profile can be either a source profile, a destination profile, or both. In this section, you'll load an existing monitor profile as a starting point for calibrating your monitor. See "Obtaining and installing source and destination profiles" on page 352 for instructions on installing such a profile.

Note: Adobe Gamma can characterize, but not calibrate, monitors used with Windows NT. Its ability to calibrate settings in Windows 98 depends on the video card and video driver software. In such cases, some calibration options documented here may not be available. For example, if you're only characterizing your monitor, you'll choose the default white point and gamma, but not the target calibration settings.

1 Do one of the following to start Adobe Gamma:

• In Windows, choose Start > Settings > Control Panel, and double-click Adobe Gamma.

• In Mac OS, from the Apple menu, choose Control Panels > Adobe Gamma.

You can use either the control panel or a step-by-step wizard to make all the adjustments necessary for calibrating your monitor. In this lesson, you will use the Adobe Gamma control panel. Any time while working in the Adobe Gamma control panel, you can click the Wizard (Windows) or Assistant (Mac OS) button to switch to the wizard for instructions that guide you through the same settings as in the control panel, one option at a time.

2 Select Control Panel, and click Next.

The next step is to load an ICC monitor profile that describes your monitor. This profile serves as a starting point for the calibration process by supplying some preset values. You'll adjust these values in Adobe Gamma to characterize the profile to match your monitor's particular characteristics.

3 Do one of the following:

• If your monitor is listed in the Description area at the top of the control panel, select it.

• Click the Load button for a list of other available profiles, and then locate and open the monitor ICC profile that most closely matches your monitor. To see an ICC profile's full name at the bottom of the Open Monitor Profile dialog box, select a file. (Windows profile filenames have either the .icc or .icm extension, which you may not see if extension display is off.) Make your choice and click Open.

- Click the Load button, and then locate and open Adobe RGB (1998).

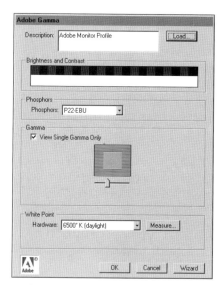

Adobe Gamma utility control panel

Setting the optimum brightness and contrast

Now you'll adjust the monitor's overall level and range of display intensity. These controls work just as they do on a television. Adjusting the monitor's brightness and contrast enables the most accurate screen representation for the gamma adjustment that follows.

1 With Adobe Gamma running, set the contrast control on your monitor to its highest setting.

Obtaining and installing source and destination profiles

When you installed your Adobe product, you installed manufacturer-supplied device profiles for some common printing presses and color spaces. You will use one of these profiles for the destination profile.

A profile for your type of monitor may already be installed on your system. You can use this profile as a starting point for the monitor characterization process, but it's not required because you'll adjust all the settings for your particular monitor anyway. If you want to obtain and install a monitor profile as a starting point, use the following procedure.

1. To minimize confusion when working with profiles, delete any profiles for devices not used by you or your workgroup.

2. Check the appropriate folder on your hard drive for your monitor profile:

• In Windows NT, open the WinNT\System32\Color folder.

• In Windows 98, open the Windows\System\Color folder.

• In Mac OS, open the ColorSync Profiles folder in the System Folder (ColorSync 2.5 or later), or System Folder/Preferences/ColorSync™ Profiles (ColorSync versions earlier than 2.5).

3. If your monitor profile is not installed, contact the manufacturer or search for the profile on the manufacturer's Web site. You can also try finding an ICC profile that most closely matches your monitor. To do this, open your Web browser and search using the text "ICC profiles." When you find the monitor profile, download it to your hard disk.

4. Copy profiles to your hard disk by doing one of the following:

• In Windows NT, copy profiles into the WinNT\System32\Color folder.

• In Windows 98, copy profiles into the Windows\System\Color folder.

• In Mac OS, copy profiles into the ColorSync Profiles folder in the System Folder (ColorSync 2.5 or later), or System Folder/Preferences/ColorSync™ Profiles (ColorSync versions earlier than 2.5). You can organize the ColorSync Profiles folder by creating additional folders within it, or adding aliases to other folders.

Note: If you use ColorSync 2.5 but have used earlier versions, some profiles may still be stored in System Folder/Preferences/ColorSync™ Profiles on your hard disk. For compatibility with ColorSync 2.5 or later, store profiles in the ColorSync Profiles folder in the System Folder.

–From the Adobe InDesign User Guide, Chapter 10

2 Adjust the brightness control on your monitor as you watch the alternating pattern of black and gray squares across the top half of the Brightness and Contrast rectangle in Adobe Gamma. Make the gray squares in the top bar as dark as possible without matching the black squares, while keeping the bottom area a bright white. If you can't see a difference between the black and gray squares while keeping the bottom area white, your monitor's screen phosphors may be fading.

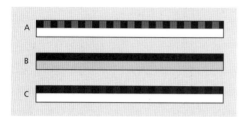

A. Gray squares too light B. Gray squares too dark and white area too gray C. Gray squares and white area correctly adjusted

Do not adjust the brightness and contrast controls on your monitor again unless you are about to update the monitor profile. Adjusting the controls invalidates the monitor profile.

Selecting phosphor data

The chemical phosphors on your monitor screen determine the range of colors you see on your screen.

Do one of the following from the Phosphors menu:

• Choose the exact phosphor type used by the monitor you are calibrating. The two most common phosphor types are EBU/ITU and Trinitron.

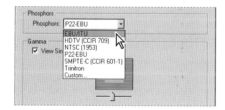

• If the correct type is not listed but you were provided with chromaticity coordinates with your monitor, choose Custom and enter the red, green, and blue chromaticity coordinates of the monitor's phosphors.

• If you're not sure which phosphors your monitor uses, see the monitor's documentation, contact the manufacturer, or use a color measuring instrument such as a colorimeter or spectrophotometer to determine them.

Setting the midtones

The gamma setting defines midtone brightness. You can adjust the gamma based on a single combined gamma reading (the View Single Gamma Only option). Or you can individually adjust the midtones for red, green, and blue. The second method produces a more accurate setting, so you will use that method here.

For the Gamma option in the Adobe Gamma utility, deselect the View Single Gamma Only option. Drag the slider under each box until the shape in the center blends in with the background as much as possible. It may help to squint or move back from the monitor.

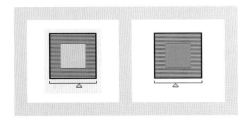

Single gamma not calibrated (left) and calibrated (right)

Make adjustments carefully and in small increments; imprecise adjustments can result in a color cast not visible until you print.

Selecting a target gamma

You may also have an option for specifying a separate gamma for viewing graphics.

Note: This option is not available in Windows NT due to its hardware protection shield that prevents Adobe Gamma from communicating with the computer's video card.

If you have this option, choose one of the following from the Desired menu:

• Windows Default for Windows systems. Leave the setting at 2.2.

• Macintosh Default for Mac OS computers. Leave the setting at 1.8.

Setting the monitor's white point

Now you'll adjust the hardware *white point*, the whitest white that a monitor is capable of displaying. The white point is a measurement of color temperature in degrees Kelvin and determines whether you are using a warm or cool white.

In this part of the lesson, you'll make sure that the white point setting matches the white point of your monitor. Do one of the following:

• If you know the white point of your monitor in its current state, you can select it from the Hardware menu in the White Point section. If your monitor is new, select 9300° K, the default white point of most monitors and televisions.

• If you started from a manufacturer's profile for your monitor, you can use the default value. However, the older your monitor, the less likely it is that its white point still matches the manufacturer's profile.

• If your monitor is equipped with digital controls for setting the white point, and you already set those controls before starting Adobe Gamma, make sure the Hardware menu matches your monitor's current setting. Remember, though, that if you adjust these hardware controls at this point in the calibration process, you'll need to start over, beginning with the procedure in "Setting the optimum brightness and contrast" on page 351.

• If you don't know the white point, you can use the Measure option to visually estimate it. If you choose this option, continue to step 1.

💡 *To get precise values, you need to measure the white point with a desktop colorimeter or spectrophotometer and enter those values directly using the Custom option.*

If you were unable to choose a hardware setting as described above, do the following experiment.

1 For best results, eliminate all ambient light before proceeding.

2 Click Measure and then click OK (Windows) or Next (Mac OS). Three squares will appear.

The goal here is to make the center square as neutral gray as possible. You'll train your eyes to see the contrasts between the extreme blue (cooler) white and warm (yellow) white, and then adjust the colors in the squares to find the most neutral gray between them.

3 Click the left square several times until it disappears, leaving the middle and right squares. Study the contrast between the bluish square on the left and the center square.

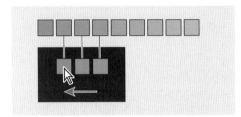

Clicking the left square will reset all the squares a shade cooler.

4 Click the right square several times until it disappears, and study the contrast between the yellowish square on the right and the center square.

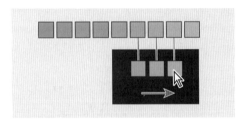

Clicking the right square will reset all the squares a shade warmer.

5 Click the left or right square until the center square is a neutral gray. When complete, commit the changes by clicking the center square.

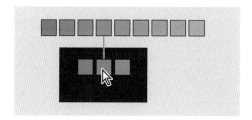

For a color version of white point adjustments, see figure 10-3 in the color section.

Setting an adjusted white point

This option, when available, sets a working white point for monitor display, if that value differs from the hardware white point. For example, if your hardware white point is 6500°K (daylight), but you want to edit an image at 5000°K (warm white) because that most closely represents the environment in which the image will be viewed, you can set your adjusted white point to 5000°K. Adobe Gamma will change the monitor display accordingly.

Do one of the following to specify a separate white point for viewing graphics:

• To use the current white point of your monitor, choose Same as Hardware from the Adjusted menu.

• To specify your monitor's white point to a target value other than the Hardware value, choose the color temperature setting you want from the Adjusted menu.

Saving the monitor profile

Now that you have calibrated for your monitor, you will save the ICC profile you have created. Applications that support color management will use this monitor profile to display color graphics. First, you'll give the monitor profile a unique descriptive name.

1 In Adobe Gamma, rename the description of the monitor profile by editing the text in the Description text box. (We used My Monitor.) When you type a description here, it appears by default when you start Adobe Gamma. In addition, applications that support color management will display this descriptive name in their color settings dialog boxes.

2 Click OK (Windows) or click the Close button (Mac OS). In Mac OS, click Save when prompted.

Now you'll give the profile a filename so you can identify it when using Explorer (Windows) or Finder (Mac OS).

3 In the Save As dialog box, type the same name you used in step 1 and save the profile in the Color folder (Windows) or the ColorSync Profiles folder (Mac OS).

Adobe Gamma makes the new monitor profile the default. You can use this profile in any application that supports ICC-compliant color management. In Mac OS, the profile information will be supplied to Apple ColorSync as the default monitor setting.

Review questions

1 What does the color management engine do?

2 What is calibration?

3 What is characterization?

4 What are the four main monitor settings you adjust when you run the Adobe Gamma utility, and why do you adjust them?

Review answers

1 The color management engine translates colors from the color space of one device to another device's color space by a process called color mapping.

2 Calibration is the process of setting a device to known color conditions.

3 Characterization, or profiling, is the process of creating an ICC profile that describes the unique color characteristics of a particular device. You should always calibrate a device before creating a profile for it.

4 Using Adobe Gamma, you adjust the brightness and contrast, phosphors (color characteristics), gamma (color contrast), and white point (extreme highlight) of the monitor. You adjust these settings to calibrate your monitor. Adobe Gamma uses those settings to create an ICC monitor profile that defines your monitor's color space for working on graphics.

Lesson 11

11 Ensuring Consistent Color

When your document must meet color standards set by clients and designers, viewing and editing color consistently becomes critical, all the way from scanning source images to creating final output. A color management system reconciles color differences among devices so that you can be reasonably certain of the colors your system ultimately produces.

In this lesson, you'll learn how to do the following:

• Specify a color management engine.

• Specify default source and destination ICC profiles.

• Assign ICC profiles in InDesign.

• Embed ICC profiles in graphics created in other Adobe programs.

Note: This lesson uses Adobe Illustrator 8.01 or later and Adobe Photoshop 5.0 or later. If you do not have those programs, you can set up default source and destination ICC profiles in InDesign, but you cannot complete the step-by-step instructions for color-managing graphics from Illustrator and Photoshop.

Getting started

In this lesson, you'll set up color management for an advertisement for a fictitious chocolate company called Tifflins Truffles. The ad will run in a variety of publications, so getting consistent and predictable color is of primary concern. You will set up the color management system using a CMYK press-oriented workflow, build the document using graphics from other Adobe products, and specify ICC profiles for individual graphics to ensure color integrity.

This lesson uses a CMYK workflow, which requires a PostScript printer. If you have a non-PostScript printer (Windows only) and want to use color management, you'll need to use an RGB workflow.

See "An RGB/LAB-based workflow" in the Adobe InDesign online Help.

Important: Successfully calibrating and characterizing your monitor as explained in Lesson 10 is a prerequisite for doing this lesson. Therefore, do not restore the InDesign default preferences in this lesson as you have done in other lessons or you will override the calibration settings and monitor profile. If you skip Lesson 10, the on-screen colors will be unreliable.

1 Start Adobe InDesign.

To begin working, you'll open an existing InDesign document.

2 Choose File > Open, and open the 11_a.indd file in the ID_11 folder, located inside the Lessons folder within the IDCIB folder on your hard disk.

Notice that the brown colors and images look muddy and lack clarity, and the overall color is saturated. This is because you have not enabled color management.

3 Choose File > Save As, rename the file **11_truffles.indd**, and save it in the ID_11 folder.

4 If you want to see what the finished document will look like, open the 11_b.indd file in the Final folder in the ID_11 folder. The ad consists of graphics created in InDesign and other Adobe applications. You will color-manage those graphics to achieve consistent color output from InDesign.

Note: Although color management is turned on for this document, the colors may still lack clarity because you have not yet set up color management for your computer or set a Preferences setting for displaying all available high-resolution image data.

A. *InDesign object* **B.** *Photoshop PSD file* **C.** *Legacy (archived) scanned file* **D.** *Illustrator PDF file*

For a color version of the finished document, see the color section.

5 When you're ready to resume work on the lesson document, choose its name from the Window menu.

Components of a CMYK press-oriented workflow

In a CMYK workflow, you work with CMYK images prepared for a specific printing press or proofing device, or legacy (archived) CMYK images. You generate a source profile based on your press or contract-proofing standard and embed it into the CMYK images or assign the profile in InDesign. The profile enables consistent CMYK printing at other color-managed sites, such as when printing a national magazine on presses in many different cities. Because you use color management, the reliability and consistency of color display improves across all of your workstations. For final printed output, you assign a separations profile that describes your contract-proofing standard or your printing press.

Setting up color management in InDesign

Color management setup involves specifying default application-wide settings for the color management engine and destination profiles, and default document-level settings for source profiles and rendering intents.

Specifying the Adobe CMS engine

Different companies have developed various ways to manage color. To provide you with a choice, a color management system lets you choose a *color management engine* that represents the approach you want to use. The color management engine translates colors from the source device or standard to the destination device or standard.

1 Choose File > Color Settings > Application Color Settings.

The color management engine and other settings you choose in the Application Color Settings dialog box are saved with InDesign and apply to all InDesign documents you work on in the future.

2 For Engine, choose Adobe CMS, InDesign's built-in color management engine.

3 Leave the dialog box open so you can use it in the next section.

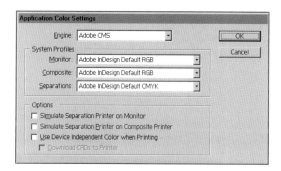

💡 *Choose Adobe CMS unless your prepress service provider recommends another engine, and then use that engine in other color-managed programs. For best results across Adobe programs, choose Adobe CMS in InDesign and Adobe Illustrator 8.0 and later. In Adobe Photoshop 5.0 and later, choose File > Color Settings > CMYK Setup, click ICC, and choose Built-In as the engine.*

Setting up default destination profiles

To complete the application-wide color management setup, you'll choose destination profiles for the devices you will use to reproduce the color, including your monitor, composite proofing device, and final separations standard. InDesign refers to these destination profiles as system profiles.

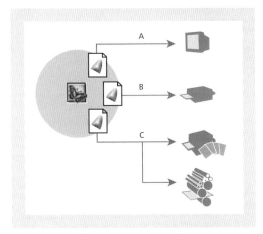

A. Monitor profile **B.** *Composite profile* **C.** *Separations profile, (which can be an output device or press standard, such as SWOP or TOYO)*

For a color version of destination profiles, see figure 11-1 in the color section.

1 For Monitor, choose the profile you created when you calibrated your monitor in Lesson 10. This profile describes the calibrated color space of your monitor.

2 For Composite, choose the profile that best matches your color desktop printer. If you don't have one, choose Adobe InDesign Default CMYK, a generic profile for a composite color-proofing device. InDesign uses the composite profile to reproduce press colors as much as possible on your composite printer.

3 For Separations, choose U.S. Web Coated (SWOP). This profile describes the CMYK output standard that determines the final colors on press.

4 Select Simulate Separation Printer on Monitor to "soft-proof" your document on your monitor. This option uses the monitor profile to reproduce the press colors (described by the separations profile) within your monitor's gamut.

In a later section, you'll set the on-screen display of images to full resolution so that InDesign can color-manage all available image data.

5 Select Simulate Separation Printer on Composite Printer, and click OK.

This option uses the composite profile to reproduce the press colors (described by the separations profile) as much as possible within your composite printer's gamut.

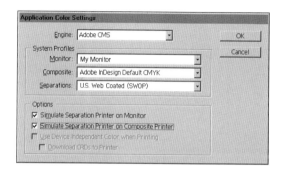

Note: *Unless you are using a product such as Adobe PressReady™, with its host-based PostScript 3™ RIP (raster image processor) and color management capabilities for certain desktop inkjet printers, the reliability of proofing on desktop printers is limited. Desktop printers don't use the same colorants (inks) or substrates (paper stocks) as a printing press.*

Turning on color management

By default, color management for the document is off, because successful color management requires that you set it up properly before depending on it.

1 Choose File > Color Settings > Document Color Settings.

The color management setting and other settings you choose in the Document Color Settings dialog box are stored with a document and can be different for each document.

2 Select Enable Color Management.

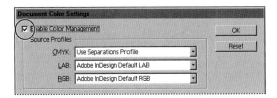

Note: *If you turn on color management after you open a document, color management settings apply only to the current document. For color management to become the InDesign default, turn it on when no documents are open.*

3 Leave the dialog box open so you can use it in the next section.

Specifying default source profiles

Source profiles describe the color space InDesign uses when you create colors in InDesign and apply them to objects, or when you import an RGB, CMYK, or LAB color graphic that wasn't saved with an embedded profile. When you import an image with embedded profiles, InDesign will color-manage the image using the embedded profiles rather than the profiles you choose here, unless you override the embedded profiles for an individual image.

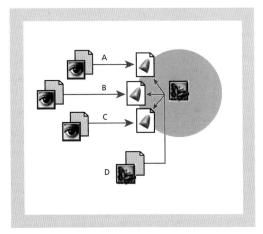

A. LAB profile B. RGB profile C. CMYK profile
D. InDesign document using appropriate profiles
for color modes

For a color version of source profiles, see figure 11-1 in the color section.

1 For CMYK, choose Use Separations Profile, which uses the same separations profile you specified when you set up destination profiles in the previous section. That way, the CMS doesn't have to map colors between different color spaces; they are the same.

Because this project uses CMYK images exclusively, and all colors in the InDesign document have been created using the CMYK color mode, you can leave the settings for LAB and RGB as they appear now.

For information on other workflows where LAB and RGB settings would apply, see "Color management workflows for commercial printing" in the Adobe InDesign online Help.

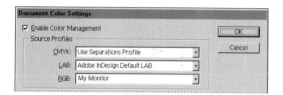

If you do not have a scanner profile and you are placing RGB scans directly in InDesign, use Adobe RGB (1998).

2 Leave the dialog box open so you can use it in the next section.

Specifying the rendering intent

The rendering intent determines how the color management engine translates colors from one device's color space to another. You'll specify the color translation method for InDesign's color management engine to apply to the graphics in the ad.

For descriptions of different rendering intents, see "About translating colors between gamuts" in the Adobe InDesign online Help.

1 In the Document Color Settings dialog box, leave Relative Colorimetric selected for the Solid Color option. This option preserves color accuracy at the expense of color relationships and is appropriate for business logos and other such graphics.

2 For Images, leave Perceptual (Images) selected. This option preserves color relationships the way the eye does and is appropriate for photographs.

3 Move the dialog box out of your way and study the colors in the ad.

Notice the heavy use of brown. You'll see a noticeable difference in the browns when you turn on color management by closing the dialog box in the next step.

4 Click OK.

Several colors change in the ad, but most noticeably the browns; they appear more distinctive.

Color-managing the display of images

Now that you have turned on color management, you can color-manage the on-screen display of images by displaying all available high-resolution image data.

1 Choose File > Preferences > General.

2 For Display, make sure Full Resolution Images is selected and click OK.

When used with color management, this option results in more reliable on-screen colors, especially in duotones.

Note: To conserve disk space, the sample files for this lesson are 150 pixels per inch (ppi), so the colors do not appear as vibrant and realistic as they would using a higher resolution.

3 Choose File > Save to save the file.

Color-managing imported graphics in InDesign

When you import a graphic, you can control its color management in your document. If you know that an imported graphic contains an accurate embedded profile with an appropriate rendering intent, you just import it and continue working. InDesign will read and apply the embedded profile to the graphic, integrating it into the CMS for the document. If an imported bitmap image does not include an embedded profile, InDesign applies the default source profile (CMYK, RGB, or LAB) to the image. InDesign also applies a default source profile to InDesign-drawn objects. You can assign a different profile within InDesign or open the graphic in the original application and embed the profile there.

To color-manage Illustrator vector graphics, save them as PDF or EPS (when using PostScript color management). You can also export vector graphics as TIFF, JPEG, or PSD, which converts them to bitmap images; InDesign will color-manage any bitmap image.

For information on PostScript color management, see "PostScript color-managed output workflows" in the Adobe InDesign Online Help."

The ad already includes two images that were saved without embedded profiles. You'll integrate those images into the document CMS using two different methods: assigning a profile within InDesign and opening the original image so you can embed the profile. Later in the lesson, you'll import two additional graphics and practice two methods of assigning a profile before you place them in the ad.

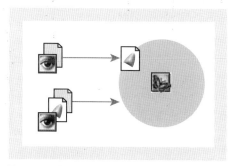

You can assign ICC profiles to any bitmap image within InDesign, or embed profiles in the original file using specific formats, depending on the application.

Assigning a profile after importing an image

When you import images into InDesign that were saved without embedded profiles, InDesign applies its default source profile to the image. If an imported image was not created in the default color space, you should assign the profile that describes the image's original color space.

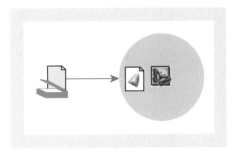

InDesign applies its default source profile to any bitmap image without embedded profiles.

You'll work with an image that was imported into InDesign before you turned on color management. First you'll confirm the default profile InDesign is using to color-manage the image. Then within InDesign, you'll assign a new profile because the image's original color space is different from the default color space.

1 Using the selection tool (➤), select the plate of truffles on the left side of the ad.

2 Choose Object > Image Color Settings.

Notice that Enable Color Management is selected and the profile is Use Document Default. InDesign enables color management for each imported image and assigns the default source profile you set up earlier in this lesson. You can disable color management for individual images using the Image Color Settings dialog box. You can also assign a new profile here. Because you are assigning the profile within InDesign, the change will apply only to the selected image in this document.

3 For Profile, choose Light GCR 280 UCR CMYK US Negative Proofing to match the image's original color space. This profile represents the color lookup tables used by the scanner operator who originally scanned this image.

4 Leave the Rendering Intent as Perceptual (Images) and click OK.

InDesign will color-manage the image using the newly assigned profile.

Embedding a profile in a Photoshop TIFF image

As a general rule, you should embed ICC profiles in files before importing the files into another document that uses color management. That way, images with embedded profiles will more likely appear as intended in InDesign regardless of the default profiles.

In this section, you'll work with a previously imported color bitmap image that does not contain an embedded profile.

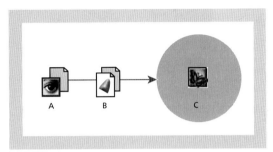

A. *Image's working CMYK color space* **B.** *Image with embedded ICC profile* **C.** *InDesign uses embedded profile*

Note: *If you don't have Photoshop installed on your system, you can use the Photoshop files provided in the lesson folder. The steps indicate when to do so.*

Setting up color management in Photoshop

First you'll define the *working color spaces* (used for viewing and editing) for the image's RGB and CMYK color modes.

1 Start Photoshop, and choose File > Color Settings > RGB Setup.

The RGB Setup dialog box defines the RGB color space Photoshop uses for displaying and editing RGB images. Because you're working in a CMYK workflow, you do not need to adjust most RGB Setup information. However, you'll make sure one option is selected.

2 Leave the settings in the top half of the dialog box as they appear now, but make sure Display Using Monitor Compensation is selected. Selecting this option instructs Photoshop to display images using the profile defined by the Adobe Gamma utility, which you set up in Lesson 10. This setting produces more reliable on-screen colors when you soft-proof CMYK images. Click OK.

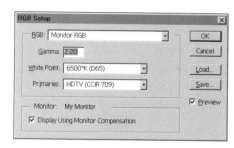

3 Choose File > Color Settings > CMYK Setup.

The CMYK Setup dialog box defines which CMYK space to use for displaying and editing CMYK images.

4 For CMYK Model, select ICC to base the CMYK color space on the ICC profile of the press standard you choose in the next step.

5 For Profile, choose U.S. Web Coated (SWOP) so that the embedded profile matches the default separations profile you specified in InDesign.

6 Leave the Engine setting as Built-In (which corresponds to Adobe CMS in InDesign), and the Intent as Perceptual (Images). Then click OK.

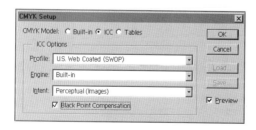

InDesign will use this CMYK color space for displaying the chocolate image.

Embedding the profile

Now that you have specified the working color spaces for the Photoshop image, you'll embed the specified profile.

1 In InDesign, use the selection tool (↖) to select the large chocolate image. Click in the upper right area of the ad.

2 Choose File > Links to display the Links palette.

3 With the image still selected, do one of the following:

• If you don't have Photoshop, you can read the information in this section and the next one, and then skip to step 2 in "Updating the image within InDesign" on page 379 to use the Photoshop file provided in the lesson folder.

• If you have Photoshop, click the Edit Original button (✎) at the bottom of the Links palette to open the image in Photoshop. The image has been converted to CMYK so you can use it in your CMYK press-oriented workflow. If the image were RGB, you would need to convert it before continuing.

4 In Photoshop, choose File > Color Settings > Profile Setup.

5 Make sure all options for Embed Profiles are selected. Leave the rest of the settings in the dialog box as they appear now—they are not needed because you are saving the file. (The other options apply to opening files.) Then click OK.

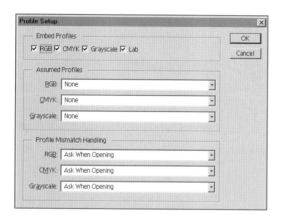

6 To embed the profile, choose File > Save As, rename the file **11_dprof.tif**, and save it in the ID_11 folder. In the TIFF Options dialog box, click OK to accept the default.

7 Close the image and exit Photoshop.

Updating the image within InDesign

Now that you've embedded the ICC profile in the Photoshop file, you can update the image in InDesign. InDesign will color-manage the image using the embedded profile.

1 In InDesign, select the large chocolate image.

2 Do one of the following:

• If you followed Photoshop instructions in the previous sections, click the Relink button (⌂⃗▥) at the bottom of the Links palette. Click Browse and locate the 11_dprof.tif file you just saved in the ID_11 folder. Double-click the file.

• If you don't have Photoshop or skipped the previous two sections, click the Relink button (⌂⃗▥) at the bottom of the Links palette. Click Browse and locate 11_dprof.tif in the Final folder. Double-click the file.

3 To confirm that the embedded profile is being used, position the pointer on the black triangle to the right of the Links palette tab and choose Link Information from the Links palette menu. In the dialog box, check that the Profile says U.S. Web Coated (SWOP).

💡 *A quick way to check profiles for all graphics in a document is by using the Preflight feature to view document components.*

Now that you have fixed existing graphics in the document, you will finish the ad by importing two additional graphics and setting options as you import.

Assigning a profile while importing a graphic

If you know a color-managed image uses a color space that is different from the color space described by the default source profile, you can assign a profile to it while you're importing the image into InDesign. You'll import a legacy (archived) CMYK image scanned without a profile, and assign a profile before you place it in the ad.

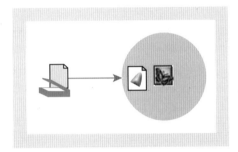

You can assign a profile while you import an image.

1 In InDesign, choose View > Show Frame Edges to show the outline of the frame for the graphic you're about to place—and the outlines for all the graphics frames in the ad.

2 Using the selection tool (↖), select the top-most empty frame in the lower right area of the ad.

3 Choose File > Place.

4 Select Show Import Options so that you can specify a profile.

5 Locate and double-click the 11_e.psd file in the ID_11 folder, located inside the Lessons folder within the IDCIB folder on your hard disk.

6 Choose Color Settings from the menu at the top of the Image Import Options dialog box.

7 Make sure Enable Color Management is selected. For Profile, choose Light GCR 280 UCR CMYK US Negative Proofing to match the image's original color space.

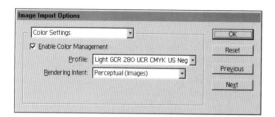

8 Leave the Rendering Intent as Perceptual (Images) and click OK.

The image appears in the selected frame. InDesign will color-manage the image using the profile you assigned.

Embedding a profile in an Illustrator graphic

InDesign can color-manage vector graphics created in Illustrator when you save them in a format that embeds profiles, such as PDF or TIFF. In this lesson, you'll save a file as PDF and then place the graphic in InDesign.

Note: *If you don't have Illustrator installed on your system, you can read the information in the next two sections, and then skip to step 2 in "Placing a color-managed Illustrator file into InDesign" on page 385 to use the Illustrator file we provide.*

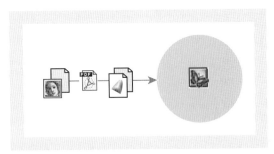

InDesign color-manages a PDF file using the profiles saved with the PDF version of the file.

Setting up color management in Illustrator

First you'll set up color management in Illustrator so that it matches InDesign's color management settings. This ensures that the on-screen colors are the same whether you're working in Illustrator or InDesign. Setting up color management in Illustrator also enables you to embed an ICC profile in a PDF version of the Illustrator file. When you place the PDF file in the InDesign layout, InDesign will color-manage the logo using the embedded profile.

1 Start Adobe Illustrator, and choose File > Color Settings.

2 In the Color Settings dialog box, select the monitor profile you created in Lesson 10 using Adobe Gamma.

3 From the Printer (CMYK) menu, select U.S. Web Coated (SWOP) for your final output device.

If you are printing a proof to a desktop printer and then printing to the final output device, be sure to select the profile for the final output device once you have printed your proof to a desktop printer.

4 For Engine, leave Adobe CMS selected.

5 For Intent, select Relative Colorimetric to leave colors that fall inside the gamut unchanged. This method usually converts out-of-gamut colors to colors that have the same lightness but fall just inside the gamut.

6 Select the Use Embedded ICC Profiles option to save the profile with the PDF version of the Illustrator file you'll create in the next section.

7 Select the Simulate Print Colors on Display option so that on-screen colors simulate the printed output. Then click OK.

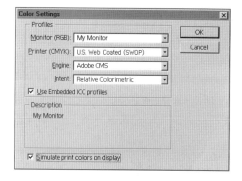

You have finished setting up color management in Illustrator.

Embedding a profile by saving as PDF

A logo gets used in a variety of corporate identity pieces—in print and on the Web— so you'll save the Illustrator document in Acrobat PDF format for its portability between computer platforms and output devices. When PDF files are created using Acrobat 4.0 technology, they can also contain embedded profiles

1 In Illustrator, choose File > Open. Locate and double-click the 11_f.ai file in the ID_11 folder, located inside the Lessons folder within the IDCIB folder on your hard disk.

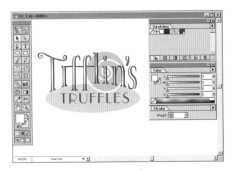

2 Choose File > Save As.

3 Name the resulting PDF file **11_Logo.pdf**, and choose Acrobat PDF from the Save as Type (Windows) or Format (Mac OS) menu. Make sure the ID_11 folder is selected, and then click Save to display the PDF Format dialog box.

4 Make sure Press Ready is selected in the PDF Options Set menu. The Press Ready option creates output appropriate for printing to high-resolution presses.

5 For Compatibility, choose Acrobat 4.0. This setting ensures that the profile is saved with the PDF file. Then click OK.

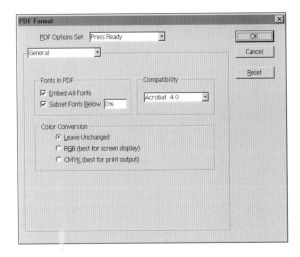

6 Close the file and exit Illustrator.

Placing a color-managed Illustrator file into InDesign

Now that you have created a PDF file of the Illustrator document, you'll place it in InDesign.

1 In InDesign, select the empty frame in the bottom right area of the ad.

2 Do one of the following:

• If you followed Illustrator instructions in the previous sections, choose File > Place and select the 11_Logo.pdf file you created.

• If you don't have Illustrator or skipped the previous two sections, choose File > Place and select the 11_Logo.pdf file in the Final folder in the ID_11 folder, located inside the Lessons folder within the IDCIB folder on your hard disk.

3 Make sure Show Import Options is selected, and then click Open (Windows) or Choose (Mac OS).

4 For Crop To, choose Content. This option places only the logo's bounding box—the minimum area that encloses the logo.

5 Make sure Transparent Background is selected so that you can see any text or graphics behind the bounding box, and then click OK.

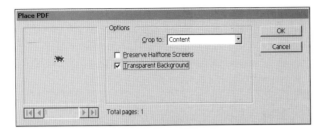

The logo appears in the selected frame. InDesign will color-manage the PDF file using the embedded profile.

In this lesson, you have learned how to set up color management across three Adobe applications—an admirable achievement. You have learned several methods for incorporating graphics so that they can be color-managed when placed in InDesign documents. Because you described your color environment to the other Adobe applications whose graphics you imported, you can expect predictable, consistent color for those graphics across the applications.

At this time, you could either hand off the native InDesign file with all the linked files, or export the InDesign file as PDF, embedding the ICC profiles you assigned. If you create a PDF file of the document, the colors in the ad will look the same across all publications that use the ad, regardless of the color-management settings used by the publication's layout application. A CMS at the press will translate the color information in the document to the color space of the press.

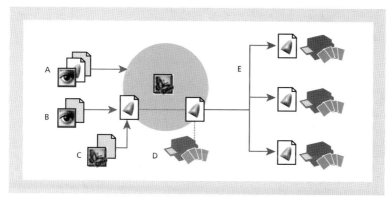

A. *Image with embedded CMYK profile* **B.** *Image with CMYK profile assigned in InDesign* **C.** *InDesign document using a CMYK profile based on D* **D.** *A separation profile* **E.** *Different separation profiles when targeting different presses*

Review questions

1 What do source profiles describe?

2 What are three ways to attach an ICC profile to a graphic so that InDesign can color-manage the graphic?

3 Why would you embed an ICC profile in a graphic?

4 Which file formats embed ICC profiles for use in both Windows and Mac OS?

Review answers

1 Source profiles describe the color space InDesign uses when you create objects using the drawing tools, or when you import an RGB, CMYK, or LAB color graphic that wasn't saved with an embedded profile.

2 You can embed the profile in the original file, assign a profile within InDesign, or use the default profile you specified when you set up color management in InDesign.

3 Embedding an ICC profile ensures that the graphic displays correctly in any application that uses ICC-compliant color management. The application that uses the graphic honors the embedded profile rather than applying a default one.

4 PDF creates portable files and embeds any ICC profiles used in the documents. Another portable format that embeds profiles in bitmap images is TIFF.

Lesson 12

12 | Preparing Documents for High-Resolution Printing

The quality and color of your final printed output depend upon the process you follow to prepare a document for print. Whether you're printing a draft of your work on a desktop printer or producing color separations to be printed on a commercial press, refining your document helps ensure that your printed results meet your expectations.

In this lesson, you'll learn how to do the following:

- Install a virtual printer for high-resolution printing.

- Perform a preflight check and correct problems in the document.

- Create a bleed.

- Trap text using a stroke to hide misregistration.

- Overprint objects to hide misregistration.

- Separate a color document into its component colors.

- Package files for handoff to a service provider.

Getting started

In this lesson, you'll work with an oversized four-color poster with a spot color and a spot varnish. The poster is mostly finished and already set up with color management. The document is at final design stage, requiring only some print production tasks for commercial printing.

Note: If you successfully calibrated and characterized your monitor in Lesson 10 and set up color management in Lesson 11, don't restore the InDesign default preferences. The project files for this lesson use the same color management settings as in Lesson 11, so the intended colors will appear more accurate if you use those settings. If you did not do Lessons 10 and 11, you can restore the InDesign defaults and complete this lesson, but the on-screen colors will be unreliable.

To restore the InDesign defaults, delete or deactivate (by renaming) the InDesign Defaults file and the InDesign SavedData file. See "Restoring default preferences" on page 2.

Using the PostScript printer driver and PPD files

InDesign uses platform-specific printer drivers to control many printing functions and improve printer performance. In Mac OS systems, for example, the Adobe PS 8.6 driver enables the InDesign printing options for color, scale and fit, graphics, page marks, and so on; without this driver, these options will not even appear in InDesign. In Windows systems, you can set the printing options without the driver, but your PostScript files will be larger and less efficient.

In addition, InDesign uses *PostScript Printer Description (PPD) files* to obtain information about the output device, including printer-resident fonts, available paper sizes, resolution, available line screen values, and the angles of the halftone screens.

About virtual printers

You'll find it useful to install a virtual printer and select a PPD for high-resolution printing so you can set options for color separations. Using a virtual printer, you can print a document to disk as a file, using the attributes of a printer you're not directly connected to. You might do this when preparing a document for printing at another location, such as a prepress service provider.

Installing a virtual printer for Windows

You will use a PPD file called AGFA SelectSet7000_ID so you can prepare the document for high-resolution printing later in this lesson.

1 Disable any virus-protection software, as it can interfere with a successful installation. See your virus-protection software documentation for instructions.

2 Insert the Adobe InDesign CD into your CD drive.

3 Do one of the following:

• If a startup screen appears, make sure Installation is selected, and then click the button for the PostScript printer driver for your system (PostScript Driver 5.1 for Windows NT 4.0 or PostScript Driver 4.3 for Windows 98).

• Use Windows Explorer to locate and open the Print Drivers folder on the CD. Depending on your system, open the Win98 or WinNT folder and double-click the Setup.exe file to begin the setup process.

4 Follow the on-screen instructions to install or update the AdobePS printer driver until the Install Printer (Windows NT) or Printer Connection Type (Windows 98) dialog box appears. Select Local Printer and click Next.

5 When the Select PPD dialog box appears, locate and select AGFA SelectSet7000_ID in the ID_12 folder, located inside the Lessons folder within the IDCIB folder on your hard disk. Then click Next.

6 Do one of the following:

• In Windows NT, in the Select Port dialog box, select FILE: Local Port.

• In Windows 98, in the Local Port Selection dialog box, select FILE: Creates a File on Disk.

Although this step is not necessary for printing to a file, it will prevent you from sending printer data to the wrong port accidentally.

7 Click Next and follow the remaining prompts to add a virtual printer that uses the PPD you selected.

8 When the Device Settings panel in the Properties dialog box appears, click Cancel. Later in the lesson, you'll reopen the Properties dialog box using the InDesign Print dialog box and change some page setup options and film requirements.

9 In the Print to File dialog box, click Cancel.

10 Follow the remaining prompts to finish installing the printer. Then enable your virus-protection software.

Installing a virtual printer for Mac OS

You will use a PPD file called AGFA SelectSet7000_ID so you can prepare the document for high-resolution printing later in this lesson.

1 Disable any virus-protection software, as it can interfere with a successful installation. See your virus-protection software documentation for instructions.

2 Insert the Adobe InDesign CD into your CD drive.

3 Double-click the Install PostScript Driver 8.6 icon on the Adobe InDesign CD to begin the installation process.

4 Follow the on-screen instructions to install the printer driver.

To enable the virtual printer options, you need to install a PostScript printer first.

5 Do one of the following:

• If you have already installed a PostScript printer, skip to step 6.

• If you have a desktop PostScript printer, open the Chooser, select the AdobePS icon, select the printer, and then click Create to set up the printer. This step selects the default PPD for the printer. To override the default PPD and select the PPD we provide, select the printer, click Setup, and then click Select PPD. Locate and select AGFA SelectSet7000_ID in the ID_12 folder, located inside the Lessons folder within the IDCIB folder on your hard disk. Then click Select. When setup is complete, close the Chooser. If necessary, click OK to acknowledge the Page Setup message.

• If you don't have a desktop PostScript printer, open the Chooser, select the AdobePS icon, and then close the Chooser. Click OK to acknowledge the Page Setup message.

You select a virtual printer from InDesign, not from the Chooser, so you'll open a new blank document.

6 Start Adobe InDesign.

7 Choose File > New, and click OK to close the New Document dialog box.

8 Choose File > Page Setup.

9 For Printer, choose Virtual Printer.

10 Also choose Virtual Printer from the menu below the printers.

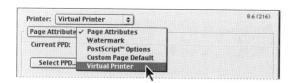

11 Click the Select PPD button.

12 Select AGFA SelectSet7000_ID in the ID_12 folder, located inside the Lessons folder within the IDCIB folder on your hard disk. Then click Select.

13 Click OK to acknowledge the Page Attributes message. Then click OK again to close the Page Setup dialog box. You'll set page options later in this lesson.

14 Close the new, untitled document without saving it. Then enable your virus-protection software.

Opening the work file

To begin working, you'll open an existing InDesign document.

1 If necessary, start Adobe InDesign.

2 Choose File > Open, and open the 12_a.indd file in the ID_12 folder, located inside the Lessons folder within the IDCIB folder on your hard disk.

The file contains outdated links, which you will update during the lesson.

3 Click OK to acknowledge the message, and then move the Links palette out of your way.

4 If you want to see what the finished document will look like, open the 12_b.indd file in the same folder. You can leave the document open to act as a guide as you work. When you're ready to resume working on the lesson document, choose its name from the Window menu.

For a color version of the finished document, see the color section.

5 Choose File > Save As, rename the file **12_poster**, and save it in the ID_12 folder.

Note: As you work through the lesson, feel free to move palettes around or change the magnification to a level that works best for you. For more information, see "Changing the magnification of your document" on page 50 and "Using the Navigator palette" on page 57.

Performing a preflight check before printing

Any time before printing or handing off a document to a service provider, you can perform a quality check on the document. *Preflight* is the industry-standard name for this process, which is analogous to a pilot's preflight check. The preflight check indicates outdated and missing components. It also provides helpful information about a document, such as inks, fonts, and print settings.

Viewing the document components

You'll run a preflight check before making final adjustments to the poster's layout and design and before specifying final output settings. When you begin the preflight process, a Summary panel appears. This panel contains warning icons if certain areas of the document require attention prior to final output.

1 Choose File > Preflight.

Note: If InDesign indicates you have missing fonts, see "Installing the Classroom in a Book fonts" on page 2.

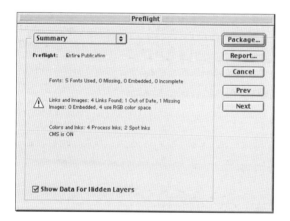

The Summary panel of the Preflight dialog box indicates there is one missing link and one out-of-date link. In addition, InDesign flags RGB images so that you know which ones to convert to CMYK if necessary. In this lesson, you'll use RGB (the original color space of these images) so you can use the document for multiple media. For example, you could convert the images to CMYK for print media or use the original RGB for online media such as the Internet, CD-ROM, or television.

2 Step through the other panels by clicking Next. Examine the current settings for each. When you get to the Colors and Inks panel, notice that the document contains the four process-color inks and two spot-color inks, a PANTONE color and a spot varnish.

3 Choose Print Settings from the menu at the top of the Preflight dialog box to examine the current print settings for the poster. The poster is currently set up for composite printing on a desktop printer. Later in the lesson, you'll specify paper options and print settings for separation-based printing.

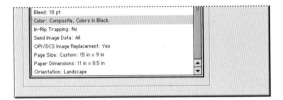

4 Leave the Preflight dialog box open so you can use it in the next section.

Repairing broken links

Using the Preflight feature, you'll relink a missing RGB image (it was renamed but not relinked) and update an out-of-date link.

1 From the menu at the top of the Preflight dialog box, choose Links and Images.

2 Select the 12_a.jpg graphic whose Status is listed as Missing.

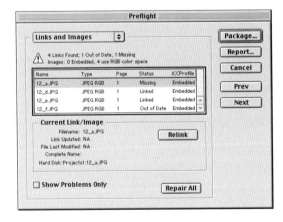

3 Click Relink.

4 Locate and double-click 12_c.jpg (the renamed file) in the ID_12 folder, located inside the Lessons folder within the IDCIB folder on your hard disk.

Now you'll update the out-of-date link.

5 Select the 12_f.jpg graphic whose Status is listed as Out of Date.

6 Click Update. The Status changes to Linked.

7 Click Cancel to close the Preflight dialog box.

You've corrected the current problems in the document. Throughout this lesson, you'll make changes to the document that affect the settings in the Preflight panels. At the end of the lesson, you'll perform a final preflight check using the Package feature to catch any remaining problem areas.

8 Choose File > Save.

About trapping

The quality of your printed document depends on how well the different inks print *in register*—that is, exactly aligned with each other. If one or more inks print out of register, white gaps may appear between adjacent objects where the paper shows through, or there may be fringes of unexpected color called *color shifts*. Commercial printers hide flaws in registration by slightly expanding one region into another, using a border strip called a *trap*.

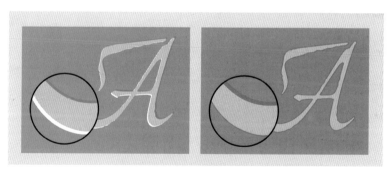

Gap created by misregistration (left); gap hidden by trapping (right)

For a color version of trapping, see figure 12-1 in the color section.

You can create a trap in InDesign using two methods: by using the In-RIP Trapping feature and by manually setting a stroke or fill value to overprint individual objects. In this lesson, you'll practice creating a few manual traps so you can see how design issues affect the way your inks print on the press.

For more information about trapping and the In-RIP Trapping feature, see "Using Adobe In-RIP Trapping" in the Adobe InDesign online Help.

Trapping spot-color text

Typically when you produce separations from a document with overlapping objects, the top objects replace, or knock out, any colors beneath them on the other separations. Another technique is overprinting, in which one ink prints on top of another. Overprinting hides the effects of misregistration, but can produce unintended blends of color. By default, InDesign knocks out spot colors.

Chokes and Spreads

There are two types of traps: a spread, in which a lighter object overlaps a darker background and seems to expand into the background; and a choke, in which a lighter background overlaps a darker object that falls within the background and seems to squeeze or reduce the object.

–From the Adobe Illustrator User Guide, Chapter 15

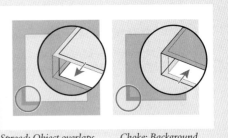

Spread: Object overlaps background

Choke: Background overlaps object

For a color version of chokes and spreads, see figure 12-2 in the color section.

In this part of the lesson, you'll use overprinting to compensate for misregistration when spot colors knock out the colors beneath them.

Note: *Because overprinting can increase the amount of ink coverage on the page and cause problems on the press, be sure to talk with your prepress service provider before setting inks to overprint.*

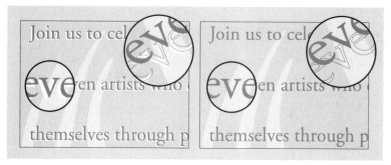

Spot-colored type set to knock out, misregistered (left); spot-colored type set to overprint, hiding misregistration (right)

For a color version of knocking out versus overprinting, see figure 12-3 in the color section.

Overprinting a stroke

Here you'll create a simple trap using two inks: black and a spot color. In the poster, the spot-color text "PHOTOGRAPHY" knocks out the black background beneath it. This would create a white gap on the press should the inks misregister.

To create a trap, you'll spread the lighter spot color into the black background by overprinting a spot-color stroke.

1 Select the zoom tool (⌕), and then drag across the upper middle area of the black object to zoom in on the "PHOTOGRAPHY" text.

2 Using the type tool, click in the "PHOTOGRAPHY" text frame and choose Edit > Select All to select the text.

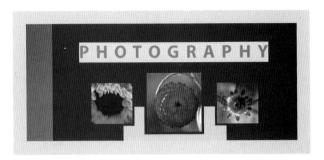

3 Click the Swatches palette tab (or choose Window > Swatches) to make the palette visible. Notice that the text is the spot color PANTONE 165 CVC.

4 Select the Stroke box (⬚) in the toolbox.

The trap requirement for the "PHOTOGRAPHY" text is .5 points. (Remember to get trap values from your prepress service provider.)

5 Choose Window > Stroke to display the Stroke palette. Choose 0.5 pt for the Weight.

Because the text includes a fill, the entire stroke weight falls outside the character outlines. See "About stroke weights" on page 404.

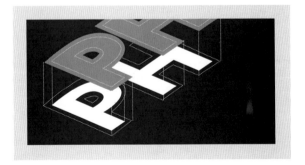

For a color version of overprinting a stroke, see figure 12-4 in the color section.

Since InDesign knocks out spot colors by default, you need to set the stroke to overprint.

6 Choose Window > Attributes to display the Attributes palette.

7 Select Overprint Stroke.

8 Choose Edit > Deselect All to deselect the text.

9 Move the Attributes palette group out of your way.

On-screen appearance (left) and printed result (right)

For a color version of results of overprinting, see figure 12-5 in the color section.

You cannot see the overprint effect on-screen, so the text looks heavy. However, when the poster is printed, the stroke will overprint and the orange spot-color ink will spread into the black ink.

10 Save the file.

About stroke weights

For objects, the weight of a stroke is centered on its path. Half of the stroke falls inside the path, and half falls outside. For text characters only, InDesign automatically adjusts stroke weights so that the entire stroke weight exists outside the character outline. This preserves character shapes by preventing a growing stroke weight from closing up the inner areas of small text characters.

Object stroke weight is always centered over the path (left). Character stroke weight grows outward from a character outline when filled (right).

–From the Adobe InDesign User Guide, Chapter 6

Overprinting a fill

When you have several small instances of spot color, such as small text characters positioned over colored areas, you may want to overprint the text, including the fill, (rather than knock out) to hide potential misregistration on the press.

The poster includes several lines of small spot-color text. You'll set the text to overprint.

1 Select the type tool (T) in the toolbox, and then scroll down if necessary to the small orange text under "Whimsy & Formality."

2 Click in the text frame. Choose Edit > Select All. This is the same spot color as the text "PHOTOGRAPHY."

3 Click the Attributes palette tab (or choose Window > Attributes) to make the palette visible.

4 Select Overprint Fill.

5 Choose Edit > Deselect All to deselect the text.

6 Choose View > Fit Page in Window.

7 Save the file.

Because the text is set to overprint, some color may show through the characters when printed. However, when working with multiple lines of small text on a light background, it's less distracting to overprint than to see misregistration or traps.

Working with black objects

By default, InDesign always overprints process black (shown as [Black] in the Swatches palette). This includes all black strokes, fills, and text characters of any size. Overprinting black-ink objects helps hide misregistration of black text characters positioned over colored areas. Using a process [Black] stroke for *keylines* (borders) around graphics helps hide misregistration of overlapping color.

Because process black is translucent, objects and colors may show through. If you do not want this effect, you can add another process color to black to achieve a more intense color, called a *rich black*.

Creating and applying a rich black

The poster includes large black display type over colored objects and a white background. You'll create a cool rich black (using 100% K, or black, and 20% C, or cyan) and then apply it to the display type to prevent background objects from showing through. Rich-black objects knock out because the cyan ink knocks out the other inks beneath it on the press.

Without cyan support screen (left) and with cyan support screen (right)

For a color version of rich black, see figure 12-6 in the color section.

Note: *A cool rich black uses cyan for its undercolor or* support screen—*the process inks used to make a rich black. A warm rich black uses magenta.*

1 In the Swatches palette, select [Black], the default process black color. (You may need to scroll in the palette.)

2 Alt-click (Windows) or Option-click (Mac OS) the New Swatch icon (⬛) in the Swatches palette to duplicate the process black color and open the New Color Swatch dialog box.

3 For Swatch Name, type **Cool Black**.

4 For Cyan, enter 20%. Leave the remaining options as they are and click OK.

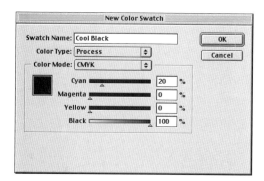

5 Using the selection tool (⬉), click "Exhibit" to select it. The text has been converted to outlines (paths) so you can no longer select it with the type tool.

6 Select the Fill box (⬛) in the toolbox.

7 In the Swatches palette, select Cool Black to apply the color to the object.

8 Save the file.

Trapping a rich black object

Rich blacks require a trapping technique called a *keepaway*. The support screen is choked back or made slightly smaller than the black area so that misregistration doesn't produce a tiny fringe of color, which is especially noticeable where black type crosses over white areas.

A fringe of cyan appears (left) when the cyan separation is misregistered (right).

For a color version of misregistered rich black, see figure 12-7 in the color section.

You'll create a keepaway by overprinting a process [Black] stroke on the Exhibit display type. The stroke will change the appearance of the type, but only slightly. In this case, the slight change in appearance is less distracting than allowing the cyan to show should misregistration occur.

1 If necessary, use the selection tool to select the "Exhibit" graphic.

2 Click the Stroke palette tab (or choose Window > Stroke) to make the palette visible. Choose 1 pt for the Weight.

The trap requirement for the display type is .5 points. For objects, InDesign always centers half the stroke inside the path, and half outside. For this reason, you need to specify a stroke weight of 1 pt.

3 Select the Stroke box ( ) in the toolbox.

4 In the Swatches palette, scroll up and select process [Black].

Now you'll use a keyboard shortcut to deselect the graphic.

5 Press Shift+Ctrl+A (Windows) or Shift+Command+A (Mac OS).

Because process [Black] overprints by default, you don't need to manually set the stroke to overprint. When you apply the stroke, the support screen of the rich black is no longer close to the edge.

Overprinting a black stroke (left) chokes back the support screen from the edge (right).

For a color version of overprinting a stroke in a rich black, see figure 12-8 in the color section.

Overprinting a varnish

You can also use overprinting for special effects. For example, you can apply a varnish (a clear spot ink) to emphasize display type or to enhance images.

The poster uses a varnish over three images and display type. To give the Exhibit display type a shiny effect with clean edges, you'll apply a spot-color varnish to a copy of the display type, and then set its fill and stroke to overprint. The varnish will fit perfectly over the display type because the silhouette is an exact replica of the Exhibit object. To prevent the varnished objects from distracting from the overall poster design, we've placed the varnished objects on their own layer, which is currently hidden.

1 Click the Layers palette tab (or choose Window > Layers) to make the palette visible.

2 Click the eye icon ( ) next to the Display Type layer to hide it. This enables you to see only the silhouette of the display type in the next step.

3 Click the square to the far left of the Varnish layer to display the eye icon.

Notice the silhouette of the display type and the three pink squares at the top right of the document. The color pink represents the varnish so that it stands out on-screen; when printed, the varnish will print on its own separations plate according to the values communicated to the commercial printer. The pink squares represent the areas where the varnish will be applied. To complete the special effect in the document, you'll also apply the spot-color varnish to the display type silhouette.

4 Using the selection tool, select the "Exhibit" graphic.

5 Select the Stroke box (⬚) in the toolbox, and then select the Varnish color in the Swatches palette.

6 Select the Fill box (⬛) in the toolbox, and then select the Varnish color in the Swatches palette.

For a color version of overprinting a varnish, see figure 12-9 in the color section.

7 With the Exhibit graphic still selected, select Overprint Fill and Overprint Stroke in the Attributes palette. This prevents the spot color from knocking out (the default).

8 Press Shift+Ctrl+A (Windows) or Shift+Command+A (Mac OS) to deselect the graphic so you can see where the varnish will be applied on the press.

Note: *Usually you don't want to overprint a trap (in this case, the stroke around the text) with a varnish. However, both the graphic and the stroke in the poster are black, so overprinting covers the entire area. Each project is unique, so consult with your prepress service provider before overprinting inks.*

9 Position the pointer on the black triangle to the right of the Layers palette tab, and choose Show All Layers from the Layers palette menu. InDesign prints only visible layers.

10 Save the file. You have completed all the overprinting and trapping tasks.

Creating a bleed

To make sure that ink is printed to the edge of the page after it is trimmed, you need to create a *bleed,* the area of the document that falls outside the crop marks. *Crop marks* define the edge of the trimmed page. The commercial printer trims the bleed after printing and assembling the document. Always contact your service provider for the exact bleed requirements.

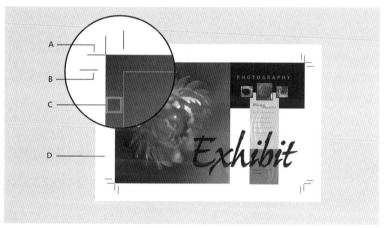

*A. Bleed mark **B.** Trim, or crop mark **C.** Bleed area **D.** Paper*

To reduce distraction during the design phase, the designer has masked the graphics to the page edge. Now that you're preparing the final document for production, you'll extend the graphics frames to accommodate the required bleed. Later in this lesson, you'll specify the precise extent of the bleed in the Page Marks panel of the Print dialog box.

1 Choose View > Show Guides. Also choose View > Snap to Guides. Ruler guides define how far to drag the graphics frames.

To see the ruler guides on the pasteboard, you'll zoom out.

2 Select the zoom tool (🔍) in the toolbox, and then press Alt (Windows) or Option (Mac OS). Click the poster until you can see the ruler guides.

3 Select the selection tool (➤) in the toolbox, and then press Tab to hide all palettes so that your workspace is clear.

4 Using the selection tool, click the large flower image on the left to select it. Drag the upper left corner of its bounding box diagonally away from the image until it snaps to the ruler guide on the top and left. Dragging diagonally extends both the top and left sides at once.

5 Now drag the lower middle bounding box handle downward to extend the image until it snaps to the bottom guide.

6 Using the selection tool, select the black box in the upper right corner of the poster. Drag the upper right corner of its bounding box diagonally away from the graphic until it snaps to the ruler guide on the top and right.

7 Select the orange rectangle at the bottom of the poster.

8 Drag the lower middle bounding box handle downward until it snaps to the bottom guide.

Note: *If you accidentally select the text frame with the date, choose Edit > Undo and select it again.*

You have extended all graphics for the bleed.

9 Press Tab to show the palettes again, and then save the file.

Setting paper options

It's important to distinguish between *page size* (as defined in the Document Setup dialog box for your document) and *paper size* (the sheet of paper, piece of film, or area of the printing plate you print on). Your page size might be US Letter (8.5 x 11 inches), but you might need to print on a larger piece of paper or film to accommodate any page marks or the bleed area.

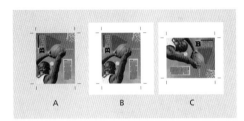

A. *Letter (tall orientation)* **B.** *Custom* **C.** *Transverse*

You'll set options for printing the poster on tabloid-size paper, which can accommodate the poster, its bleed, and all page marks. Follow the steps for your computer platform.

In Windows:

1 Choose File > Print and make sure AGFA SelectSet7000_ID is selected at the top of the dialog box.

2 In the Print dialog box, click Properties, and then click the Page Setup (Windows NT) or Paper (Windows 98) tab.

3 Choose Tabloid from the Paper Size menu.

4 Make sure Landscape is selected and click OK.

In Mac OS:

1 Choose File > Page Setup. Make sure Virtual Printer is selected in the Printer menu at the top of the dialog box.

2 For Paper, choose Tabloid.

3 For Orientation, make sure Landscape (▣) is selected.

4 Leave the rest of the options as they are and click OK.

Creating color separations

To reproduce color documents on a printing press, you must first create individual pieces of film (the separations) for each of the component inks: cyan, magenta, yellow, and black, and any spot colors, if applicable. The process of breaking composite artwork into its component inks is called *color separation*.

The poster is composed of process colors and two spot colors. If you were to print color separations at this point, you would have six pieces of film: one each for the cyan, magenta, yellow, and black plates, and one plate for each of the two spot colors. You can print separations using process colors or spot colors, or you can use a combination of both.

Important: *Each print job has specific requirements that you'll need to discuss with your prepress service provider before setting separation options.*

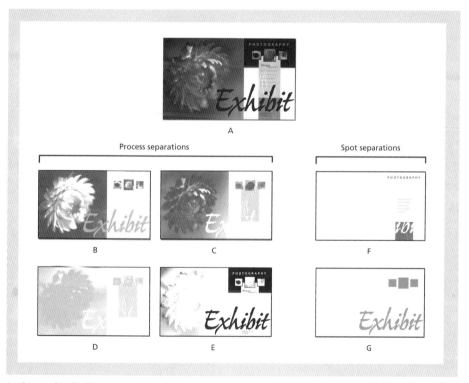

*A. Composite B. Cyan separation C. Magenta separation D. Yellow separation E. Black separation
F. Spot color separation G. Spot varnish separation*

For a color version of color separations, see figure 12-10 in the color section.

You'll specify separations in the Color panel of the Print dialog box using the high-resolution options available in the PPD you installed with the virtual printer.

1 Choose File > Print.

2 Make sure AGFA SelectSet7000_ID (Windows) or Virtual Printer (Mac OS) is selected at the top of the dialog box.

3 Do one of the following:

• In Windows, click the Color tab.

• In Mac OS, choose Color from the menu under the printer name.

The ink functions are grayed out because Composite is selected by default.

4 Select Separations. The poster's colors are represented by their component inks in the ink list on the Color panel. The printer icon to the left of the ink names indicates that a separation will be created for each ink.

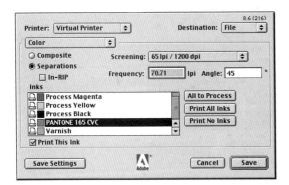

💡 *If you need to reprint a single separation (for example, if you changed the content on a certain separations plate), click Print No Inks to select all of them, and then double-click the printer icon next to the ink you want to print.*

5 Leave the dialog box open so you can use it in the next section.

Note: For convenience, you can preserve applicable print settings for all applications that use the same printer by clicking the Apply (Windows) or Save Settings (Mac OS) button. The current print settings will be saved for the selected printer.

Specifying the screen frequency

The relationship between *device resolution* and *screen frequency* determines the quality of the printed output. Device resolution is the number of printer dots per inch (dpi) produced by an imagesetter or laser printer. Screen frequency is the number of lines per inch (lpi) of *halftone cells*, dots of varying sizes used to simulate shades of gray on the printed page. Depending on the selected PPD, more than one screen frequency value may be available. Your prepress service provider will direct you to select the screen frequency appropriate for your document.

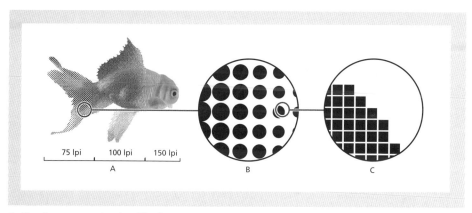

A. Continuous tone simulated by line screen **B.** *Line screen consisting of halftone dots* **C.** *Halftone dots consisting of printer dots*

⬛ For more information about device resolution and screen frequency, see "Specifying the screen frequency" in the Adobe InDesign online Help.

For this exercise, you'll select one of the preset screen frequencies and printer resolution combinations for the virtual printer.

1 In the Color panel of the Print dialog box, choose 133 lpi / 2400 dpi from the Screening menu. The first value, 133, represents the screen frequency (lpi), and the second value, 2400, represents the output device resolution (dpi).

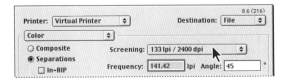

When you select inks in the ink list, the values in the Frequency and Angle text boxes change, showing you the optimum screen frequency and angle for that ink. For this exercise, do not change the values.

2 Leave the dialog box open so you can use it in the next section.

Setting graphics and fonts options

Using the Graphics panel, you can specify ways to print bitmap images, EPS graphics, and PDF pages most efficiently to PostScript printers. In addition, you can specify how InDesign downloads fonts to the printer. The options you choose determine how big the resulting PostScript file is.

1 In the Print dialog box, do one of the following:

• In Windows, click the Graphics tab.

• In Mac OS, choose Graphics from the menu under the printer name.

The default options for graphics are appropriate for printing this document to a contract proofing device, so you won't change them. However, you'll select one additional font downloading option.

2 In the Font Downloading section, select Download PPD Fonts. This option ensures that your version of the fonts in the document are downloaded to the output device, even if those fonts reside in the printer's memory. This prevents line wraps due to outline variances, and is usually worth the larger PostScript file and longer printing time.

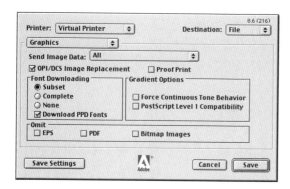

3 Leave the dialog box open so you can use it in the next section.

Adding page marks

You'll set the exact bleed area for the bleed you created earlier in this lesson, in addition to a variety of markings that print outside the page bleed boundary. Service providers use these *page marks* or *printer's marks* to align separation films when producing contract proofs, to measure film for correct calibration and dot density, to trim film to size, to align colors on the press, and so on.

A. Crop marks B. Registration marks C. Page information
D. Color bars E. Bleed marks

1 In the Print dialog box, do one of the following:

- In Mac OS, choose Page Marks from the menu under the printer name.

- In Windows, click the Page Marks tab.

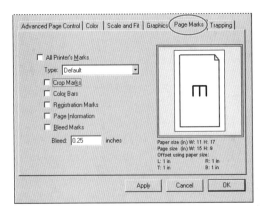

2 Select All Printer's Marks to select all marks at once.

Because you chose Tabloid for the paper size earlier in the lesson, the page marks fall within the paper size.

3 In the Bleed text box, type **p9** (9 points). Page marks will stand off from the bleed.

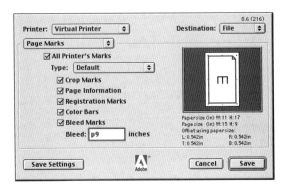

For more information about printer's marks, see "Printing page marks" in the Adobe InDesign online Help.

4 Do one of the following:

• In Windows, leave the Print dialog box open so you can use it in the next section.

In Mac OS, make sure File is selected for Destination at the top of the Print dialog box, and click Save. This saves the printer information so that the Package feature can read it later in the lesson. Then click Cancel to close the Print dialog box; you'll specify settings using the Page Setup dialog box in the next section.

Proofing options

As a general rule, the closer the proofing method mimics the conditions of the actual printing press, the more reliably it indicates the final product's quality. The following are proofing steps you can take to ensure that your files print as you intended.

Black-and-white proofs *Before printing your separations to a high-resolution output device, it's a good idea to print a set of separations on your black-and-white desktop printer. Using black-and-white proofs, you can make sure the correct number of separations prints; you can check the bleed size and page marks. You can also check for surprises in overprinted versus knocked-out objects.*

Adobe PressReady color comp or Adobe PDF file *Adobe PressReady is a powerful proofing and printing system for color inkjet printers. Using PressReady, you can produce press-quality color comps on select color inkjet printers using Adobe PostScript 3 technology. You can also create and send color-calibrated PDF files to clients for approval.*

Contract proofs *Color proofs that you sign off on, sometimes called contract proofs, indicate to the commercial printer the color you expect in the final document. Your service provider can provide color proofs based on actual pieces of film (called separation-based color proofs, or analog proofs) or digital CMYK proofs (with or without halftone dots). Next to proofs made on the printing plates themselves, the most accurate proofs are separation-based color proofs, and are regarded as the industry standard. Digital proofing can achieve high quality, but most digital proofs do not show moires and trapping errors.*

–Adapted from the Adobe Print Publishing Guide, Chapter 3

Identifying film requirements for high-resolution printing

Now you'll set emulsion direction and indicate whether you want positive or negative film for the imagesetter whose PPD you chose when you installed the virtual printer at the beginning of this lesson. Follow the steps for your computer platform.

Note: In your work environment, ask your service provider how they intend to print the film. In most cases, they will print negatives, right-reading and emulsion side up. In other words, the black and white areas are reversed, and the text on the page is readable (not mirrored) when the emulsion side of the film is toward you. Once you know what your service provider wants, ask what settings are best to achieve this result. Some service providers will want you to specify settings in the software, others will set either their RIPs (raster image processors) or recorders to do this.

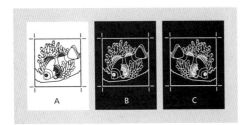

*A. Positive image **B.** Negative **C.** Negative with emulsion side down*

In Windows NT:

1 Make sure AGFA SelectSet7000_ID is selected at the top of the Print dialog box. Then click Properties and click the Advanced tab.

2 Navigate through the option tree until you come to Document Options\PostScript Options\Mirrored output, and then select Yes.

3 If necessary, click the + (plus sign) next to Printer Features.

4 To print negative pages, select RIP Negative Output and then select Negative.

5 Click OK to close the Properties dialog box.

6 Make sure Print to File is selected at the top of the Print dialog box and click OK.

7 Leave PostScript selected for Save as Type, and save the 12_Poster.ps file in the ID_12 folder. This saves the printer information so that the Package feature can read it later in the lesson.

In Windows 98:

1 Choose File > Print, click Properties, and click the Graphics tab.

2 To print negative pages, select Print as a Negative Image.

3 To print emulsion side up, select Print as a Mirror Image.

4 Click OK to close the Properties dialog box.

5 Click OK to close the Properties dialog box.

6 Make sure Print to File is selected at the top of the Print dialog box, and click OK.

7 Leave PostScript selected for Save as Type, and save the 12_Poster.ps file in the ID_12 folder. This saves the printer information so that the Package feature can read it later in the lesson.

In Mac OS:

1 Choose File > Page Setup.

2 Choose PostScript Options from the menu under the printer name.

3 To print emulsion side up, deselect Flip Horizontal and Flip Vertical.

4 To print negative pages, select Invert Image. Then click OK.

Packaging files for handoff

Packaging an InDesign document is similar to the Collect for Output (QuarkXPress®) or Save for Service Provider (Adobe PageMaker) features. InDesign gathers the files you've used, including fonts and linked graphics, for easy handoff to a service provider.

You don't need to perform a final preflight check manually before packaging. InDesign automatically performs an up-to-date preflight check before gathering the files. If it detects problem areas, InDesign displays a dialog box. Because the poster includes RGB images, you will see this dialog box.

1 Choose File > Package.

2 Click View Info to open the Preflight dialog box, where you can assess or correct any remaining problems.

3 Do one of the following:

• If the only problem area is the RGB images, click Package from the Preflight dialog box to begin the packaging process again. You don't need to convert these images to CMYK.

• If you have other problem areas, such as broken links, fix them before continuing or your package may not be complete. (See "Performing a preflight check before printing" on page 397.)

4 When prompted to save the document, click Save.

InDesign displays the Printing Instructions dialog box, where you can provide contact information. The filename at the top of the dialog box is the name InDesign gives to the report it generates for service providers; you can rename the report. This report, which is saved in the default text editor format, includes the information in the Printing Instructions dialog box; a list of all used fonts, links, and inks required to print the document; and print settings. The report is stored in the same folder as the other packaged files.

For this lesson, you'll skip the exercise of filling in the printing instructions.

5 Click Continue.

InDesign creates a new folder for the packaged files.

6 Rename the folder **12_PosterPack,** and make sure ID_12 is the current folder.

In the packaging dialog box, the options for copying fonts, copying linked graphics, and updating graphic links are selected by default. Leave those options selected. InDesign copies the fonts and linked graphics to separate folders named Fonts and Links in the package folder. By updating the graphic links at the time you package the document, you'll ensure that the links are maintained.

7 Select Include Fonts and Links from Hidden Layers, and also select View Report.

At this time, you could fill in or update the Printing Instructions by clicking the Instructions button. Then click Continue to return to the packaging dialog box.

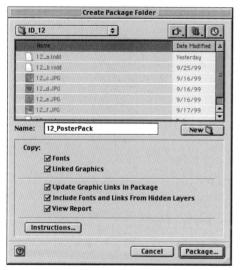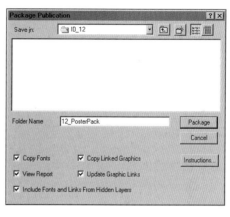

Mac OS (left) and Windows (right)

8 Click Package.

9 When the Font Alert dialog box appears, read the text. If you agree to the terms, click OK.

10 When the service provider report opens in your default text editor, review the print settings you specified in this lesson, such as separations and bleed. Then examine the File Package List (at the end of the report), which describes the components of the poster.

11 Exit from the text editor.

In addition to copying the service provider report, fonts, and linked graphics, InDesign copies the InDesign document to the package folder.

You've finished the lesson. In a typical workflow, you would now be ready to send your document to a service provider. Include proofs of color separation setups when you send your electronic file to a service provider. Also tell your service provider about any traps you created in the document. You could also send a press-optimized PDF file from Press-Ready, for example, to your service provider for final production. Keep in mind that you must remain in close communication with your printing professional for each print job.

On your own

Now that you have learned how to overprint objects to hide misregistration, and install printers and set print settings, you're ready to apply these skills on your own. Try the following tasks to improve your trapping and printing skills.

1 Hide all layers except the Special Trap layer to see how to trap an object that crosses multiple colors.

2 Try printing proof separations to a desktop printer. When setting up the printer, be sure to use a PPD for a PostScript level 2 or higher output device. If the poster doesn't print on a paper size your printer supports, set scaling in the Scale and Fit panel of the Print dialog box (not the printer driver dialog box).

3 Create a .5-point trap on the "PHOTOGRAPHY" display type by choking it. First, set up an example to choke by reversing the colors on a copy of the start file. Change the black background to the orange spot color, and apply a dark blue to the text. (Don't use black, or you would just overprint it.) Then bring the light-colored background into the dark-colored foreground. Unlike the spread example on text, you work with a duplicate text frame directly on top of the original, which has a stroke but no fill. That way, the stroke will center on the path and therefore overlap the inside of the original character outline. Duplicate the text, remove the fill, and set the stroke to orange. Use the Attributes palette to make this orange stroke overprint. Give the duplicate a 1-point stroke. A 1-point stroke equates to .5 (trap value) on either side of the path.

 To create a duplicate text frame, press Shift+Ctrl+V (Windows) or Shift+Command+V to get the Step and Repeat dialog box, and set one copy with an offset of 0,0.

Review questions

1 Why should you use the PostScript printer driver supplied on the InDesign CD?

2 What does a preflight check reveal?

3 What is meant by the term *bleed*?

4 What is overprinting? What is knocking out?

5 Why do you overprint a process [Black] stroke on rich black objects that cross over white areas? What is this technique called?

6 In which area of the print dialog box do you specify screen frequencies and output device resolution?

Review answers

1 The printer drivers control many printing functions and improve printer performance. For example, the driver for Mac OS systems enables the InDesign printing options for color, scale and fit, graphics, page marks, and so on. In Windows, the PostScript files will be smaller and more efficient.

2 The preflight check warns of problems that may prevent a document from imaging correctly, such as missing fonts or outdated or missing files. In addition, the preflight check provides information about a document, such as the inks it uses, the first page on which a font appears, and print settings.

3 A bleed is a printed area that extends beyond the crop marks of the page.

4 With overprinting, a second ink is applied on top of the first ink on the page. With knocking out, the first ink is not applied to the area (called the knockout) where the second ink will appear.

5 You overprint a process [Black] stroke to hide flaws in registration on the press. This technique is called trapping.

6 You specify screen frequencies and output device resolution in the Color panel of the Print dialog box.

Index

Production Notes

This Adobe InDesign 1.0 Classroom in a Book was created electronically using Adobe InDesign and Adobe FrameMaker. Art was produced using Adobe InDesign, Adobe Illustrator, and Adobe Photoshop. The Minion and Frutiger families of typefaces were used throughout this book.

References to company names in the lessons are for demonstration purposes only and are not intended to refer to any actual organization.

Images

Photographic images and illustrations are provided in low-resolution formats and are intended for instructional use only.

Photography credits

Adobe Image Library: Quick Tour (red armadillo, from volume 6, Objectgear/Culturals; ceramic sun, from volume 6, Objectgear/Culturals; skeleton, from volume 5, Objectgear/Amusements; pinata, from volume 6 Objectgear/Culturals; tin fire heart, from volume 6, Objectgear/Culturals;); Lesson 7 (pear, from volume 5, Objectgear/Amusements).

Bob Bringhurst: Lesson 5 (bike riders).

Julie Brockmeyer: Lesson 11 (chocolate shavings, truffles, and packaging).

Paul Carew: Lesson 5 (Bad Clams eyes).

Bonnie Lebesch: Lesson 2 (paper iris and paper fortune); Lesson 3 (paper armadillo, paper sparrow, paper fortune, paper sea lion, paper crane); Lesson 5 (bicycle crank, bicycle seat); Lesson 6 (bicycle spokes, bicycle tire); Lesson 7 (searching hands, clasped hands); Lesson 12 (pink flowers, yellow flower, orange flower).

Susan Bari Price: Quick Tour (pressed tin, blue moon, ceramic angel, el paraguas, beaded moon).

Typefaces used

Adobe Garamond, Adobe Jenson™, Myriad, and Trajan® were used throughout the lessons.